WE CAN DO BETTER

Dr Maja Göpel is a political economist and an important voice for a sustainable transformation of society, working at the intersection of the economy, politics, and society. From 2017 to 2020, she was secretary-general of the German Advisory Council on Global Change, and in 2019 was appointed honorary professor at the Leuphana University of Lüneburg. She is a member of the Club of Rome, the World Future Council, the Balaton Group, and the German government's Bioeconomy Council, and a co-initiator of the Scientists for Future network.

For Mimi
I have had the privilege of learning so much from you

CONTENTS

Part III
Who are 'We'?

Prologue

Humanity's greatest adventure

'Hope locates itself in the premises that we don't know what will happen and that in the speciousness of uncertainty is room to act. When you recognise uncertainty, you recognise that you may be able to influence the outcomes — you alone or you in concert with a few dozen or several million others. Hope is an embrace of the unknown and the unknowable, an alternative to the certainty of both optimists and pessimists.'[1]

REBECCA SOLNIT, AUTHOR

The world is changing; it always is. We all know that. Some of the changes are easy for us to accept, while others we lament or resist. Some changes can't come soon enough for us, and we do everything in our power to hasten their advent. Others are devastating, leaving us feeling profoundly insecure. But whatever the nature of the change, we like to think we have a sense of the

1

typical speed and scope of such changes. We have come to expect the familiar, prior situation to be restored largely unchanged after a certain time. When we turn on our phones in the morning, we do not expect to find that the world as we know it has become skewed overnight. But that is precisely what appears to have been happening with increasing frequency for some time now.

Suddenly the world economy is in jeopardy due to the collapse of an American bank, laying bare just how vulnerable the international financial system is. A nuclear power plant in Fukushima, Japan, is flooded by a tsunami, and the whole question of how we will meet our energy needs in the future is opened up again. The people of Britain vote to leave the European Union, and an entire continent's history of political integration is called into question. Fires rage across entire regions of Brazil, Australia, and Russia; violent floods kill hundreds of people in Germany, Belgium, and the Netherlands. Supporters of Donald Trump storm the US Capitol, willing to use violence to prevent his election defeat from being officially recognised. The world is brought to a standstill by a virus that apparently spread from bats to humans somewhere in China. Russia invades Ukraine, and war is once again a political instrument in Europe.

But also: a previously unknown Swedish schoolgirl suddenly persuades millions of people all over the world to take to the streets to demand action on climate protection. Movements such as Black Lives Matter and #MeToo shine a spotlight on issues that were suppressed, silenced, or just accepted for years or decades. For the first time, industrialised countries such as Germany report that more electricity is being produced from wind and solar power than from coal and gas. Internal combustion engines are recognised as harmful products, and moves are made to ban them or phase them out unless they run on alternative carbon dioxide–neutral fuels. Germany's Constitutional Court rules that the government must do more to protect the climate, justifying its decision with the argument that the freedoms of future generations must be given as much legal weighting as our freedoms today. Demands begin to rise for the United Nations and international courts to recognise ecocide as a crime. The people of Europe take in and, for the most part, welcome millions of people fleeing wars and crises.

Such momentous developments are not an everyday occurrence, and they take place in some parts of the world more often than in others. But the point is that we no longer consider it impossible that such significant developments *might* take place every day. We no longer see them as rare exceptions that we can brush off as isolated cases whose effects will be gone by tomorrow without leaving an impact on the way we live our lives. We can no longer put our faith in the principle that the state of things the day after tomorrow will be only slightly different from the state of things today. Sometimes, that can be too much for us to deal with, and we long to return to normality as quickly as possible. But our idea of what that normality is, or should be, is growing increasingly unsteady.

Is it not the case that all the crises we're seeing now are an indication of the fact that all cannot have been well, or stayed normal, before?

Do we really wake up in a different world after such events? Or is it perhaps just the same old world in which we used to deliberately disregard gradual changes until they became impossible to ignore, or, if we did notice them, would refuse to pay sufficient attention to them? In our world today, we feel almost on a daily basis that the pressure for change in many areas of our lives has increased to such an extent that simply carrying on as before is no longer an option. When we take an honest view, many beliefs, routines, and supposedly self-evident facts begin to look completely outdated. And we see that crises can also open up opportunities to finally tackle long-observed risks and much-discussed problems.

Changing our energy supply structure, for example, or re-organising our systems for mobility, restructuring agriculture, or redistributing the financial burdens that come with living in a society.

No longer conflating progress and economic growth.

And striving to achieve a world order that might actually accomplish the fair-development goals touted so prominently in all the international declarations and charters.

For many people, the fact that the status quo has begun to falter is not only a threat, but also a signal for a new beginning. However, with societies now digitally linked around the globe, it is difficult to predict precisely what kind of a normality such a new beginning might eventually lead to. There are many possible answers to the question of which path towards that end is best: some believe technology will save the day; for others, the answer lies in cutting consumption, or in market forces, or in state intervention. These views are often in competition, rather than conversation, with each other.

When the future appears so unclear and so wide open, it is often difficult for us to imagine our place in it. That can make us feel insecure or anxious, or sometimes even angry. A common way of dealing with such feelings is to look for someone to blame and then distance ourselves from the 'guilty' party, from those who get rich from the system and those who have made sure the existing structures provide maximum profit for themselves. But also from those who have recognised the imminent dangers, and therefore want to change the old structures, and, in doing so, call privilege and comfort into question. Or from those who have a very different view of what is right, or even disagree on what the most pressing issues are.

On the one hand, many human beings now have more stuff, more opportunities, and more freedom than any previous generation. On the other hand, we are now depleting the planet's resources faster than they can regenerate. At the same time, many of the well-documented inequalities between rich and poor, North and South, Black and White, and men and women are not decreasing, and in some cases are on the rise again. The greater concerns become that we might really be reaching the limits of growth, the more difficult it appears to be for us to share resources. Rather than sharing, we continue to increase production, leaving no time for regeneration—of both humans and nature. The social imbalances that result from our way of life are like the mirror image of the environmental damage it leaves behind. We are not in equilibrium. We are stuck in a system that promises us freedom but offers us no way out.

But we do have ideas about how we can change the way we live, interact economically, consume, and cooperate. In my last book, *Rethinking the World*, I issued an invitation to take a closer look at those ideas, and to rethink some of the old beliefs that continue to shape our societies today. Those beliefs may have been appropriate for the realities and challenges at the time they were formed around 250 years ago, but now, with almost eight billion inhabitants on the planet, and us consuming resources at a rapidly growing rate, they are the cause of many of the crises we see around us. That's why I wanted to show that we need to rethink our world.

In this book, I want to focus on the action that can—and, I believe, must—grow out of that new way of thinking. I want us to stop staring into the rearview mirror and turn our gaze towards the horizon, to focus on hope, and to switch our inquiring spirit into overdrive so that, together, we can become something greater than we are today. I strongly suspect that it is not ideas for the world of tomorrow that we lack, but the belief that those ideas can be implemented. It may be the case that we lack both the confidence to take the first steps and the conviction that many others are ready and willing to join us on that journey. Or we may lack the courage to change the deep-rooted structures and key political parameters on which our societies are based. But that is to underestimate our own powers. And to ignore the fact that things started to change some time ago, and that it's time for us to intervene.

Our societies are in the midst of changes whose significance in the history of humankind can only be compared to the upheavals of the kind brought by the invention of agriculture, the emergence of feudalism, the arrival of the Industrial Revolution, and the development of capitalism. Those are all examples of what we call 'Great Transformations'. They are the focus of a research movement in which colleagues from a wide range of disciplines are pooling their knowledge of past upheavals of a similar scale in order to manage those we face today in a more strategic way. Their insights can help us avoid feeling overwhelmed by their increasing complexity and just passively accepting change, and help us, rather, to find ways to anticipate and navigate change better. And to move away from always looking for ways to patch up worn-out old structures, and muster the strength to find solutions that may well involve difficult restructuring in the short term, but that will be all the more suitable for the future.

'The true criterion of reform,' wrote the philosopher and social psychologist Erich Fromm, 'is [...] its realism, its true "radicalism"; it is the question whether it goes to the roots and attempts to change causes—or whether it remains on the surface and attempts to deal only with symptoms.'[2]

I have chosen the radical path. This book, which is the result of that decision, is divided into three parts, which, by and large, progress from the big picture to the level of the individual, guided by three key questions.

How, in the complex world we live in today, can we turn things around? And how can academic research help us develop solutions for the 21st century?

Where must we start the process of changing our present structures to make them more expedient to the achievement of our goals, rather than standing in our way?

Who can provide the impetus for these changes? Politicians? Business? The so-called elites? Who is the 'we' everybody talks about when they talk about implementing change?

A Great Transformation to a better world is humanity's greatest adventure. It will be made up of many small steps—but it will not succeed without a clear orientation and tireless enthusiasm for achieving what it is possible to achieve. This is what I have learned from all the letters, suggestions, and notes I received in reaction to my last book and my work for the Scientists4Future initiative. They have shown me how much is already possible in real terms, and how many people are already on the starting blocks and raring to get going. This book is also the product of the exchanges I have had with the many people I've had the privilege to meet along the way. None of those people claimed that the times we live in are simple, or that social change is easy to achieve. But they all share the conviction that we sometimes have to let go of things in order to make room for something new. We just need to do some things better. And we can do that.

Part 1

Our Operating System

'In complex systems, relationships are key. Connections or relationships define how complex systems work; an organisation is its relationships not its flow chart. And this perception is crucial in understanding how complex systems differ from simple or complicated systems.'

FRANCES WESTLEY, BRENDA ZIMMERMANN, AND MICHAEL QUINN PATTON, TRANSFORMATION RESEARCHERS[1]

1

The story of Tanaland

'Everything we do or don't do affects the whole. We are all co-creators. Of course, we can't deliberately bend the world to our will, but, with the decision we make, we contribute to the whole. It is from this participatory experience that our unbreakable responsibility to preserve this world grows.'

HANS-PETER DÜRR, PHYSICIST[1]

Tanaland is a region somewhere in East Africa. A river runs through the area and widens into a lake. Some of the area is covered with forest, but the dominant landscape is grassland. It is home to zebras, leopards, monkeys, and two villages housing two different ethnic groups, the Tupis and the Moros. The Tupis are farmers. Their village on the shore of the lake is surrounded by vegetable gardens and fruit trees. The Moros are herdsmen. They spend their days out on the plain, driving their herds of cattle and sheep between watering holes. They also sometimes hunt. Life in

Tanaland is tough, but not impossible.

In the mid nineteen-seventies, the German psychologist Dietrich Dörner gave twelve students the opportunity to improve the situation in Tanaland as development workers, and afforded them a great deal of freedom to do whatever they thought best. They could clear the forest, dig wells, build dams, buy tractors, use artificial fertilisers and insecticides, employ doctors, or electrify the entire area if they believed that would improve the situation. The students included agricultural scientists and biologists, as well as psychologists and law students. Despite their wide range of specialisations, all the students' actions were successful initially.[2]

Better medical care reduced the infant mortality rate, and the population grew. Fertilisers increased agricultural yields, meaning everyone had more to eat, and, since the introduction of the intense hunting of the leopard population, the herds were thriving. After just a short time, the rookie development workers seemed to be in control of the situation and to have solved the most pressing problems. So it was all the more surprising when devastating famines soon set in and the population shrank. After some time, life for the Tupis and the Moros was far worse than it had been before the students' interventions. Eventually, almost all the students left Tanaland in a far worse state than any colonial exploitation could have done, as the German news magazine *Der Spiegel* noted back in 1975.[3] Of course, this was the complete opposite of what the students intended.

You've never heard of Tanaland, you say?

And nor could you have. Tanaland is nothing but a computer simulation used by Dörner to investigate how good humans are at solving complex problems, and when they fail — as the students did all-too-clearly in Tanaland — why that is. Determining the causes of failure was the great puzzle of this experiment.

Why do things that initially show amazing success suddenly stop working? Why does every attempt to solve a problem of this kind always start to make things worse at some point?

We can all think of examples of this 'logic of failure' as Dörner called it. When couples are newly in love, they often manage to resolve any difference of opinion with understanding and affection, or to write them off as unimportant. But for many couples that works increasingly less well over time. And many people who find themselves rising rapidly up the career ladder at the start of their professional lives — as long as they are prepared to work around the clock — realise a couple of years down the line that such behaviour is more likely to lead to professional burn-out than to a promotion. The saying 'the more, the better' is of little help here.

Take fossil fuels, for example: There is no doubt that we have generated an amazing level of prosperity in the 200 years since we started burning coal and oil to produce our energy; but, at the same time, exploiting those energy sources is propelling us ever faster into ever-deeper crises. First boom, then bust.

Why is that?

The students who failed to guide Tanaland into a stable future did not fail because they lacked any particular essential ability. Rather, the point of the computer simulation was 'the ability to apply ... common sense to the circumstances of a given situation', as Dörner put it—in the same way we often do to solve problems in our daily lives.[4]

When the students realised that one of the reasons for the terrible food-supply situation in Tanaland was that some of the crops were being eaten by monkeys and mice, they tried to control the pests with poison. But once the monkeys and mice that the native leopards had previously preyed on were gone, the big cats began to kill the sheep. When the students then killed the leopards and sold their skins to buy more cattle, the much-increased herds overgrazed the grassland. Also, the mouse and monkey populations exploded once again. When the students drilled wells to water the fields, the crop yields increased and the population grew, leading to the need to drill more wells. This resulted in a drop in the groundwater level, drying up the wells and causing crops to wither in the fields and the people to starve.

Just as the students in the experiment did, most people around the world act according to learned routines that seem obvious to them. And then they are constantly surprised when today's solution leads to tomorrow's problems.

Sounds like a vicious circle?

If it were a vicious circle, we would have no possibility of breaking free of it. We would be doomed to fail. But there is no such thing as an unchangeable vicious circle. Rather, there are complex, or even highly complex, problems—and often it is not until things really start to rattle and shake that we learn to see and react to them as such. We perceive them as a vicious circle only if we fail to do precisely that. When we fail to solve a complex problem, following the same strategy, only more efficiently, will often not lead to success. It is then time to rethink the strategy. And, perhaps even more crucially, to rethink the very way we understand the problem.

This is precisely what the Tanaland experiment teaches us.

At first, the students took their time in making decisions. They asked questions, tried to get their bearings and understand the interconnections, and they were successful. However, the longer they played the simulation, the less they thought things through and the fewer questions they asked, while the number of decisions they were making, and the rate at which they were making them, increased dramatically. At some point, they decided they would no longer deviate from the plan they had adopted, no matter what they were told about the situation of the people in Tanaland.

One participant, for example, decided to irrigate the grasslands to turn them into agricultural fields. To this end, he decided to build a long canal to carry water from the river. He encountered countless obstacles to his plan — for example, a lack of building materials, or bad coordination. When famine eventually arrived, the man had invested so much in his idea that he ignored the starvation that his plan was originally meant to prevent. Now he had other problems: he was determined to finish the construction of his canal. Indeed, many of the students increasingly received the recurring reports of famines caused by their decisions with indifference, or even cynicism. Eventually, some of them believed it was the Tupis' and Moros' own fault that they were starving. Others suspected their professor of having programmed the simulation deliberately to make the problem unsolvable. Either way, they no longer had the feeling that the solution to the problem lay in their hands.

Knee-jerk reactions, followed by confusion and anger when they did not have the desired effect. This resulted in endless unrealised projects, accusations, inflexibility, or a retreat into conspiracy theories. Sound familiar? Take just one look at our modern society, and it's clear to see: Tanaland is everywhere.

So what's the way out of this so-called vicious circle?

When dealing with a complex problem, we are used to taking an analytical approach. We break the problem down into its constituent parts, examine each one in isolation, and identify the weak point. We then replace any parts that are broken, put everything back together, and expect the fault to be fixed. This is also the way we like to see the world. We break it down into its components in the belief that once we have understood all the individual parts well enough, and/ or have 'repaired' them, the whole will behave like the sum of its parts — and its behaviour will therefore be predictable. But, unfortunately, that's not the way it works.

A political party changes its leader again and again, but no matter who is heading the party, it's simply no longer capable of winning elections. A new road is built to relieve the traffic load on other routes, but it is soon gridlocked without easing the congestion elsewhere. A company executive checks into a clinic to cure his burn-out, but, as soon as he looks at his busy schedule on his first day back at the office, already feels ready for a holiday.

In all these examples, the problem is not located in
one individual part, which is why it cannot be solved
by a detailed analysis that aims to put the cause of the
problem down to a faulty or missing component. It is the
relations between individual parts, the way they interact
with each other, that promotes a certain dynamic and
produces undesired results or failures. If you want
to change that, you first have to understand those
interactions. Otherwise, you will fail to see the wood for
the trees.[5] Or the traffic for the cars. Or the society for
the people. Individual elements, but not the interactions
among them. However, it is from those very interactions
that the quality of the individual elements emerges, and
which determines the direction they will develop in.
Individuals and single elements are important, of course.
But development processes are born out of the relations
between them. And a group of interconnected relations
is what we call a system.

Donella Meadows, one of the pioneers of our
understanding of complex systems, describes a
system as 'a set of elements or parts that is *coherently
organised* and interconnected in a pattern or structure
that produces a characteristic set of *behaviours*, often
classified as its "function" or "purpose".'[6] Her landmark
work, *Thinking in Systems*, provides a constant point of
reference throughout this book.[7]

We encounter complex systems everywhere in
our day-to-day lives. We often do not notice them

until they stop working. We use phrases such as 'the economic system', 'the financial system', 'the ecosystem', 'the healthcare system', and 'the cardiovascular system'. But only when they fail—as in a recession, a stock market crash, a collapse of the bee population, a need to triage patients, a heart attack—do we realise that our existence is maintained and supported by something that continues to function in the background as a matter of course. In the case of cars, it's a breakdown; in our relationships, it's a fight with our partner; in a democracy, it's radicalisation; and in ideological matters, it is doubt—*if* we succumb to it.

Once you know what to look for, you begin to see systems everywhere—and realise you are a part of those systems yourself.[8]

Where does all the water, food, and oxygen that keeps our bodies running come from? How are the substances then excreted by us humans transformed back into clean water, healthy food, and oxygen? That certainly could not happen without the systems we like to call collectively 'the environment', which we are now systematically polluting and destroying.

Although the existence of systems is such an obvious fact, we have lost our knowledge of them over time. It has been replaced by a reductive approach that picks the world apart in ever-more specialised ways. The holistic view, which prevailed before the Enlightenment and the Age of Modernity, disappeared, and only gained increasing traction once again in Western science after the Second World War, with the advent of ever-more powerful computers.[9]

Computers have made it possible to model even very complex systems, to feed those models with huge amounts of data, and to run them to test their reactions to different interventions. However, for scientists and societies used to thinking reductively, viewing the world as a collection of systems means taking a broader perspective and increasing the set of patterns we use to interpret and organise our coexistence. And, in some cases, to make a radical reappraisal of them. Like any fundamental change or paradigm shift, such a reappraisal cannot happen overnight, and it feels far more difficult than sticking with short-term solutions to a problem that we believe we understand well. However, the rewards for making such a change are all the greater: breaking out of the vicious circle.

In many academic disciplines — from medicine to sociology, and from environmental science and pandemic control to digitisation — it has become commonplace to investigate problems or failures in the context of the systems they are embedded in. But this still appears to be a difficult pattern of behaviour for societies to adopt. As societies, we continue to break down the big picture into its individual aspects and force them to fit supposedly universal templates. The market or the state. Growth or no growth. Environmental goals versus social goals. The global North versus the global South. This reduces many conflicts to an either-or issue, a partisan zero-sum game.

In this book, I would like to show the value of systemic thinking both in the discussions we engage in every day, and in the way we analyse and organise the structures of our society. Incidentally, systemic thinking also entails thinking beyond limits and limitations—simply remarking 'everything is connected' is little help if we want to take strategic action. But a systemic view is one that constantly evolves, which means that as a matter of principle it takes into consideration the fact that the future can develop dynamically in many different directions, and that any given moment is just one of many equally possible moments. This means that limits are not hermetically sealed, but variable. We infer them from the description of any given problem, and even—as we will see—actively seek them out. Thus, systemic thinking neither pretends there are no limits to certain developments since anything can be replaced somehow, nor does it make explicitly quantified, long-term linear predictions about results. Rather, an evolving study of systems seeks to understand and influence possible development patterns.

Taking a systemic approach therefore changes our perspective on where we should intervene to make changes to complex problems or their root causes. And, along with that new perspective, our ideas about how that might be possible also change. It broadens our spectrum of possible strategies and solutions. And, perhaps most importantly for me, it begins to draw our attention to the structures through which we organise interactions, and the way we influence the behaviour of individual parts or elements of those structures. This helps us to avoid apportioning blame to individual parts, and instead to identify the so-called system traps that make us believe we are stuck in a vicious circle.

Such system traps are present in all areas of our lives, and they are the focus of the second part of this book. The third part takes us back to the place where change begins: ourselves. According to my view of the world, it will not be artificial intelligence or technological revolutions that shape our future in a positive way. They also depend on the possibilities of human imagination. Artificial intelligence can only perform the tasks for which it is programmed by humans — and, on the occasions when it is switched off, that is also the work of humans. Thus, the roots of social development lie within ourselves. Understanding them is also a far more exciting endeavour than seeking our salvation in machines. It is full of vitality. And learning. 'We can't impose our will on a system,' writes Donella Meadows, but 'we can listen to what the system tells us, and discover how its properties and our values can work together to bring forth something much better than could ever be produced by our will alone. We can't control systems or figure them out. But we can dance with them!'[10]

That may be a sobering thought in these crisis-ridden times, as management and control are precisely what we yearn for when things get out of hand—I'm put in mind, for example, of the much-vaunted return to 'normality' during the pandemic. If we take a systemic view of the present, however, we see that this normality is also a dynamically evolving structure made up of different developments.

The issue of whether the extent of the social and environmental side effects of something is 'normal' is a political one. From a scientific point of view, any condition existing in the present will inevitably be different in the future. A temporary state of stability in the running of routines and processes should not be mistaken for the working of a machine. Societies don't work like machines, not even very complicated ones. And complex systems that, to a certain degree, have a life of their own are not the same as complicated systems.

This systemic perspective teaches us that it is 'normal' to expect the solutions of today to become the problems of tomorrow. That there are no universal blueprints, no great plan that, once forged, will work forever and that must be defended against change at all costs. Systemic thinking also teaches us that it makes sense to begin as early as possible gradually adapting structures to the goals we ultimately want to meet—while, incidentally, always questioning precisely what those goals are. It also teaches us the limits of forecasting, management, and control, especially when we have paid too little attention for too long, or when we have failed to recognise growing problems, leading us to feel we are caught in a vicious circle. This takes us away from the vain illusion that everything is possible and towards greater humility. From a zero-sum game to coevolution. From division to connection. From system traps to dancing with systems.

That's all well and good, I hear you say, but even dancing requires some rhythmic and choreographic rules. Aren't there any guidelines at all?

Yes, there are. Anyone who deals with complex systems—as defined by Donella Meadows—should keep three things in mind in particular: their networked nature; their dynamic changeability over time; and their purpose. Any complexity researcher would call this a massive oversimplification, but I consider this trio of characteristics to be a good starting point for understanding the essential ideas behind what has variously been termed a profound paradigm shift, an epochal turning point, a second renaissance, or a Great Transformation.[11]

This amounts to nothing short of a reconfiguration of our core ideas about learning and progress, our use of technologies, and the design of our public administrations. A vision of a world population living in mutually cooperating states arose in the 20th century, but today's crises mean that goal is slipping out of sight. We cannot face the upheavals of the 21st century using the same patterns of cooperation that were often the cause of those very upheavals in the first place. The next three chapters examine more closely the three features of complex systems mentioned above. If we keep them within our sights, we will be in a far better position to understand systems and how they function, what rhythms they follow, and where they can eventually lead us. And then we will see more clearly which features require an update.

2

Networked: everything is connected

'A complex system is dynamic, it moves, it changes, it evolves, it is, in a certain way, "alive".'

UGO BARDI, CHEMIST[1]

Peter and Paul are two nondescript lakes in northern Michigan. Like a pair of wings, they sit on either side of a gravel track leading through an almost-deserted area. There is little other than lakes, forests, and gravel for miles around. The two lakes would be difficult to find in this wilderness even with a map. They are simply too small—just two pinheads in the middle of nowhere. And yet there are few places in the world that demonstrate more clearly than Peter and Paul Lakes what it means for systems to be fundamentally networked.[2]

The US ecologist Stephen Carpenter selected the two lakes as the subject for an experiment in the summer of 2008. At that time, they were typical habitats for small, planktivorous fish such as minnows and golden shiners, whose diet consists mainly of water fleas, which in turn feed on algae. Carpenter is a biologist specialising in freshwater habitats, with a particular interest in the ecological balance in inland waters. He investigates the processes that lead to the development of such an equilibrium in lakes.

For this experiment, Carpenter and his team of researchers released twelve largemouth bass into Peter Lake — a species that preys on other fish and that can grow to a length of up to a metre. The team repeated the procedure a year later, this time releasing thirty bass into the lake. The scientists then documented the fish population in Peter Lake over the next three years. They placed fish traps by the shore and monitored them daily, counting the fish before returning them to the water. After three years, the population of the small prey fish was only a fifth of its original quantity. By contrast, the predatory fish population had increased by a factor of twenty.[3]

The appearance of Peter Lake also changed considerably. Before the experiment, the lake had a green glint to it, due to algae in its waters. The introduced predatory fish reduced the population of the prey fish so much that the lake's water flea population exploded. That boom rapidly led to an almost complete eradication of algae from the lake, after which the water fleas had no source of food, causing their population to quickly collapse again. The experiment left the water of Peter Lake clear and transparent. The neighbouring Paul Lake, which the researchers had left untouched as a control, was still as green as ever.

In Peter Lake, Carpenter had transformed *a set of elements that is coherently organised in a way that achieves something.* He had changed that 'set' to such an extent that it turned a lake dominated by prey fish into something quite different: a lake dominated by predatory fish.

The story of Peter and Paul Lakes is a powerful illustration of the way that systems are always more than the sum of their parts. Their parts or elements are interconnected to form a single unit in such a way as to create a shared development dynamic. This explains why none of the constituent parts can be replaced without there being consequences. If an element is added, or an existing element is changed, the whole system changes. And, over time, so do the elements themselves. That may be innocuous at first, but the more often, or the more deeply, you intervene, the more noticeable the response from the other parts of the system becomes, until the behaviour of the entire structure eventually changes.

Viewing systems as mere collections of individual parts blinds us to this evolving interplay, and we simply see a mass. That can be sufficient when dealing with more or less lifeless masses. For example, I can move around small piles of sand as much as I like without it having a great effect on the nature of the sand or the environment it is in. But if that sand develops into a dune, hosting plant and animal life, and is subject to the influence of wind and water, what was just a mass of sand becomes a system. It is the life that develops on the dune that makes the difference.

By the same token, people also do not form small individual masses, but living systems — whether as families, companies, or societies. The interplay between their members engenders something bigger than each individual is or can ever be. In families, for example, we see that the actions of individuals within the network of relationships always have an impact on the other members of the family. If we care about the wellbeing of the system, we take the others into consideration. If we don't care about it, then, at some point, the family's everyday life — between the breakfast table, work trips, and parents' evenings — is likely to become less harmonious.

Even if you went to live in a forest in absolute isolation, you would soon realise that knowledge of the plants and animals living there is pretty important for your survival. The German physicist and epistemologist Hans-Peter Dürr therefore says that we should not speak of parts or elements in living systems, but of participants.[4] And, when talking about systems made up of human beings, he suggests that we should speak of effectors. We have an effect on each other, whether we want to or not. Our actions influence the subsequent reactions in a system; everyone's behaviour has an effect on the people around them.

Try it for yourself.

For a day, react to everything you encounter with interest and openness. Even on social media. Instead of responding with 'You must be out of your mind!', try something like 'I've never looked at it that way, tell me more!' Then watch what happens when you act as an effector. Even if you fail to find any common ground with the other person, the experience both of you have will probably be a different one — and it may influence your reactions to other things for the rest of that day.

In other words, positivity and civility are just as infectious as negativity and verbal abuse. Positive experiences shape what we call reality just as much as negative ones do. Which simply means that the state of the world is partly shaped by the way we view it. This is because that view shapes the way we approach, understand, and form the world around us. This realisation opens up huge opportunities. It is the gateway to changing our social systems.

Let's take our common notion of cause and effect. We are all great fans of the idea that we can achieve precisely the effect we desire if we take the right action—problem seen, problem solved. That was precisely the attitude of the students who wanted to save Tanaland. They were thinking reductively—that is, in a highly oversimplified way—ignoring any complexity or connectedness, and striving fiercely for one thing: to find the one solution that would work. This way of thinking is also particularly popular today, because the competitive, performance-oriented society we live in principally favours those who come up with the quickest and easiest solutions. At the expense of all others.

'We are constantly driven by the determination to hold an even bigger piece of the world in our hands,' writes Hans-Peter Dürr. 'And that is how competition and competitivity became the guiding principles of our age. Competition means we must always run faster than the rest. The direction we run in is of secondary importance; the main thing is to finish the race first.'[5]

Unfortunately, such an approach usually leads us to tackle individual symptoms, rather than getting to the roots of a given problem. As we saw clearly with Tanaland and Peter Lake, we can never make adjustments to one thing without also affecting others, and every intervention has multiple side effects, some of which can be undesirable. It's basically what's printed on the leaflet inside every pack of drugs. Of course, the human body is also a complex system, and every time we take medicine, we are intervening in that system and affecting not just one element of it, but all of them. When we take antibiotics to cure a case of bronchitis, the medication kills not only the bacteria responsible for the illness, but also the microbes that live in our gut and help support our body's immune system. If we rely too heavily on antibiotics because they work so well, or take them even for a slightly sore throat, for example, it can lead over the long term to bacterial resistance, and the medication that cured our bronchitis the last time will no longer work. Less can sometimes be more: it was not for nothing that the United Nations Environmental Programme declared the rapid increase in resistance to antibiotics to be a global threat in 2017.[6]

Thus, if we want to keep a system in the desired state, or, on the contrary, to change it, we must learn in as much detail as possible how its parts are connected—and that brings us to the first of our three features. That knowledge enables us to judge how the system is working at any given time and which parts are connected to which others, be they fish, fleas, and algae—as in the case of Peter and Paul Lakes—or bacteria, resources, people, money, or other information. If we go too far in reducing a problem's complexity by intervening within a system, we will lose sight not only of important causes, but also of equally important effects. That is why it is helpful always to question what elements we consider relevant for the understanding of any given problem.

———

With his experiment, Stephen Carpenter wanted to find out not only how a problem can become so bad that it leads to the transformation of an entire system; he also wanted to find out whether it is possible to predict when a system will reach that stage. He scoured his collected data for anything that might have indicated before it was too late that the lake was approaching a tipping point.

Were there any signs that such a change was imminent? Precisely how many fish did it take to push the lake over the edge?

Some time prior to his experiment at Peter Lake, Carpenter was sitting around after a conference with some colleagues who were also interested in such transformations. One was an ecologist who was researching a species of insect whose caterpillars regularly caused huge damage to forests. The caterpillar population seemed to explode as if out of nowhere every few years. They ate their way through the trees, stripping hectares of woodland bare of leaves, and there seemed to be no way of predicting the population booms. The only indication that such an outbreak was imminent was the fact that, shortly before such a boom, large numbers of caterpillars would suddenly appear in some parts of the forest, while in other parts very few were present. Carpenter observed precisely the same phenomenon at Peter Lake. A few days before the lake reached what he later recognised as a tipping point, the distribution of prey fish in its waters suddenly became uneven and erratic. Some of the researchers' traps would be teeming, while others were almost empty.

The two scientists found no explanation for this pattern of behaviour. But an economic mathematician who also happened to be present at the gathering was listening to their conversation. He told them about an interesting phenomenon called 'critical slowing down'.[7] It is often seen in systems that are approaching a tipping point. In such a phase, they require longer and longer to recover from disturbances and to return to their formerly stable state of equilibrium. They need to find a new balance. And if that is not possible with the system's old structure, the only option is structural change — that is, transformation.

The critical slowing-down model is very useful in many branches of research. It also occurs in social transformations. Long before critical slowing-down phases were described as such, the Scottish anthropologist Victor Turner referred to them as 'liminalities' — periods between 'no longer' and 'not yet'. And the Italian philosopher and political economist Antonio Gramsci referred to such a phase as an 'interregnum', an interim period in which 'the old is dying and the new cannot be born'.[8]

Isn't that precisely the situation we find ourselves in right now?

The discovery of the fact that systems show patterns of critical slowing down before undergoing radical change is important because the number and scale of the indications can work like an early-warning system: a clustering of unusual events and an increase in extreme fluctuations indicate that a system has already come close to its tipping point.[9] Any further disturbance in the system's equilibrium can have an enormous effect. There is no other time when the likelihood of events gaining an unstoppable momentum is greater. Suddenly, what seemed unthinkable only a short time ago becomes eminently possible.

The irrigation canal in Tanaland and the events at Peter and Paul Lakes are not isolated examples of this — it is also evident in humanity's interactions with the Earth as a whole.

In 2009, a group of Swedish climate scientists led by Johan Rockström came up with the concept of planetary boundaries. The idea rapidly gained traction far beyond scientific circles, becoming a central point of reference not only in the field of Earth system science, but also in the debate over international sustainability policies.[10] The concept is based on a view of the entire Earth as one complex system. Within that system, the scientists defined nine processes that were distinct but all interlinked. Each one is critical for life on Earth. They are the foundations on which human existence is built.

The nine areas cover not just climate change and the state of the oceans, but also freshwater use, biodiversity loss, and the parts of the Earth that are covered with forests, wetlands, and grasslands. They also include less well-publicised issues, such as the biospheric nitrogen and phosphorous cycles, which are of fundamental importance to all life on Earth. Without nitrogen and phosphorous, and their compounds, there can be no plant growth. That's why they are used as agricultural fertilisers. When they are employed in large amounts, they flow down rivers to the sea, where they can cause widespread algal blooms that deplete the water's oxygen, creating huge dead zones where life is all but impossible. By 2019, 700 such dead zones had been identified in the world's oceans. They had almost doubled in number in the previous ten years.[11]

The researchers applied a simple question to each of these areas: where are the absolute, non-negotiable boundaries of natural cycles within which the disturbances caused by humans can remain without throwing the nature of the entire Earth system out of kilter?

Or, in even more simple terms: how much more can we heat up the Earth's climate? How many more animal and plant species can we allow to go extinct? How much more forest can we clear, how much more fresh water can we use, how much more can we acidify the oceans—until the ecological system as we know it undergoes radical change?

The answer turns out to be: Not much more.

We have already overstepped five of the nine planetary boundaries, taking us out of what the Johan Rockström and his research team call a 'safe operating space for humanity'. These are the boundaries of climate change, biodiversity loss, the nitrogen and phosphorous cycles, land use, and, as of only recently, 'the release of new entities in the biosphere', which includes plastics and other chemical pollutants.[12] Each of those areas is now in increasing—or already extreme—danger of collapse, because they have become too fragile to absorb any more human interference. If we are to prevent their collapse, the researchers say, we urgently need to change our way of life, our economic behaviour, and our level of consumption. And time is running out. If we fail, an unstoppable process of destabilisation will set in. The eventual result will be a system with different structures and qualities.

We get the same message from the metaphor of the much-mentioned tipping point—which will be the focus of the next chapter—when we examine the dynamics of how our trio of features develop over time. In view of the networked structure of systems,

we can already see the importance of developing
strategies to avoid such tipping points and to think in
the same networked way as the problem to be solved
is structured. If we break the problem down into too-
detailed parts — that is, if we think reductively — we
will miss the core of the issue. And most probably
provoke the next symptom.

Let's take the issue of mobility. At present, we might
believe we are moving closer to saving the world if we
run our cars on electricity, rather than on diesel or petrol.
But if we are really to slow down climate change — it
is, after all, the strategy we are discussing to achieve
that goal (and the third of our three features) — that
electricity must not come from coal-fired power
stations. This will require the installation of far more
wind turbines and solar panels. However, producing
them will require the extraction and processing of huge
amounts of iron ore, copper, bauxite, and so-called rare
earths — and they will need to be mined and transported
using machinery that also runs on green electricity, so
that we don't end up still heating up the climate, but
by the back door. That might not be impossible, but to
extract those ores, forests will again need to be cleared,
grasslands ploughed, and swamps drained — all natural
sinks for the very carbon dioxide we are trying to stop
being emitted by technological means. Not to mention
the fact that the mining of ores destroys water cycles,
biodiversity, and natural habitats, putting pressure on

the other parts of the Earth system that we heard about above in the context of planetary boundaries. While energy can be sourced in a sustainable and carbon-neutral way from solar, wind, and hydro power, that isn't necessarily the case for the hardware required to harvest it, or for the production of all the necessary electric vehicles, batteries, and charging stations. If we want to assess the value of electric vehicles for the mobility revolution and climate protection, we must look beyond just the automobile emissions saved. We must include the emissions and other environmental impacts caused by the manufacture of those cars and the infrastructure necessary to run them. They cannot be ignored if our assessments are to be honest.

Simply switching out the combustion engines in our cars for electric motors is a case of what the inventor of Tanaland, Dietrich Dörner, called the 'preoccupation with immediate goals'.[13] It means that we become too fixated on solving the problem that seems most pressing — an example of this in the context of electromobility is the preoccupation with removing greenhouse-gas emissions from the traffic and transportation system. It's a typical case of treating the symptoms while ignoring the big picture. That is borne out by the consequences of such behaviour. For example, a massive increase in the number of electric vehicles in our cities would leave even less space for cyclists and pedestrians. It would not lead to the creation of any new parks or green areas. There would still be congestion, but now with added pressure to build more roads and parking spaces. That would do little to improve the attractiveness of the urban environment, and people would continue to move to the suburban countryside and commute far too often to the cities. In a nutshell: in solving one problem, we would again be creating or exacerbating others.

Reducing the mobility revolution to the introduction of electric cars is a good example of our habit of stopping asking questions far too early about the root causes of the problems we wish to solve. And of how we easily lose sight of the long-term goals we wish to achieve with our many gradual investments and innovations.

Do we want to preserve our traditional traffic and transport structure as the masses of vehicles continue to grow — and, if so, at what price is that even possible?

Or do we want to preserve something of value and create new structures that solve as many problems as possible at once?

If so, we must stop fixating on cars and the infrastructures built for them, and turn our attention to the problem of how to bring about reliable, individual, and sustainable mobility. The question then becomes one of what the needs for mobility are and how they can be met with the fewest side effects possible. It then also becomes important to examine why we want to be so mobile at all. No one enjoys commuting constantly. Urban and land-use planning that reflects those needs, the use of automated shuttles or high-speed and night-train networks, or even the adoption of reduced working hours and more time spent working from home are examples of very diverse strategies to reduce traffic volumes, as is making alternatives such as cycling as attractive as they are inexpensive.

According to a study published by Lund University in Sweden, every kilometre travelled by car costs society around 27 eurocents.[14] This is not a reference to buying fuel — that's paid for by motorists themselves — but to the cost of building and maintaining roads, and repairing the damage caused by accidents, noise, and air pollution. Those costs are borne by every one of us, even those who don't drive. By contrast, every kilometre travelled by bike saves society a good 30 cents, not only because most of the costs involved in driving are not incurred. It also takes into account the fact that cycling is simply healthier, and so reduces healthcare costs that would otherwise have been borne by society.

To constantly question the cost of investing in a different future is to fail to recognise that it has now increasingly become more costly to leave things as they are. Maintaining the status quo can be a real money pit.[15]

The case of the electric car is enough to illustrate the fact that the transformations we must bring about go far beyond technological innovations. They concern more than just replacing one type of motor with another. The necessary changes go far deeper. They must reconcile social, environmental, and economic aims. At its core, the transformation we must tackle is a cultural one. Let's face it: this is about nothing less than our future—how we want to live, who we want to be. It sounds like a big question, but it is one that helps us examine the goals or purposes to which we have aligned our social systems until now. In uncertain times, in an interregnum, that higher purpose is the guiding star by which we must navigate towards the future.

Does that sound esoteric? Well, it is precisely the premise upon which economic models and the primary goal set out in the constitutions of nation states are based: achieving the greatest happiness for the greatest number of people, or pursuing the wellbeing of the population. If the circumstances we live in change radically, the means by which we seek to achieve those aims will also have to change radically. Of course, when it comes to implementing that change, there will be uncertainties, resistance, distribution problems, and disputes. That should come as no surprise—it is perfectly natural.

Yes, but you may ask, aren't our societies already overwhelmed by the upheavals that loom on the horizon? Won't resistance inevitably increase as the pressure continues to rise?

First of all, from a systemic perspective, resistance against change is simply a sign that a system is robust and/or stable. The interaction of its parts and the relations between them are designed to be self-sustaining. However, that interaction is always adaptive, meaning it develops continually over time. Therefore, overly powerful resistance in one part can cause resistance across the entire system to decrease. In the case of societies, that does not mean the adaptations will all be immediately obvious, or that they will provide no cause for concern, or that they will come easily. And there is always a range of several possible developments, so evolving an appropriate and shared understanding of the problems is a good start towards turning an interregnum into a new understanding, in turn leading to the creation of something new that involves and enjoys the support of many people.

So there is one thing we must avoid if we are to come to a new understanding of problems: a culture of one-upmanship and domination. I will return to this point in more detail in the second part of this book. In times of upheaval, we must get to the root of problems in order to retain a good, well-functioning compass. We can find examples of how that can be done in the behaviour of toddlers. They keep on asking 'why?' about something, and don't give up until they have finally understood it. They stick with their questioning until they reach something like the ultimate reason. *Does it really have to be this way?* opens up a direct path to innovation. For me personally, at least, remembering the supposed naivety of toddlers often helps when I start to feel disheartened by endless and fruitless project-planning, finger-pointing, and blaming, or professional inflexibility and abuse of power, rather than problem-solving.

Try to imagine what it would be like if our inner cities were redesigned to promote quality of life, human interaction, and safety, health, and biological diversity, rather than the smoothest possible flow of motor traffic. That would solve several problems at the one time. We would be turning a development that has caused problems at several different levels into one that creates improvements at several levels. Rather than concentrating on a single element of the system, we would open up the perspective to take in the whole picture.

Under such conditions, would we still speak of 'sacrificing' our cars? Or might we feel freed from the necessity of maintaining an expensive and resource-guzzling, but underused or often-gridlocked, vehicle?

From multiple crises to multi-solving.[16] That is the prospect opened up to us by systemic thinking.

What is the *actual* issue? Engaging with that question lifts our view of any situation. It opens us up to causes and connections. When that happens, maybe we will begin to speak less of sacrifices and proscriptions, and more about responsibilities, capabilities, mediation, behaviour, and communication. And that will lead to completely new ideas and alliances. We will see cycles that are not vicious circles, stop finger-pointing, and start feeling the rhythm of change.

The structure of our reality is one of complex systems that are networked, both internally and among each other. Therefore, if we want to stop just treating the symptoms and achieve lasting change, we cannot simply replace the individual parts of those systems. We need to understand the connections. The starting point is to identify the actual problem to be solved and understand its makeup. Along the way, we must expect to encounter unforeseen side effects. And remember: if something looks like a vicious circle, sometimes the devil is not in the detail, but in the circle itself.

3

Dynamics: how little things grow big

'When we speak of the end of the world, we must consider what the world actually is. That's a difficult question. In any case, the end of the world doesn't mean the end of all worlds. The crux of the whole matter is that when one world ends, a new one begins.'

ROBERT FOLGER, APOCALYPTIC STUDIES RESEARCHER[1]

The Gorge Amphitheatre is one of the most spectacular venues for open-air concerts and festivals in America. It is situated on a small elevation above a kind of canyon with the Columbia River flowing majestically through it. Festival-goers have two stages before them, so to speak. Bands play on the smaller stage, while the landscape plays out on the larger one behind. It was against this backdrop that one visitor to the *Sasquatch!* music festival in May 2009 happened to shoot a video that would later be shown at many a management seminar and academic lecture, because it provides a wonderful example of what happens when social systems reach a tipping point.[2]

The video shows a young man dressed only in a pair of shorts dancing away to himself. The heavy beats of a song that appears to be called 'Unstoppable' can be heard coming from the stage, but the festival seems to be going through a relatively quiet phase. Other festival-goers can be seen sitting or lying on the grass, staring drowsily at the landscape, while the young man in their midst wildly jerks his limbs around to the music, as if lost in a world of his own. After a while, he's joined by a second man, whose dance moves are even more unconventional. When yet another man eventually joins in, it starts to resemble one of those festival scenes where you wonder whether you're seeing right, or if you might have caught too much sun. But what happens next is astonishing.

Within seconds, more and more people start joining the dancers. Five at first, then ten, then more than you can count. People flock in from all sides. They come running, eager not to miss out. They cheer as they melt into the crowd, which has soon swollen to fill the entire camera frame. Almost no one is left sitting or lying on the grass. Everyone seems to want to join the dance party before the song is over. People are magically drawn to the spot where, just minutes before, a lone man was lost in a solitary dance. Now, he's surrounded by so many revellers that he's no longer visible amid the mass of bodies. The situation has changed completely in the space of less than a minute. What was just a sleepy group of people moments ago is now a dancing, jumping, cheering crowd.

That is a tipping point.

A tipping point is reached when an interaction that begins as unorganised individual behaviour becomes a collective development. It occurs when an ever-more powerful wave develops in a set of seemingly independent and unconnected movements. It is not important whether the individuals involved intended such a development from the outset. No one knows whether the first people to join the dancing man did so with the aim of spreading an ecstatic frenzy to almost everyone present, or if they were only thinking of their own experience. What is important is what happens to the system as a whole. When a system reaches a tipping point, its condition, its pattern of development changes, and—crucially—that change is not steady, but takes place in an erratic and often-unpredictable way. A dancing man motivates another man to dance, then another, and so on until a critical mass is reached and being one of the dancers no longer sets a person apart, but becomes normal for the situation.

I, too, was first shown the video of the dancing crowd during a leadership seminar. The seminar was not focussed on any specific method or formula according to which one person shows others what to do. The point was to understand the amount of persuasive work necessary if systemic change is to be not just prescribed, but also achieved in real life, and why that is so. Contrary to what we might think, the decisive factor here is not just the person who starts the dance, but also the first person who joins in. It is the first follower who shows others how to follow. Only followers can turn those who are courageous enough to try out new things into leadership figures. Without them, such people continue to be considered crazy freaks.[3]

When more and more people join a new trend, being part of it becomes more attractive to others, and the probability of feeling like a freak is reduced. The dynamics of this process are well illustrated by the dancing guy video. The trend catches on, the mood changes from laid back to ecstatic — and the system enters a new, different state. So a tipping point could also be described as a qualitative turning point.[4]

The term was coined by the American economist Thomas Schelling in 1971 when he was trying to come up with a scientific explanation for why a population group that forms the majority in a certain residential area starts moving out of the neighbourhood — even though they still form the majority — when more people from other groups start moving in.[5] He used the example of Black and White Americans, but the same effect can be seen with other distinguishing factors such as income or political affiliation, and it is not limited to the case of residential areas. In all these instances, the behaviour of a group that is significantly smaller than the majority is enough to change the entire situation.

The term tipping point did not gain real traction until nearly thirty years later, when the Canadian science journalist Malcolm Gladwell took it as the title of a book he wrote about the phenomenon. *The Tipping Point* topped the bestseller lists in many countries around the world for many years.[6] In it, the author investigates the astonishing and puzzling way that certain ideas, products, or behaviours can suddenly and without warning become a trend.

Gladwell asked himself how some restaurants are considered insider tips soon after they open, with barely a table available for weeks. Or: How did *Sesame Street*—a children's educational show, after all—manage to become such a TV favourite for generations of viewers? Why did Hush Puppies—an American brand of suede shoes considered staid and uncool until the midnineteen-nineties—suddenly start appearing on the catwalks at major designers' fashion shows, causing sales to explode just before the company was about to go under? How did the crime rate in New York go from being among the highest in America at the start of the nineties to less than half that rate within just five years? Could it really have been due to the fact that the courts suddenly started coming down hard on petty criminals such as fare-dodgers on public transport or sidewalk tricksters?

Gladwell showed how something very small is sometimes all it takes to trigger a real turnaround, but it has to be the 'right' little thing. The concept was very fitting for the time. The new millennium had just begun, and globalisation was picking up pace. A wave of new digital start-up companies hit the stock markets, buoying share prices to previously unseen heights. Those who managed to seize the golden moment became rich overnight, rather than through gradual accumulation of wealth, as was previously the case. The difference between success and failure was apparently no longer a question of luck or hard work, but of whether a person knew which levers to pull, and when, to get the most return for the least effort. At the dawn of the new millennium, it appeared that humanity had found that golden moment, and that place was the 'tipping point'.

Just a couple of years later, the German climatologist Hans Joachim Schellnhuber used the term with reference to the climate.[7] Like some other scientists, Schellnhuber did not expect that the changes to the Earth's climate triggered by human activity would continue to take place as gradually as they had seemed to until then. He believed that at a certain point, some elements of the climate system would become very sensitive to global heating — or, to put it more simply, they would change unexpectedly dramatically. Those elements included the huge ice sheets in Greenland and Antarctica, the Amazon rainforest, coral habitats such as the Great Barrier Reef off the coast of Australia, the monsoons in Asia, and the Siberian permafrost. Each of those elements is as important for the stability of the Earth's climate as an individual organ is for the healthy functioning of the human body. According to Schellnhuber, the collapse of one of these elements can trigger a chain reaction that cannot easily be stopped This was a climatological formulation of the idea that would resurface a little later as the concept of planetary boundaries.

The meaning of the phrase 'tipping point' has changed completely within a short space of time. With Malcolm Gladwell, humanity had entered a new millennium in which the tipping point promised a radiant future. Now, with Hans Joachim Schellnhuber, it had arrived in a future in which the tipping point seemed more likely to herald the end of the world. From fabulous success to Biblical apocalypse — and all explained by the idea of the tipping point.

But isn't that a contradiction?

Not at all.

Complex systems have a tipping point at which they transition to a different state quite abruptly and irreversibly — see, for example, the sluggish mass of festival-goers, as well as the global climate, which seemed so stable for so long—and that is, in the first place, just a fact, neither good nor bad. It simply points to the second of our trio of features, namely that which we encounter when we want to anticipate, compensate for, or accelerate change—the dynamics of change in a system over time.

An examination of the dynamics of a system reveals more than just the way it is networked at the present moment; we also see patterns of change over time. We see how it functions over a certain period, and what sources and resources it requires, and we can observe the size and quality of its inventory (that is, its stock of those resources at any given time), and how it develops as they are utilised. We are familiar with this from our own households—we can only only keep a sensible supply of food at home if we keep track of the contents of our fridge and pantry. And observing those patterns of change can reveal why systems sometimes appear to remain unaffected for so long before suddenly and violently reacting—assuming the system is in a condition to do so.[8] It is this dynamic momentum we are questioning when we ask what happens over time.

Let's take Greenland's ice sheet as an example, and view it as a system. More than 80 per cent of Greenland is covered by ice, making it the second-largest area of permanent ice cover in the world, after Antarctica. The ice shield is up to three kilometres thick in some places. If all of Greenland's ice were to melt, global sea levels would rise by around seven metres over several hundred years.[9] Such a scenario was long considered unthinkable. The system seemed to be stable. The glaciers shrank every summer when the temperature rose, but were replenished by the winter snowfall. There was a dynamic equilibrium between growth and shrinkage.

However, since the turn of the millennium, more of Greenland's ice has been melting each summer than is replaced by fresh snow in winter. This is because climate change has caused not only Greenland's summers to get warmer over the past thirty years, but, in winter, precipitation that used to fall as snow now falls as rain. More and more land is thawing as a consequence, and some branches of industry have already spotted an opportunity to exploit the oil reserves and other mineral resources that lie beneath the ice sheet. There is, however, a different and more interesting effect at play here, too. It has to do with the ability of surfaces to reflect light. The scientific term for this property is 'albedo'. When land is covered with ice or snow, the bright white surface reflects back incoming radiation from the Sun. When the reflective cover melts, the darker surface of the land is revealed, which absorbs the Sun's radiation rather than reflecting it. The ground warms up as a result, further accelerating the melting process.[10]

This is an example of what we call a feedback loop.

'Feedback' also describes the interactions between different parts of a system. And since living systems are not hermetically sealed off from each other, feedback effects can also include the way a system reacts to an input—in the example of the ice sheet, that input would be the constant rise in temperature due to climate change. If the system's feedback *reinforces* the effects of the input, an ever-increasing trend results. If the feedback *dampens* the input's effects, the trend is counterbalanced—in the case of the ice sheet, that would be the replenishing effect of the winter snowfall.

If one of the feedback effects is removed from a system, or if one of them increases significantly in intensity, the pattern of dynamic behaviour between the elements will change over time. That means the state of the system will also change. In the case of the Greenlandic ice sheet, the reinforcing (positive) feedback loop accelerates the melting process. As long as the glaciers maintain a certain thickness and thus height, a portion of their snow cap will protrude into colder atmospheric layers. When the glaciers melt, part of their snow cap sinks to where the air is warmer, which further accelerates the thaw. Meltwater is not as efficient at reflecting sunlight as ice, which weakens a dampening (negative) feedback loop, further warms the glaciers, and causes them to lose ice at an accelerated rate.

This may go unnoticed for a long time because the ice sheet is so thick that it has a huge buffer. But every tonne of water that is lost to the system reduces the size of the buffer, while the melting process increasingly accelerates due the various feedback effects. In systemic terms, lots of small changes that would not make much difference to the system individually are no longer added to each other, but begin to multiply. What was a gradual change becomes a rapid one, and what was a linear progression becomes non-linear or even exponential. At some point, the same input begins to have a strikingly different effect. Once critical slowing down is reached, a single additional drop of meltwater — or, if we think of Peter Lake, one additional fish — will be all it takes. The interesting aspect of this pattern, however, is the fact that the *slowing down* of an entire system's ability to absorb shocks and to regenerate often results from an *acceleration* of individual feedback loops. We might call this 'critical speeding up'. Adaptation becomes destructive transformation. The system's buffers are exhausted, and its processes permanently disrupted. And once the trends have gained non-linear momentum, they cannot easily be halted. Complex systems have no stop button to bring all their feedback loops to an immediate standstill. They have a braking distance.

We are all familiar with this effect from the Covid-19 pandemic, when the curves would sometimes skyrocket. Suddenly, there were far more new infections, hospitalisations, and deaths than the day before. In such a situation, immediately imposing a lockdown does not instantly remedy the situation. Frequent contacts between people who are infected but do not yet show symptoms means they will continue to spread the disease without that being reflected in the infection-rate curves. And today's infected people are likely to become next week's patients. The time delay between infection and symptoms means the upwards trend will initially continue, even when isolation regulations are strictly adhered to. The illness is ahead of the visible symptoms. And even if we go into reverse gear immediately, there will be some delay before we actually start moving backwards. Thus, the right moment to limit social contacts is before the situation has deteriorated too dramatically and the spread of the virus is still within tolerable limits.

Exactly the same is true of climate change—with the important difference that there is no vaccine against climate change. Promises abound that we are on the verge of some technological developments that will enable us to remove large amounts of carbon dioxide from the atmosphere, but those promises have been around a long time, and it is still very uncertain whether they will ever be delivered on. The window of opportunity for the necessary reduction of massive quantities of carbon dioxide in the atmosphere is the next eight to ten years. So our priority must be on making rapid use of the already-existing potentials for reducing it. When it comes to climate change, there is a much bigger time gap between cause and effect than with the pandemic. And so its braking distance is also longer.

We saw in the previous chapter that the networked nature of complex systems means they often behave contrary to our expectations. Their non-linear dynamic shows that there doesn't even have to be a balance between inputs and outputs in a complex system. Making many changes to the system does not mean it will change massively at once. Making a small number of changes does not necessarily mean that the resulting changes in the system will be limited in scale. And something that worked well yesterday will not necessarily work tomorrow. We can't simply make predictions about the future behaviour of the system based on what happened in the past.

If there is one lesson we can learn from the pandemic, it is that we have the reserve capacity to deal with a rising number of infected people over the short time—both in terms of the healthcare system and the economy—but not for an extended period, and not beyond a certain number of infections. There is a limit to the number of patients our system can treat. Not to mention the fact that healthcare workers' reserves are also limited, and that at some point their tank is empty.

If they are not able to regenerate sufficiently for an extended period of time, they will eventually reach a tipping point and break down. If too many people are off sick at the same time, the care system will also start to tip over.

Taking a systemic approach to crises therefore means behaving proactively, learning to be aware of future developments, and acting before they occur. That's why system scientists did not try to calculate precisely how many fish could be released before the tipping point of Peter Lake was reached. There is in fact no reliable way of doing that, especially if we are concerned with the long-term future, or if there are so many fish in the lake that they cannot accurately be counted. And so scientists such as the ones who investigate planetary boundaries observe changes in trends, and recommend urgent interventions before the effects of an imminent tipping point are felt and while it can still be avoided to some extent.

Human beings are equipped with the ability of foresight and alternative thinking. We are able to prioritise the desirable aspects of any adaptive changes we encounter. Sometimes that can lead to a breakthrough, and sometimes it can prevent a collapse. And that's something we should celebrate. So the next time someone tells you that all the prophets of doom out there just want to make your life harder, arguing that the hole in the ozone layer has shrunk again and that acid rain did not kill off our forests, just tell them about the prevention paradox: we set priorities, took a threatening trend seriously, banned chlorofluorocarbons, and introduced catalytic converters, and it was precisely that early intervention that lessened the impact of those dynamic changes. This would not have been the case if we hadn't acted to reverse the trend.

And Greenland's ice sheet? What will happen if we don't set the right priorities there? Of course, Greenland won't be ice-free by the day after tomorrow. But it does mean that the melting process will become unstoppable, once the system passes its tipping point. Some scientists believe the tipping point for Greenland's ice sheet may already have been passed.[11]

But isn't it already far too late?

This question crops up again and again in public debate. I am often asked it myself, commonly by people who feel discouraged or even panicky when they hear the scientific forecasts about the negative impact on the environment of our way of life, of doing business, and of consuming. But we also see evidence every day of how quickly the world and our social systems can react. Humanity has often surprised itself with its creativity, courage, and determination in the face of looming danger. And there's no reason it can't do that again.

There is another important aspect of tipping points and the question of whether it is too late to act: tipping points don't work like a switch with which a certain development can be turned on or off—apocalypse *on* or apocalypse *off*.

If the world warms by 1.6 or 1.7 degrees—so, more than the 1.5 degrees agreed by the world community in Paris in 2015—that won't yet be the end of the world, of course. Such a world would still be more friendly to human life than one that warmed by two, three, four, or five degrees. That's what scientists mean when they say that every tenth of a degree counts when it comes to global heating. There is not a particular point at which pursuing a transformation agenda for a future with a stable climate suddenly becomes futile. Its aim is to reverse a destructive trend and to ensure as much as possible that humanity will be able to meet its needs in the future. So the effectiveness of a scientific forecast is not measured only by how accurately it predicts what will happen. It is also measured by how well the message reaches and changes the thinking of those who decide whether that predicted future will come to pass or not—and that's all of us.

The name Severn Cullis-Suzuki is probably not familiar to you. At the age of twelve, she made a remarkable speech in front of a large international audience. 'Coming up here today, I have no hidden agenda,' she told the delegates, 'I am fighting for my future. Losing my future is not like losing an election, or a few points on the stock market. I am here to speak for all generations to come. […] In my life, I have dreamt of seeing the great herds of wild animals, jungles, and rainforests full of birds and butterflies, but now I wonder if they will even exist for my children to see. Did you have to worry about these things when you were my age? […] I'm only a child and I don't have all the solutions. I don't—I want you to realise, neither do you. You don't know how to fix the holes in our ozone layer. You don't know how to bring the salmon back up in a dead stream. You don't know how to bring back an animal now extinct. And you can't bring back the forests that once grew where there is now a desert. If you don't know how to fix it, please stop breaking it.'[12]

Sounds like Greta Thunberg?

Well, Severn Cullis-Suzuki made her speech almost thirty years earlier.

When the twelve-year-old spoke at the United Nations Conference on Environment and Development in Rio de Janeiro in 1992, politicians from almost every country in the world were meeting for the first summit since the end of the Cold War to discuss environmental matters. It was the first time the international community had discussed concrete cooperation mechanisms to coordinate the global effort to protect the environment. Severn spoke for just a few minutes. The audience applauded, some reportedly with tears in their eyes. Her speech was clear, simple, and powerful.

But it was not followed by any demonstrations, political movements, or waves of protest through society. Neither Severn herself nor the speech she gave received much attention beyond the limits of the conference hall.

When Greta Thunberg spoke at the United Nations Climate Action Summit in 2019, the picture was completely different. On a single day in the run-up to the summit, more than four million people took to the streets in almost every country in the world to call for more climate protection — probably the biggest political demonstration in human history.

Why was Greta able to trigger that reaction, when Severn was not able to do so three decades earlier?

To answer that question, let's take fossil fuel use — the foundation upon which our modern civilisation is built — and view it as a complex social system. That system is now 200 years old. It arose along with industrialisation — or industrialisation arose with the system — and it worked extraordinarily well for humanity as a whole for a very long time. Indeed, the prosperity in today's world basically rests entirely on the use of coal, oil, and natural gas to provide supposedly cheap energy. Almost every state around the world is part of this system, no matter how different their politics or economics may be, and that is due to the fact that the use of fossil fuels appeared to have no downsides. Until the nineteen-seventies, barely anyone could conceive of any negative effects of fossil fuels, beyond localised pollution. The advantages were simply too great. The global economic growth powered by coal, oil, and gas was just too impressive, and it cemented the powerful positions of those who were the winners in this system. Their success seemed to validate the system.

Studies showing the dangers of climate change were questioned or even actively opposed, even as it was becoming increasingly difficult to deny that their predictions were increasingly coming true. However, some people still pushed ahead with the search for alternative ways to provide humanity with energy. Some were even so bold as to ask whether our hunger for energy really needed to keep growing incessantly. For a time, it seemed as if technology would provide the solution. If we could get our machines to give the same or a better performance with less fuel, we would be able to slow down global heating, save the system, and avoid a major upheaval. That was the hope. But that vision has now been rebutted. The underlying trends have not changed. We still emit increasing amounts of carbon dioxide — albeit much more efficiently now. But there is no getting around the fact that the amount of carbon dioxide that the atmosphere can absorb without it resulting in rapid climate change is limited. That's why our future will be decided in the next decade.[13]

That realisation is slowly getting through to people, which explains why Greta Thunberg managed to do what Severn Cullis-Suzuki did not. For a wide variety of reasons, the system based on the use of fossil fuels has lost legitimacy in the almost-thirty years between their two speeches, and it is now ripe for change.

Ripe for change: depending on how you look at it, that can be a case of 'critical slowing down' or the right moment for renewal. In management-speak, the strategic preparation of a country—or a state—to replace outdated structures is known as 'system readiness'.[14] Transformation researchers who work on sustainable development speak of 'unlocking the lock-ins'—by which they mean proactively changing social conditions that are found to accelerate damaging trends.[15] Whether they are prepared for or come about due to lack of preparation, upheavals such as that described as an interregnum affect even systems whose structures are so deep-rooted that they encompass the entire world.

Of course, the first study to prove that our use of fossil energy sources is heating up the planet's atmosphere was not going to lead to the establishment of a permanent global-climate discussion forum such as the Intergovernmental Panel on Climate Change. But the 100th might, and that does not mean the first is any less important. It takes more than just a few warnings from scientists, just one hot summer, or just one demonstration for a society to develop an awareness of the fact that it is heading towards some very big problems. But those scientists *did* issue their warnings; the summers *have* become hotter; people *did* take to the streets to demonstrate; international conferences *were* held; and states *did* agree to concrete climate goals. Support for Green Parties has grown, and we should not forget the pioneers—the engineers and entrepreneurs—who have shown us that energy can also be harvested from the wind and from sunlight, proving that alternative energy sources for the future do exist. Finally, we have also seen the rise of social media, which can now be used to spread both scientific information and calls to mass protest extremely quickly.

Many of the changes instigated as yet may not go far enough, fast enough, but we should not underestimate the incredibly huge changes that have taken place over the past thirty years, and we should not overlook the fact that the decarbonisation project has now been generally adopted, with timetables set and power granted to courts to sanction countries and companies that do not comply. Decarbonisation is at least now seen as an official project for the future, with overarching strategies such as the European Commission's Green Deal.

None of these changes were enough on their own, but together they have prepared the fossil-based system for a fundamental change. It is only because of this that a girl who refused to go to school in protest about climate change was able to spark a worldwide movement that now calls for 'system change'—meaning a comprehensive transformation of the way we run our societies. The aim is to restore the balance between the input and output of our ecosystems so that the changes they undergo become less extreme.

In addition to the moral outrage at Putin's war crimes, the international shock triggered by his war of aggression against Ukraine showed very clearly that environmental issues are anything but mere 'green' or 'soft' issues, and actually form the foundations of life on Earth. It has become obvious to all that an interruption in the reliable supply of energy, water, and food destroys the conditions for the peaceful and healthy development of the biological species called humans. Such an interruption may be caused by acts of war or by natural processes, when ecosystems are no longer able to regenerate reliably. In responding to the disruptive shock caused by this war, it would therefore be very unwise to lose sight of the long view when it comes to those trends — neither the climate nor our biodiversity goals 'can wait'. Ecosystems have never heeded such slogans, and they never will.

Climate change does not come out of nowhere. No one acts in a vacuum, isolated from what came before or from the activities of others. Try to keep that in mind when someone tries to convince you that your actions will make no difference in the grand scheme of things because you are too small, too insignificant, or too few in number. Like when they say the factory-farming system won't be impacted by your decision to eat organically raised meat. Or that it won't make any difference to the pollution in our oceans if you stop buying anything packaged in plastic. Or that it won't make any difference to democracy if you use your vote or not. Or that what you do in our country will make no difference to staving off climate chaos because you are only responsible for a small percentage of global carbon emissions. Or that it doesn't matter what some child says about the future. You have the power to make a difference—for example, by saving energy, and by doing so demonstrating that you accept the scientific and technological bases of our existence. Another effect of your actions will be to reassure politicians and policy-makers that calls to engage in similar behaviour are not seen as edicts from an eco-dictatorship, but are pure and simple *realpolitik*.

The US environmental activist Paul Hawken once put it this way, 'When asked if I am pessimistic or optimistic about the future, my answer is always the same: If you look at the science [...] and aren't pessimistic, you don't understand the data. But if you meet the people who are working to restore this earth [...] and you aren't optimistic, you haven't got a pulse.'[16]

So don't be deceived. Take action whenever you're no longer convinced the existing situation is good, or when you feel drawn to change it. Be an *effector*. Talk about your ideas and experiences, your motivations, and your wishes for the future. And about your doubts—but remain friendly. Cooperation and collaboration are key to creating a new reality.

Tipping points are the stages when the processes in a system undergo a fundamental change. Such tipping points should be categorically avoided in the ecological systems that provide humans with the bases for their lives. However, we can use our knowledge of tipping points to expedite the necessary changes to human-made structures that are holding us back from sustainable living. Remember: even if it doesn't register immediately, seen over time, every step is a change that, if it's made at the right moment, can swiftly have a great effect.

4

Purpose: the *actual* concern

'Myth matters. Narratives sustain us. They create our thought-worlds and shape our social conversations. They legitimise political power and underwrite the social contract. [...] Sometimes myths work for us, sometimes they work against us.'

TIM JACKSON, ECONOMIST, *POST GROWTH: LIFE AFTER CAPITALISM* [1]

When Hans-Dietrich Reckhaus took over his parents' business, which had been producing household insecticides in Bielefeld for forty years, he had no intention of shaking up the industry—at least not in the way he was later to do. He had studied business administration at the elite university of Sankt Gallen in Switzerland, spent a semester at Harvard, and completed his PhD, even though his father deemed it unnecessary for the business. Reckhaus was more interested in art, science, and literature than fly paper, moth traps, and ant bait, but there was never any question that he would take over the family business. When the time came for him to do so in the mid nineteen-nineties, he still held out hope that he could divide his attention between running the company and pursuing his interest in writing and reading. But he was wrong.

Hans-Dietrich Reckhaus turned out to have a talent for the business. Soon, the company became the exclusive supplier of insecticides not just to specialised local retailers, but also to the big discount supermarkets and drugstore chains, which sold his products under their own brand names. It had already achieved an annual turnover of 25 million euros, with a workforce of sixty people, when Reckhaus had an idea for a new kind of flytrap. His innovation was to produce a flytrap in which the sticky surface had a decorated cover, so that householders were spared the ugly sight of a paper stuck full of dead flies. It was unique on the market. Reckhaus patented his idea — the first patent in the company's history. He had high hopes for the new product, which he planned to manufacture under the company's own name. But he needed an innovative campaign to publicise his new flytrap.

As the manager of a medium-sized company, Reckhaus did not have a huge advertising budget, so he approached two Swiss conceptual artists whose work he admired. Years earlier, the twins Frank and Patrik Riklin had turned an underground bunker near Sankt

Gallen into an elaborate art project that they marketed under the name *Zero Star Hotel*.[2] Perhaps they would have an idea for marketing his new flytrap? Full of expectation, he travelled to Switzerland, explained his invention to the artists, and enthused about its potential. But, contrary to his expectations, they were not very impressed.

'Your products are just bad,' they told him, 'What is the actual value of a fly to you? Instead of killing insects, you should be saving them.'[3]

The two artists suggested that Reckhaus develop a kind of cat flap for flies that caught them without killing them so that they could be released again outside. Reckhaus was nonplussed. He needed an advertising campaign for his flytrap, not for a fly flap. But as he travelled back home, the artists' question kept going round in his head.

What if they were right?

What if his products were harmful?

What if what he was doing was wrong?

That was in summer 2011, and no one outside of expert circles had even heard of such a thing as a decline in Germany's insect population. There was no public discussion of the phenomenon at the time: the alarm was not sounded until 2017.[4] It would still be years before Bavaria became the first region in Germany to hold a referendum on increasing the protection of species. Reckhaus had no idea whether his products really were harmful or, if so, what kind of harm they might cause. He was unable to find any scientific information about how many insects were killed by his company's flytraps, moth paper, insect sprays, and ant bait every year, or what value the insects might have had for nature or even humans—but he estimated that his products were responsible for the deaths of several hundred million insects a year.

But why should that bother him?

Wasn't he a businessman? Isn't the customer always right? And if customers want to get rid of insects, why shouldn't he provide them with an inexpensive means to do so? Didn't the profit he was making prove that he was doing the right thing? And if he didn't make the products, wouldn't someone else just do it instead?

Reckhaus had expected the meeting with the two Swiss artists to lead to an idea for his advertising campaign—not to an idea for a new direction for his life. But that is exactly what happened. The meeting had shaken some of the core beliefs that gave meaning and orientation to his thoughts and actions as a businessman.

In short: it challenged the purpose of his system.

Looking at the purpose or function of a system—the third feature in our trio—can help us understand why change in a system is so slow to get going, and why it appears to be so fraught with resistance. If we abide by Donella Meadows' definition, a system's purpose is the function around which it is constructed and which it is designed to fulfil. How well a human-made system fulfils its purpose is a measure of how justified, credible, or legitimate it is.

The common purpose of a company, for example, is to sell as many goods or services as possible so as to maximise profits. At least, that is what very many people consider forms the core of business activity, and that did not come out of nowhere. From at least the nineteen-seventies, under the influence of the economist Milton Friedman, the phrase *the business of business is business* became set in people's minds, creating a direct equivalence of the maximisation of profit with good business performance and development.[5] And it was according to this principle that Reckhaus ran his company.

But ten years after his meeting with the two artists that initially left him so perplexed, Reckhaus's business had changed radically. The packaging for his products now prominently displays graphic warnings that using them leads to the annihilation of valuable insects. On the back of the packages, customers can now find extensive information about the value of insects and the threats they face, as well as recommendations for how to prevent insects from entering residential spaces in the first place. Reckhaus believes that prevention advice is one of the best ways of reducing the overall market for insect-control products. A fixed amount from the sale of each product is invested in offsetting the insect losses it causes. *Kill with care* became the company's slogan. Reckhaus's first idea was to breed millions of insects and to release them into the wild. But then he was convinced by a biologist that it would make more sense to create ecological compensation areas, where insects could breed naturally. The first such area was installed on the company's roof, which was sown with more than thirty local plant species and furnished with piles of deadwood and rocks, creating an insect-friendly habitat that had not been there before.

Reckhaus had begun to turn around his business model. His activities were no longer focussed solely on what he could get out of the system, in which he was integrated, to grow his sales figures. He was now concerned at least as much with what he could put back into that system — and how that affected the system itself. 'Yesterday: earn as much money as possible, and do good in the process. Tomorrow: do as much good as possible, and earn money in the process.' That's how Reckhaus describes the change in purpose of his company.[6]

'From inside-out to outside-in' is how Katrin Muff and Thomas Dyllick-Brenzinger have described such a change in perspective. The two researchers are interested in matters of management and sustainability. Their work focusses on the question of what conditions are necessary for individual companies to be able to make a real and effective contribution to sustainability that is also verifiable — since many such company declarations remain merely that: declarations. And that has been the case for decades. They are not made the aim of company practice, nor are they used as a measure of company success. This has prompted many brilliant minds to try to create a business-based case for a sustainable economy: a more efficient use of resources also brings financial rewards, for example, or a responsible brand image breeds customer and employee loyalty. But such advances are far too little. They cannot halt the trends towards breaking our planet's boundaries.

The two researchers wanted to understand this 'big disconnect' between the sum of improvements made by businesses and the improvements to the overall economic system that are necessary. In the course of their research, they found two points to be particularly relevant. First, strategies at the micro-level (the company) and the macro-level (the entire system) do not mesh sufficiently. The decisions taken by companies are simply too disconnected from the overarching strategies at a societal level, in both planning and execution. It appears that, in practice, barely any attention is paid to the question of whether the sum of a company's actions really leads to its declared goal.

The second thing they noticed was that companies

treated their so-called Key Performance Indicators (KPIs) — performance figures that are centrally defined and usually financially expressed — separately from their indicators for sustainable development. Far more attention is paid to financial figures, while the sustainable development indicators are treated as a desirable but not necessary accessory.

In short: when causing social and ecological damage costs nothing, it is not reflected in a company's accounts. And nor is the extent to which its ability to continue doing the same business in the future depends on a stable supply of resources, and well-trained workers with their purchasing power. Perhaps the origin of the big disconnect lies precisely in Friedman's idea that business must see itself as disconnected from the world around it? This is more or less the conclusion that Dyllick-Brenzinger and Muff came to when they evoked a new stage in the development of business sustainability — a stage they call 'business sustainability 3.0' in their model.[7]

The key to escaping the 'big disconnect' lies in a 'big reconnect': companies must ask themselves how they can contribute to solving the problems of sustainability — socially, ecologically, and economically in equal measure. That is what it means to take the 'outside-in' view. It entails taking action even if it cannot be justified in terms of a direct reduction in financial expenses and risks. And it must go much farther than just reducing the environmental and social damage caused by a company's existing products and current business model. In stage 3.0, companies must reorient their knowledge, experience, resources, and competencies in such a way as to create a repertoire of products and services that enable the economic system as a whole to reach sustainability goals: aligning the purpose or goals of the company with the purpose or goals of social development.

That is precisely what Hans-Dietrich Reckhaus did. He asked himself whether the profit generated by his business came at a cost to the resources of the society that he is part of, and the honest answer he came to was that the market for insecticides was already too large to be compatible with the maintenance of sufficient populations of insects. He saw that if we are not able to reverse that trend rapidly, we will no longer be able to rely on insects to fulfil the functions they have performed until now in our ecosystems. In facing this challenge today, it helps to take an outside-in view and consider such questions as whether there really is a need for hundreds of thousands of insect traps, when there is already a shortage of insects to pollinate our plants; or whether a few remaining flies and mosquitos will be much of a nuisance when we have nothing more to eat.

Reckhaus's activities now include educating the public about the central role that insects play in providing for humans' needs. Pollinating, decomposing waste, maintaining soil quality, producing textiles, and providing a source of food, medicine, and chemicals—all of these rely at least in part on insects. That's why Reckhaus's company has a scheme to enable other companies and organisations to compensate for the damage they cause to insect populations. One of Reckhaus's ideas for reconnecting his company's objectives with the overarching social goal of creating insect-friendly habitats has now taken hold in Germany, Austria, and Switzerland. All manufacturers who not only compensate for the damage they cause but also include warnings on their products about the risk to insects are entitled to carry the 'Insect Respect' quality seal, which Reckhaus's company has developed in collaboration with scientists.

All of these things cost money, of course. Reckhaus's company initially lost a quarter of its turnover and three-quarters of its return on investment. That was until public awareness of the decline in insect populations grew, Reckhaus began winning awards for his ideas, and the big retail chains eventually discovered the problem and started stocking his products. It took a lot of patience and staying power on the part of Reckhaus, during a time when he had nothing to rely on but the feeling that he was doing the right thing. Selling up never entered his mind. Even though he was no longer invited to industry events, he had no intention of leaving the system. Rather, he was keen to find out what the *real* problem is when it comes to sustainability, to redefine the meaning of 'success', and to realign his company's purpose. And to make use of his company's entire repertoire of knowledge, experience, resources, and competence in doing so.

Among the list of what she calls 'leverage points' for changing a system, Donella Meadows considers the system's purpose to be one of the most effective.[8] The only thing placed higher are paradigms — the science-based mindset and worldview, but also moral convictions and normative narratives — in other words, all the stories we tell to shape and describe the reality we live in.

Stories — that sounds like something you might read to children at bedtime. Or something made up. Certainly, something that isn't true. But say that to any child, and they will instantly tell you otherwise. A story is true as long as people believe it.

Some of the stories we tell are indeed with us from our earliest childhood. Our view of reality is shaped by our gender, skin colour, and nationality, as well as by our social background and our family. Whether you were born in a Mumbai slum or a suburban housing estate in North Rhine-Westphalia simply *does* make a difference. What our parents tell us about the way the world works influences the way we approach that world, before we even realise that much of what they tell us is a story that our parents were in turn told by their parents. That doesn't mean we have to remain our parents' children forever. We can change the stories. We all do it. We have experiences of our own, see different things, or see the same things differently. That changes our view of the world. Sometimes it happens without us even noticing. And sometimes it takes a profound shock or a crisis. That depends on the meaning the story in question has for us.

The stories—social scientists often call them 'narratives'—that prompt people to act are pivotal in understanding what drives social development at a deep level. They create the space and the boundaries for what versions of the future we consider possible. What are considered proven facts today were for a long time no more than imagined ideas.[9] Since much of today's world is the product of our insights and narratives from the past, and since our experiences in that world influence what stories we consider to be right, wrong, convenient, dangerous, convincing, or absurd, our freedom to predetermine our future is shaped from the outset—preconstructed, so to speak.

In their book *Erzählende Affen* (*Story-telling Apes*), the writers and communication experts Samira el Ouassil and Friedemann Karig collect and evaluate around 500 pages' worth of stories that have influenced both us and our social structures: 'They carry subliminal messages across the world: supposed origins, effects, connections, conflicts, which we are seldom aware of, but which we are told over and over again and which we go on to retell'.[10]

Once we look carefully, we can see that many standard assumptions are in fact social constructions. The assumption that money represents the true value of things — and therefore that less-well paid people create less value and are therefore ultimately worth less themselves — is just such a story. The idea that an ever-more analytically understood natural world is simply a pool of resources that can be torn apart and plundered by humans to satisfy their needs without consequences is a story. The belief that women are the weaker sex, or that some of the world's cultures are less developed than others, and that the White Man in the global North created the best of all civilisations are all stories. And they become more durable the more they are written down and repeated.

In this way, the stories shared between humans become sets of rules of conduct and construction manuals. They are the source of our ideas about appropriate behaviour, and they serve as a frame of reference whenever we develop new products and services, or plan collaborations and infrastructures — and, of course, our business models.

With all the talk of stories, we must not forget that there are other ways of creating images of the world and its development—some more substantiated, sophisticated, and intelligible than others. Scientific evidence is not the same as an opinion—an argument that cropped up with increasing frequency during the heated Covid-related debates in recent years. And even before the pandemic, it was becoming increasingly clear to me that science can, and perhaps must, play a role that is both responsible and occasionally thankless.

I noticed that science plays this role as I increasingly found myself being asked to announce uncomfortable scientific findings at industry gatherings. At first, I was surprised that companies' sustainability departments would invite speakers from outside to point them in the right direction. I reasoned that my hosts had far greater and better knowledge of the specific situation in their industry or their company than I did—as someone who tends to explore the bigger contexts and connections. But then I discovered that annual congresses devoted to the overarching issue of sustainability were a new thing. Of course, there had been events dedicated to sustainability for some time. But for an entire branch of industry to place climate and environmental issues so actively and prominently at the top of the agenda at their public events was new. It was a megatrend, so to speak, which gained added momentum after the founding of the Fridays for Future movement in 2018. So it was no wonder, in fact, that companies now wanted to show themselves to be 'on trend'.

Let's take the travel industry. It has a great interest in ensuring that important destination countries such as Mauritius, for example, and other island nations, are not swallowed up by rising sea levels, or that they are not ravaged by ever-more frequent and ever-more violent storms. It is no secret that flights to and from such destinations account for a large proportion of the carbon emissions generated by tourism, and that taking many short trips and long-haul flights has a very different effect on our carbon footprint than travelling less frequently and using slower forms of transport. However, the fact that this knowledge played no part in the established business models of the airlines operating those flights did not appear particularly problematic to their bosses. After all, their customers kept demanding ever-longer flights or ever-more frequent short trips, rather than choosing more sustainable alternatives. So why not continue pursuing the usual annual benchmark for growth in passenger numbers, which ranged from 4 to 6 per cent in Germany? And when that trend was broken for the first time in 2019, causing the German Airports Association's statistics service to flash red, the airlines stuck to their policy, aiming to restore the old normality.[11]

The companies wanted to square the circle of rising flight numbers, profit maximisation, and sustainability by doing one thing above all: they told the story of the options of carbon compensation and their use of synthetic fuels. That was the point at which I understood my role. It was to exert a corrective force on the company managers' stories about the future by using my legitimacy as an external expert. For those in the company who dealt with the issue of sustainability on a daily basis as part of their jobs, it was becoming increasingly difficult to live with the discrepancy between their company's *declared* purpose and its *lived* purpose. The gap between the slogans claiming to take the climate crisis and the sustainability megatrend seriously, on the one hand, and the managers' insistence that the company's financial performance had absolute priority, on the other hand, had become too great.

The employees felt trapped in an internal company 'big disconnect', and needed outside help to have any influence at all on the finances-trump-sustainability hierarchy. As an external expert, I was able to provide academic research on the limits of carbon compensation, and to set the facts straight on the market readiness for synthetic fuels and the available volumes of such fuels and those in development.[12] My role also allowed me to highlight two further points: the production of such fuels must also be a low-emission process, and it must not use massive amounts of water; otherwise, the 'solution' will be nothing more than a postponement of the problem.[13] And I also pointed out that reducing carbon emissions is a very pressing matter if we want to meet the climate goals we have set ourselves.

So what the company sustainability officers already knew, but were either not allowed to say out loud or were ignored when they tried, was that the science-based forecasts do not match the prevailing story in the industry that technological progress will enable the number of passengers to keep on growing indefinitely without consequences. When reality and the picture we paint of it become disconnected, it becomes even more difficult to take timely action than is already the case.

Thus, if we are to understand why it is so difficult for us to let go of some stories, we must get to the root of the *purpose* that is deeply anchored in our modern systems. In that endeavour, it can be helpful to ask the question: What drives us? Just like unearthing the roots of a problem—what is the *actual* issue?—we may have to dig around a little here, since the more that something depends on one of those stories that drives us, the longer it has been seen to work well, and the more we have invested in it, the stronger our attachment to it is.

It is for that reason that this conflict tops Donella Meadows' list of 'leverage points' for intervening in a system, while adapting subsidies standards, and technological standards is at the bottom of her list. The purpose is the driving force. And as long as the purpose continues to be dictated from the inside out, the 'big disconnect' will not go away. Those with alternative proposals are often pushed to provide long, complicated justifications for their suggestions, until it becomes apparent that the old stories can no longer fulfil their promise of providing a meaningful explanation of reality. That is when they begin to falter and fall apart — and, with them, the systems whose purpose is expressed in those stories.

That is the interregnum.

That is transformative change.

And it is already happening almost everywhere.

Suddenly, we have started to see the undeniable rise in the frequency and intensity of heatwaves, wildfires, and flooding all over the world as effects of anthropogenic climate change, rather than putting them down to short-term caprices of the weather.[14]

Suddenly, multinational oil companies such as Shell, and also Germany's federal government, are being taken to court to face the charge that their climate goals and protection measures are insufficient and will therefore leave future generations with such a burden to bear that they will be unable to lead the kind of lives we do today.[15]

Suddenly, the governments of 130 countries are planning a global minimum tax rate for large international companies, in order to curb the bottom-feeding competition among the most unscrupulous tax havens.

Suddenly, there is a growing movement towards regenerative business practices, which directly confronts the problem of the internal company 'big disconnect', labelling it 'corporate schizophrenia'.

Suddenly, calculations are being developed to vastly improve the way the social and environmental effects of a business model—both positive and negative—are reflected in companies' balance sheets.[16]

Thus, anticipating the apocalypse also gives rise to insights and new stories for us to be guided by. It's the end of the world—making room for a new one. Disputes over the stories, institutions, identities, technologies, and roles it is built on will necessarily be highly political, as every different world has a different distribution of privileges, power, and vested interests.

Can't we just decide we'd rather not bother with this transformation?

No, we can't. We can't not transform.

The question is not *whether* great changes are coming. The question is how we influence those changes, give them direction, absorb the breakages, shape the transitions, and take our fate into our own hands. We have the ability to do all that. If we redefine the purpose of a system, the search for solutions will also be oriented to the new direction. We are just as responsible for the consequences if we opt to cling on to the old purpose. And if everyone continues to hide behind everyone else—claiming they are only doing what everyone has always done—the transformation will eventually be imposed on us.

But if we have the courage to implement the much-vaunted goal of a sustainable economy in a way that is equal and binding for all, we will need to worry far less about what others will think of it. In his article on behaviour during tipping points, Thomas Schelling put it this way: 'People acting individually are often unable to affect the results; they can only affect their own positions within the overall results.'[17]

If we reset the rules of the game and redefine the Key Performance Indicators for the success of strategies and solutions, those who are talented, innovative, courageous, compassionate, and interested in successful business models can promulgate very different innovations than before. In this way, we can both conserve values and transform structures. Then we will stop fixating on demise and work on what will arise.

'Where attention goes, energy flows, and where energy flows, life grows,' a systemic coach once told me. The things you often think about, and/or believe are important, direct what you spend your limited amounts of attention, energy, and time on — and lead to different outcomes.

We are bursting with potential to improve the quality of our lives and, most importantly, to maintain that improvement over the long term. The problem until now has been that we have not taken the foundations of a good quality of life seriously, nor have we earnestly considered the positive effects of changing our consumer behaviour.[18] They are rarely taken into account in our descriptions and measurements of success, freedom, and progress. They are simply not valued in that way. This keeps our concept of what is or can constitute successful progress and a good quality of life artificially small. And it keeps our concern that there is not enough to go around for everybody artificially large.

During the shaky time around the emergence of a tipping point, letting go of that which has outlived its purpose can often be more important than having 100 per cent certainty about what will come in its place. We are only free when we are in a position to stop doing something—even if at first that only involves opening up our imagination to new normalities and consigning the stories that are no longer credible to the scrapheap.

We humans, the only species capable of reflection and intention, have the ability to take conscious action with our heads, hearts, and hands. That's the difference between transforming and being transformed: somewhere between evolution and progress.

The good news is that humanity has done this successfully several times in its past. Transformative processes 'entail co-evolutionary changes in technologies, markets, institutional frameworks, cultural meanings, and everyday life practices'.[19] We've seen it all before. The Renaissance and the Enlightenment are examples of periods in Western history associated with progress. However, the birth of the civilisation we like to call normal today was far from straightforward or minutely planned. It was a searching process, shaped by new scientific knowledge and technological possibilities, new groupings of agents and fresh alliances, and wrangling over the distribution of power and legitimate institutions.

Pioneering figures in the history of ideas of classical liberalism such as René Descartes or Thomas Hobbes described that search process as a classic interregnum: new insights and ideas about the individual, nature, the state, and the economy, combined with new technological inventions and groupings of agents, brought about a 'total collapse of order', as the Danish sociologist and anthropologist Bjørn Thomassen put it.[20]

That period resembled a 'desperate search for new ordering principles', in which many pioneering thinkers were persecuted as radicals while they were destroying the order created by feudal and clerical stories and structures. Irrespective of whether such a collapse was supported by some, while others wanted to prevent it, fundamental questions came to the forefront in this period. Questions such as how we see ourselves and who we want to be. The potential of the human species lies precisely in our ability to build a compass from such questions to navigate times of upheaval. As apocalypse-studies scholars remind us, what we are talking about is the end of *a* world, not the end of *the* world.[21]

Humans are purpose-seeking and cooperative beings. Human societies are built on stories, which create a world and explain it, as well as provide the basis and justification for the decisions we make. If those stories begin to falter, entire systems that have arisen around them change. In such times, it is important to set clear priorities and find new stories to give us an orientation for what we want and what is possible. Those stories also add meaning, and are apt to spread quickly. If we stop staring into the rearview mirror and turn our eyes to the road ahead, letting go becomes much easier. And remember: from every demise, something new can arise.

Part II

Changing the Operation

'No one deliberately creates those problems, no one wants them to persist, but they persist nonetheless. That is because they are intrinsically systems problems—undesirable behaviours characteristic of the system structures that produce them. They will yield only as we reclaim our intuition, stop casting blame, see the system as the source of its own problems, and find the courage and wisdom to restructure it.'

DONELLA MEADOWS, PIONEER OF SYSTEMIC THINKING[1]

5

What *Monopoly* teaches us about the rules of the game

'The economic rules we take for granted are human inventions. We must decide which economic rules we want to keep and which we want to leave behind ...'

RIANE EISLER, SOCIOLOGIST AND CULTURAL HISTORIAN[1]

At the beginning of the last century, a young shorthand typist called Elizabeth Magie wanted to raise awareness among the American public of an economic problem that she believed explained the difference between rich and poor. So she invented a board game. The object of the game was 'to obtain as much wealth or money as possible', according to the application she filed with the American Patent Office.[2] Players had to buy the plots of land that were lined up around the perimeter of the board. If a player landed on a plot that already belonged to another player, they had to pay rent to the owner. The player who had amassed the most money by the end of the game was the winner.

Elizabeth Magie took the inspiration for her game from the ideas of the economist and social philosopher Henry George, who had gained prominence in the last quarter of the nineteenth century. He had died a few years earlier, but his ideas were still popular, even far beyond the borders of the United States. George was of the opinion that the misery, hardship, and economic crises he saw on the streets of New York resulted from the unequal distribution of land ownership. In his 1879 book, *Progress and Poverty*, he wrote that it was fundamentally unjust that a few people could take ownership of the land 'on which and from which all must live', and that this was 'separating modern society into the very rich and the very poor'.[3] The rich could grow ever richer on the income and speculative profits from the land and real estate they owned, while the poor were dependent on selling their labour to survive. To escape this trap, George suggested what he called a 'single tax' on the ownership of land and natural resources, and the abolition of all other taxes on production — that is, work — and consumption. He hoped this would have a corrective effect on a development that created ever-increasing imbalances, whose origins lay in the simple fact that some people owned land and real estate while others did not.

Elizabeth Magie also saw that inequality as key. To illustrate its effect, she deliberately designed her board game so that players who owned land always had an advantage over those who did not. While some players grew richer and richer, and soon owned railway stations or utility companies, others stumbled from rent payment to rent payment, and could only hope to avoid bankruptcy before they passed 'Go' and received a kind of wage from the bank. Every circuit of the board made them poorer — the difference from reality being that they could now finally see why.

'In a short time, I hope a very short time, men and women will discover that they are poor because Carnegie and Rockefeller, maybe, have more than they know what to do with,' Elizabeth Magie told a reporter in an interview in 1906.[4]

What Magie was basically highlighting with her game was the fact that a system functions according to certain rules, and that those rules influence the freedom of participants differently over time. She wanted people to recognise and think about those rules, instead of believing that everything they did, every result of their actions, was dependent solely on their personal abilities. This realisation was so important to her that she even included it in the game's instructions: she wrote that the game was 'based on present prevailing business methods. This the players can prove for themselves; and they can also prove what must be the logical outcome of such a system, i.e., that the land monopolist has absolute control of the situation.'[5]

Today, the name Elizabeth Magie is as little known as that of the game she invented. She called it *The Landlord's Game*. But her idea formed the basis for one of the world's most popular board games: *Monopoly*.

Players move around the squares on a board. There are streets, cards, railway stations, a jail; the square called 'Free Parking' was originally meant to represent a public park with no charge for landing on it. In essence, *Monopoly* still works today the same way as the original of more than 100 years ago did. The later addition of the option to build houses and hotels on the streets to drive other players into bankruptcy more quickly did nothing to change that. On the contrary, in fact. *Monopoly* represents a world in which winners have a structural advantage, and losers have a structural disadvantage. In other words: *He that hath, to him shall be given.*[6] Cases when the rules create a situation like this are what we call 'system traps'.

System traps are particular, recognisable system structures that lead to problematic behaviour patterns, and so are damaging to the system as a whole over the long term. An example of this is any kind of addictive behaviour in which ever-increasing doses of the source of the addiction are necessary to maintain the same state—whether they are drugs, fertilisers, or profits. There are many such system traps. We encounter some of them regularly as part of our daily lives. We often tend to place the blame solely on individual actors or events when the harmful development is unstoppable, despite all attempts to correct it. However, the real fault is within the system itself, in its feedback loops—that is, in the way it typically reacts to stimuli. If the problematic developments in the system are not recognised as early as possible, they drive people to behave in a way that results in an outcome that nobody wanted.

In her book *Thinking in Systems*, Donella Meadows gives a summary of the most common archetypal system traps, their effects, and how they can be escaped.[7] In the chapters that follow, I will apply some of those archetypes to the way we live on our planet, the way we run our economies, and the way we behave towards each other. My aim is to show how we came to be in the situation we currently find ourselves in, and how we can change it. My hope is that an awareness of the way system traps work will make us less likely to get stuck in supposed vicious circles.

'System traps can be escaped,' Meadows writes, noting that, although they perpetuate development trends, they can be changed gradually, which is why she calls these archetypes 'not just traps, but opportunities', if they are recognised in advance.[8]

Let's look at the system trap that awaits *Monopoly* players. Meadows calls this archetype 'success to the successful'. Such a system allows winners to use their winnings to ensure that they will win more in the future. This is a self-reinforcing feedback loop with no counteracting feedback to dampen its effects. The winnings just keep getting bigger and bigger — as do the losses on the other side of the equation.

Is there a way out of this trap?

Donella Meadows lists some strategies for escaping it. Losers could be given the chance to withdraw from the competition that is harming them, and start afresh somewhere else: that is the strategy of diversification. A limit could be placed on the amount one competitor can own: that is what antitrust laws aim to do. Or a periodic 'levelling of the playing field' could redress situations that have become unfair over time. Inclusive education and inheritance taxes are mechanisms without which children's opportunities in life are massively dependent on the wealth accumulated by their ancestors. Whatever the case, if we want to change the results, we need to change the rules under which the system functions. And that was what Elizabeth Magie had realised.

Very early on, she came up with a version of *The Landlord's Game* that included an optional feature called The Single Tax Rule.[9] In this version of the game, which was played on the same board, players had to pay all land rents to the public treasury. When the coffers were full, the money was used to buy railway stations back into public ownership and to provide free public transport. Certain squares remained permanently in public ownership, where free schools could be built. If the treasury continued to grow, it was used to increase wages, which were paid out on passing 'Go'—a square that Magie rather tellingly named 'Mother Earth'. There was also no longer any need for players to buy themselves out of jail. The 'Poor House', which was in the same corner of the board as the public park, was abolished. It was still the same game, but played under a different set of rules, and the outcome was quite different. The original version of the game played in this version also ended with one monopolist winning, but almost all the other players also became richer during the game.

After Magie was awarded a patent for *The Landlord's Game* in 1904, she tried to sell it to the games manufacturers Parker Brothers, but they rejected it as too political and too complex.[10] So she marketed the game herself, but without great success. However, unlicensed, hand-made copies soon started circulating, which developed into several different versions. It was one of those versions that was used by a professor at the University of Pennsylvania to teach his students about capitalism. Other copies circulated among the Quaker communities in the north-eastern United States. In 1933, an unemployed domestic-heater salesman named Charles Darrow got hold of a copy, and—as the journalist Michael Prüller puts it—recognised the potential of a game that would allow players to feel rich, if only briefly, at a time when they were going through the worst of the Great Depression.[11] He changed the game's visual design, and sold it Parker Brothers. From that moment on, *Monopoly* began to take over the world.

Almost 280,000 game sets were sold in the first year, with six times that many going over the counter in the second year. More than 250 million copies have now been sold around the world, making *Monopoly* one of the highest-grossing games of all times.[12] Charles Darrow was the world's first millionaire games producer. Magie was delighted to see her teaching game about economic inequality reaching a mass audience, and she agreed a price of $500 to sell the patent to Parker Brothers. Her original intention in inventing the game was not recognised at that time. And it remained so until the nineteen-seventies, when an American economics professor published an alternative to the game, which he called *Anti-Monopoly*. When he was sued for copyright infringement, he became interested in the origins of the game, and discovered the true story. The game that has become a by-word for greed and soulless moneymaking was originally designed to teach us that we can do better.

6

Responsibility: learning better

'Any guarantees for the human future can be sought nowhere else
but within ourselves. What is needed is for all of us to learn how to
stir up our dormant potential and use it from now on purposefully
and intelligently.'

AURELIO PECCEI, CLUB OF ROME COFOUNDER[1]

The first financial crisis of the new millennium had
been rocking America badly for some time when it
reached Europe in late 2009. At first, it appeared that
Greece was the problem, but it soon became clear that
the crisis, which was soon dubbed the 'euro zone crisis',
affected the whole and not just one of its parts. Europe's
top politicians gathered for ever-more hurriedly
organised summits. News items were full of phrases
such as sovereign debt, rating agencies, and bailouts.
Billions had to be mobilised to save some countries
from bankruptcy—but even that was not enough to

prevent real economic crises from breaking out in some states. Unemployment among young people in Greece and Spain rose above 50 per cent, while in Italy and Portugal one young person in three was jobless. People spoke of a 'lost generation'.[2]

Faced with this situation, the European Commission came up with a strategy called *Europe 2020*, which outlined an economic growth agenda for the next ten years, naming seven so-called flagship initiatives. They covered innovation, industrial policy, digitisation, and resource efficiency, but also included a strategy for addressing the concerns of young Europeans. It was called 'Youth on the Move'. Its stated aims including reducing the high school dropout rate in Europe to 10 per cent, and raising the proportion of young people with university qualifications above 40 per cent. 'Europe's future prosperity depends on its young people,' a European Commission memo on the initiative explained. 'Their skills and abilities will be decisive in achieving the Europe 2020 goal of smart, sustainable and inclusive growth.'[3]

At that time, I was working at the World Future Council in Brussels. It is a German non-profit organisation that gathers a wide variety of people from all over the world to develop, share, and support policy proposals for peace and sustainable development. One of the focusses of its work is the rights of future generations. I was working intensively on strengthening the issue of future justice in our institutions, and so, when the European plans for young people were published, we invited someone from the commission, as well as several members of the European Parliament, to a podium discussion. We also invited all political parties and many non-governmental organisations (NGOs), as well as representatives of young people. After all, the event was about improving the future for young people.

In the Brussels jungle, organising such an event can be a frustrating experience for a rather small and less well-known foundation, because many similar events take place all the time. In the business of politics, attention is a scarce commodity. At least I had realised by then the importance of stating on the invitation that free finger food and drinks would be on offer — or, even better, free canapés and champagne. And that it was important for the panel to include representatives from several EU institutions and as many political parties as possible. Eventually, our invitations were accepted by people with diverse views of the issue of future justice.

I was in the moderator's chair, the event was well attended, and at one stage the representative from the commission stressed the importance of improving the employability of young high school or university graduates so that they would be better suited to the jobs offered by industry. He said that the way to achieve this was for universities to work even more closely with companies. A young woman in the audience raised her hand. She was from one of the youth organisations, and spoke in an impressively direct way, saying that although she was supposed to be the target group of this strategy, she couldn't see the point of it, from what she'd heard so far.

'I don't know what world you're living in,' she said, 'but I look at the situation we're in, and I'm struck by very different issues.'

In her view, it was not the task of education to simply prepare people for the jobs the existing economy needed at any given point. 'I see real chaos ahead. And it is your job to prepare me to deal with that,' she said, 'instead of training me to become a cog in the system that created the chaos in the first place.' She told the panel the issue was to decide which ideas, capabilities, and solutions could help make our future less uncertain — and to learn how to organise those opportunities and identify the necessary policies, economic models, and social changes. Those were the issues she would like to be taught the skills to deal with.

After the young woman's interjection, the room fell silent. Everyone knew that she was right. I have often experienced such moments in my time working at the interface of politics, academia, and the public when someone says, loudly and clearly, 'No!' In an ideal world, a comment like that would spark a joint discussion about whether a certain political strategy for solving a given problem is really likely to be able to do so. Or whether it perhaps misses the mark and is ripe for change.

However, in the real world—as we all know—such comments are often treated like the elephant in the room. Everyone tries not to notice them, so they can return to the order of the day. The same happened that day in Brussels, although I invited several of our panellists to answer the woman's question.

The representatives from the commission and the parties wanted to talk about education. But what the young woman had asked about, in a moment of crisis and with an uncertain future looming, was not education, but learning.

Learning is often seen as the result of trial and error. When we are faced with a problem, we try to solve it. The experiences and insights we gather as we do so influence our future decision-making: if it works, we stick with it, because we believe it will work again in the future. This is how people, groups, and societies learn and develop their educational canon, which creates a store of knowledge for coming generations. Or, at least, that is the notion behind this widespread, linear understanding of learning, in which each improvement is built on the next in a strictly straight line, so to speak. We learn from the past for the future, because we assume that predictions about the future can be, to a greater or lesser extent, based on the past.

But what if that notion has now become outdated?

Around the turn of the millennium, the British physicist Stephen Hawking was asked whether he thought the next 100 years would be the century of biology, just as the previous 100 years had been the century of physics. His answer was no.

'I think the next century will be the century of complexity,' was his reply.[4]

Today we see how right we was. No previous generation had to deal with a world whose crucial systems — the natural ones we live off, and the cultural and social ones we live in — were interconnected in such a complex way and with so many different mutual interactions as ours today. Climate change has shown us that fossil fuel use is not just a national problem, and the financial crisis revealed that the same is true when it comes to rescuing large banks. The pandemic proved that we must think of health in global terms, otherwise viruses will mutate in countries where the people are less well protected by vaccines, and those mutation will make their way back to us.

That global interconnectedness underlies the sanctions with which some parts of the world have reacted to Russia's current war on Ukraine. We are only just beginning to learn the consequences of living in such a complex, networked way, and of the way that affects the course of things. For the first time, in rich countries at least, we are feeling the direct, tangible effects of the fact that while we can keep increasing financial capital endlessly, that does not necessarily make goods and services more available. It is not money that is scarce, but labour and resources. Limits are being readjusted, ranging from special immigration rules for crop pickers during the pandemic to the creation of new blocs in the global political order.

'The world has now entered the Planetary Phase,' writes the American physicist Paul Raskin in his extended essay from early in the new millennium, *Great Transition*, in which he and a group of academics from various disciplines attempt to pin down the effect of such complexity on our future civilisation. 'A global system is taking shape with fundamental differences from previous phases of history.'[5]

This is encapsulated by the phrase 'the Anthropocene'—a term popularised by the atmospheric chemist Paul Crutzen: humanity has entered a new epoch in which it has itself become the central force of change in the natural cycle of the Earth system.[6] In such an era, it becomes important to actively re-examine and re-assess past certainties and assumptions. 'Effective planetary stewardship requires updating our Holocene mindset. We must act on the urgency, the scale, and the interconnectivity between us and our home, planet Earth,' wrote a large group of Nobel Prize laureates in *Our Planet, Our Future: an urgent call for action*, published at the conclusion of their summit in 2021.[7]

What capabilities will be required for us to live well and, more importantly, to live well *together* in this new epoch, the Anthropocene? How can we ensure that the 'human era' remains habitable for humans?

The Jacobs Foundation, now based in Switzerland but originally established by a member of the Jacobs Coffee dynasty in Bremen, northern Germany, focusses on creating a better future for young people. In 2020, it commissioned a study to investigate the possible changes to our way of living and working in the coming decades, and to determine the skills that children and young adults would need to tackle those changes — hence the title of the study, *Future Skills*.[8] The central questions were: what might the future look like, and what can we teach younger generations to prepare them for it, without knowing for certain whether that predicted future will actually come about? The study outlined four scenarios for Switzerland, one of the world's richest countries, up to the year 2050. It also singled out two features shared by many countries of the global North — wealth and freedom — and examined how they intersect with each other. This matrix resulted in four different futures, characterised either by abundance or scarcity, in connection with restrictions or no restrictions on people's freedoms.

The first scenario is 'Collapse'. As a result of climate

change, the world experiences a series of abrupt disruptions. Extreme weather events trigger wars and mass movements of refugees, which in turn leads to the closing of borders and thus to a collapse in international trade. The financial system breaks down, currencies lose their value, and nation states descend into regionalism. People are largely cut off from the outside world. Travel becomes almost impossible due to the scarcity of energy, crumbling infrastructures, and a widespread mistrust of strangers. Cities become depopulated as people move to the countryside, where essential resources such as water, timber, and land are easier to come by. Industrial production is virtually non-existent, almost all supply chains are broken, and people have to rely on repairing goods or acquiring them locally. This is a scenario of scarcity, in which freedom is also restricted, since so many things are simply no longer possible. The important skills are practical and manual: those necessary for survival. However, the real challenge faced by people is to secure their own existence without becoming radicalised and falling prey to short-term strategies such as theft or war, which only make the situation worse.

The second scenario is what the authors call the 'Gig Economy Precariat'. It depicts a world in which technological progress leads to mass unemployment. Machines have replaced human workers so quickly and extensively that the unemployed can no longer be absorbed by the labour market or the welfare state. Companies have used digitisation to create a system in which services are no longer provided by salaried workers, but are outsourced globally via job platforms. This creates a mass of digital day-labourers who are in constant competition with each other, some of whom do the same job as before, but for lower pay. In this future, the international wealth gap is smaller, since poorer countries now also have access to the labour market—most work can be carried out from anywhere. But the wealth gap within societies has grown. Many people are living at subsistence level. Money can be earned by teaching machines to perform human tasks, or by those who disclose their personal data, or by those who covertly advertise products among their friends. Entrepreneurship and the ability to adapt to an ever-more dynamic market are paramount. State services are almost non-existent; many have been privatised. The movement of goods, payment transactions, the job market, and communications take place via a single online platform, which has become a kind of digital operating system for the world. Freedoms are not officially restricted in this scenario, but are *de facto* only enjoyed by a small elite.

In the third scenario, called 'Net Zero' by the authors, for good reason, the world attempts to react sustainably to climate change. Once it becomes clear that the solution cannot be provided by technology alone, people choose to take more drastic measures. There are no material shortages in this scenario. But people do have to accept the loss of some of the conveniences that we have become used to. Flying has become a rarity, individual motorised transport also takes place only on a small scale, and the cars that still exist are shared. Solar and wind power are the main sources of energy generation. Any excess energy is put towards producing hydrogen as a way of storing it. International trade mainly uses modern sailing ships; but, in general, the movement of both people and goods is greatly reduced. Many goods are produced locally, repaired, or recycled. In some ways, this is similar to the 'Collapse' scenario, and the skills required for this scenario are also comparable. The main difference is that the restrictions on freedom and wealth are not forced on people by circumstance, but are a deliberate choice. The challenges of this scenario are the facts that the effect of the restrictions in mitigating climate change are not felt immediately and that, for them to take effect at all, everyone must adhere to them, with no one taking advantage of others by refusing to shoulder their fair share of the restrictions.

The fourth and final scenario is called 'Fully Automated AI Luxury'. This also describes a world where machines have taken over the work otherwise performed by humans; but, unlike in the scenario where this benefits only a small elite, everyone benefits.

State intervention has managed to prevent digital monopolies from emerging. There is not one single platform that collects and controls information. Instead, there is a decentralised network in which anyone can access almost any information, thereby rendering the data commercially unusable. No one needs to work for money in this world of open information. Robots take care of people's basic needs. Property is no longer a status symbol. Prestige is gained by those whose creativity goes beyond what artificial intelligence can produce, and who share their creative output with others. This is the scenario in which there are no restrictions on freedom, and prosperity is widespread. An understanding of technology is useful, but the real challenge for humanity in this scenario is finding meaning in life when it is far easier to let computers and machines shape that life than doing it yourself.

One study: four scenarios. None of them seem totally far-fetched, even though they are so different. Apart from gardening, which is considered useful in all four scenarios — for self-sufficiency, or as a physical pastime, or as a way of gaining personal affirmation or showing solidarity — there appears to be no single skill that is necessary in all four scenarios. But, for all their differences, the four scenarios do have something in common: they all describe a possible future.

Scenarios can simulate very different versions of a possible future, depending on the kind of results that those who set them up are interested in. Unlike freely imagined utopias and dystopias, they try to trace a path between today and the day after tomorrow — a journey towards plausible versions of the future. Vision meets trend selection; imagination meets dataset, so to speak. The chance to react to these scenarios and to adapt to them, meet them head-on, or navigate around them, depends on taking action that is ahead of the possible consequences. Thinking in terms of different scenarios opens up new horizons. It prepares a multitude of different responses that we can turn to when crisis hits. It enables discussions over what responses appear not only realistic, but also positive — and allows us to discover and explore alternative courses of action before problems and faults emerge.

Thus, thinking in scenarios invites us to debate the values that underlie desirable versions of the future. It also reveals the places where perceptions of realistic futures diverge.[9] When we take a long view, and ask ourselves at what point we can and should make changes to create a world for our children, we are able to monitor trends and to change them proactively, rather than being taken by surprise and panicking when they suddenly become exponential, or when they unexpectedly disappear.

Do you remember what a feedback loop is? It is the reaction of a system to a stimulus.

Better learning means being able to 'feed forward'

rather than relying on feedbacks. It is the ability to consciously influence the future before it happens.

Whether, and in what way, a given scenario comes about, or whether it turns out to be mistaken, is not down to fate, but to social change. A few years ago, the British futurologist and innovation researcher Bill Sharpe developed his 'Three Horizons' approach to help us improve our understanding of the social processes that constitute the future, as well as to make us more aware of our own role as we navigate the phases of liminality, and show how we can use them as a springboard into the world of tomorrow.[10]

'The three horizons,' he writes, are 'three possible patterns in which the present might play out into the future. All three are always present, in any conversation and indeed in our own thinking. Being able to identify them and work skilfully with them, in groups, communities, nations, and within ourselves, is a practice that we can all develop. It restores our sense of agency in the face of a future that is, and always has been, radically open.'[11]

Horizon 1 refers to the dominant system at present, the status quo, or 'business as usual'.[12] A better understanding of this horizon requires the knowledge of 'engineers', that is, those who are able to say precisely how the prevailing system works and what is required to keep things ticking over. But as the world changes — due to insights and developments resulting either from crises or from innovation — aspects of business as usual begin to feel out of place or no longer fit for purpose. As the inadequacies of the system become increasingly obvious, this horizon is superseded by Horizon 2.

Horizon 2 describes the phase when it becomes increasingly clear that the dominant system no longer dictates the future. This is the horizon of the 'entrepreneurs', who ask themselves how the old system can be improved or even replaced. When their innovations work better than the existing system, a point of disruption has been reached, a tipping point at which the relevant actors must decide whether to continue protecting the system's status quo or invest in innovations that could replace it.

Beyond the necessary innovations, ever-more radical ideas for renewal are developed and tested on a small scale. They can generally be recognised by their experimental nature and the fact that they appear so far removed from what we perceive as 'normal'. They are the domain of the 'visionaries', who often work with fundamentally different premises and do not aim to improve what currently exists, but look to create something completely new. Behind the scenes of our everyday lives, they work on possible futures that have the ability to prevail against today's 'normal'. That is Horizon 3.

The three horizons describe different ways of relating to and influencing the future. Futurology, which, among other things, examines how we do that, suggests three different types of future that fit well with the Three Horizons approach. 'Probable' futures occur when we continue with Horizon 1, with no transformative changes. 'Plausible' futures appear possible in view of present trends, if transformative changes are initiated in Horizon 2. 'Desirable' futures begin at Horizon 3 and act as targets for us to work gradually towards, even if not all the necessary measures and solutions are yet on the table.[13] These three perspectives are always available to every one of us, and social progress emerges from a productive tension between them. Thus engineers, entrepreneurs, and visionaries are always all necessary to change the direction of the present towards a desired future without losing touch with what is probable. The important thing is to recognise early enough when continuing to hold on to the status quo places too many limitations on 'feed-forward' loops and means disruptions are more likely to bring about an end than lead to a new beginning.

In short: dealing consciously with disruptive times means keeping Horizon 3 in our sights.

The first major attempt to approach this task systematically was published by the scientists of the

Club of Rome. Their 1972 report, *The Limits to Growth*, caused a worldwide sensation, as it was the first time that computer-aided simulations had been used to show that the future of humanity hinges on certain long-term trends. The research team extrapolated five of those trends—population growth, food production, industrialisation, the depletion of non-renewable resources, and environmental degradation—to create a version of the future in which humanity instigates no transformative change. One of the twelve resulting scenarios, dubbed 'standard run', corresponds to 'business as usual', and results in an exponential acceleration of those trends, until they reach an abrupt tipping point in the early-to-mid 21st century. The same result occurred even in the scenario with twice the amount of available resources as were currently known of at the time. Only extensive political intervention was able to turn the pattern around.

Of the twelve scenarios presented in the report, only two led to a sustainable future—and it was those in which the effects and, most importantly, the drivers of trends were taken into account together, and in which appropriate political measures were integrated. Those measures concerned resource efficiency, sustainable agriculture, and the stabilisation of population growth, energy sufficiency, and food distribution, as well as a move away from a focus on material consumption and towards quality of life.

Despite the criticism that has been levelled at details of the report since 1972, its basic findings have never been refuted.[14] Even today, in all large-scale studies of sustainability, the 'business as usual' scenario is never a particularly attractive one. It is important to remember that large scenario-based analyses are never intended as tools for predicting the future precisely; they are concerned with investigating patterns of change and their drivers.[15] An analysis of this kind was an absolute innovation in 1972, especially with regard to its global scale and long-term perspective. The report's real success was in showing that trends which had always been viewed individually were actually in constant interaction with each other, so that 'it would never again be possible to look at problems such as population, food production or energy in isolation,' as Aurelio Peccei, co-founder of the Club of Rome, wrote in his autobiography.[16]

I am not concerned with judging whether Peccei was right, although one of my motivations for writing this book was the impression that there is room for improvement in that regard. However, far more important for the way forward are the conclusions that the scientists drew from their report. They also pondered how the necessary level of political and social will could be mobilised for transformative change. To explore how humanity might deal successfully with their findings, they published a second report seven years later, under the title *No Limits to Learning*, which was discussed by an illustrious group of researchers and decision-makers.[17] After the previous report had explored the outer limits of growth, this one attempted to sound out the inner scope for action available to humanity as it headed towards the future. To this end, the authors compared two different kinds of learning, which they called 'maintenance learning' and 'innovative learning'.

To put it in academic terms, what they call maintenance learning works well for a prolonged period in the mode of relatively stable feedback loops. As long as the current system reveals only little frictions, maintenance learning reacts to challenges in a routine and rules-based way, and responds to problems with familiar procedures, implementation schemes, roles, and models. When many people are familiar with it, social cooperation becomes far easier, and society functions well. People can get a grip on minor aberrations with adaptive or corrective measures, and the processes of the system are thus dynamically stabilised.

Innovative learning, by contrast, becomes important when the familiar routines no longer bring about the desired results, or are no longer available. Or when shortages — of labour or natural resources, for example — become so severe that 'business as usual' can no longer be maintained. In such cases, innovative learning prepares the way for real change, and the 'entrepreneurs' need to orient themselves towards

Horizon 3. Figuratively speaking, innovative learning does not lead to the umpteenth improvement in candle-making; it invents the light bulb. Take gas deliveries from Russia, for example. Since we suddenly realised how problematic those supplies are, renewable-energy sources have been rebranded as 'freedom energy', and prior resistance and objections to them now have less validity. The result is a clear mission, a social tipping point. We now know that a new system must be set up, and this knowledge makes the collaborative work of the 'entrepreneurs' of the second horizon both faster and more effective.

Under the Club of Rome's description of learning, the aim of education is not to measure the standardised performances of individuals and to compare them in detail. Instead, learning as described by the Club of Rome places the focus on the creative skills and effective cooperation of a society, including the expertise of future visionaries. That is how progress works. And that is how we can reinvent ourselves if it becomes necessary — or if we just want to, and it makes sense to do so.

The precise form of the transition from the present to a desirable future, and how long it takes, will depend on the strength of our commitment to pursuing the new and to abandoning the old. Of course, we could reboot coal power, subsidise petrol prices, and reward car drivers — tearing up our climate goals and delaying behavioural change in the process. Or we could conserve energy, use shared electric taxis, and provide social support, without encouraging carbon-intensive behaviour.

Ideally, of course, the transformation to the new should take place proactively. According to the authors of *No Limits to Learning*, if a society clings on to 'business as usual' for too long, it is in danger of severely limiting its freedoms and its range of options. If change is only ever triggered by crises, many possible alternatives will fail to be systematically planned, tested, and promulgated in good time. Then we will have no choice but to learn very fast. This 'learning by shock' generally results in innovations that challenge us more than do transformations that we consciously shape ourselves.[18] The authors conclude from this that education and academic systems should always include sufficient teaching of innovative learning, including awareness of our own role as an *effector*.

That is precisely what the young woman at the panel discussion in Brussels was demanding. She was asking for an educational strategy focussing on how to get off the beaten path. Even Plato's allegory of the cave shows that it is always important to question oneself and abandon illusory certainties.

So what is it that drives us? And what does the long-term perspective look like?

When I attended my first professional conference as a sustainability scientist in 2014—I had previously mostly attended conferences on political economics and international relations—I was impressed by the range of different types of event. As well as the usual scientific papers and poster sessions, there was music, an exhibition, and a session called 'participatory forum theatre'. I attended a debate hosted by a group of young colleagues from the Stockholm Resilience Centre, which was set up with the explicit aim of gaining a better understanding of socio-ecological systems and developing recommendations for sustainability transformations. Since sustainability issues have, by definition, an environmental, a social, and an economic aspect, working in interdisciplinary teams was the norm at the Stockholm Resilience Centre. But that was also a cause for concern for the young academics. Not only is completing a Master's or PhD programme with interdisciplinary research designs challenging, but it is also professionally risky for young would-be academics. Fixed-term, project-based positions are available, but it is difficult for 'interdisciplinarians' to access the classic funding, publishing opportunities, and prestigious awards in higher education that are so important for their future careers—because their work just doesn't fit into the traditional faculty system. They are literally 'undisciplined', and fall through the cracks in the very system they are supposed to work in.

Together with some colleagues, one of the researchers at the Centre, Jamila Haider, decided to make this innovation dilemma a research subject in itself, in part to raise awareness of the researchers' status as misfits, or as 'entrepreneurs', whose questions and interests fall between all stools. Rather than ignoring or abandoning 'what can sometimes be an uncomfortable space in education and research', they launched a survey at the conference, and eventually published an academic paper that put not only their position within the system (the lack of sufficient career opportunities), but also the rules of the system itself (the means of knowledge production) officially on the agenda.[19]

Their criticism was motivated not only by concerns about their own position in the system, but also by the question of whether they could work effectively within it on the issues of the future that were important to them.[20] After all, mainstream politics is increasingly committed to sustainability transformations. Particularly in times of transformation, friendly undisciplined behaviour can help to recognise and actively unlearn illusory certainties, worldviews, and self-perceptions that do not, or do not any longer, correspond to reality and the challenges it poses.[21] In this way, the structures of learning do not lag behind its challenges, but are ahead of them.[22]

In his book *The Evolution of Science*, the historian of science and director of the Max Planck Institute for the

History of Science, Jürgen Renn, summarises more than two decades of empirical and comparative research. He puts it this way: 'We must descend into the machine room of science and take part in the daily struggles to turn the Anthropocene into a liveable environment for humanity.'[23] The academic system is plagued by a tendency to maintain the status quo, even though research is often portrayed as a relay race, in which brilliant ideas are continually passed on and refined. As Jamila Haider showed, academia is not exempt from operating within a system. That's why scientific results are always also an expression of the structures, rules, and stimuli amid which they are created.

'Even the most fundamental aspects of the classical image of science — proof, experimentation, data, objectivity, rationality — have proven to be deeply historical in their nature,' Renn concludes.[24] And so, over time, many insights that once appeared objective and rational entered the history books as certainties that turned out to be temporary. Who writes those history books, and when, why, and by whom they are altered, is always an expression of power relations. The case of Galileo Galilei, who was condemned by the Catholic Church for his uncomfortable thinking, is perhaps the most famous example of this.

Therefore, we must take care, and pay attention to the way we create knowledge, as knowledge provides the basis for a society's agency. Knowledge, education, and technological development cannot therefore be viewed separately from a society—quite the opposite, in fact. They are its organised learning process. They must always be viewed in the context of the present and the developments that led to it. They do not produce neutral results, but they do produce the closest answers to our questions.[25] If we don't change the questions along with the changing times, or if we don't change them enough, we can expect no transformative answers, only adaptive ones. If our questions are too superficial, we will not learn to call anything into question. That is why misfit experiences, while uncomfortable, are valuable. They are often a step towards desirable versions of the future.

'[A] lack of desirable but plausible futures may be contributing to the malaise that can be found across much of the world,' writes the British innovation researcher and government adviser Geoff Mulgan, 'It's certainly linked to a sense of lost agency and a deepening fear of the future.'[26]

We must get to the bottom of that malaise if we want to avoid the mistakes of the students in the Tanaland experiment. And having done this, we must learn to both re-read and rewrite the future. A useful aid in doing so, according to UNESCO's *Social Sciences Report* for the year 2013, is something called 'futures literacy'. That is '[the] capacity to imagine futures that are not based on hidden, unexamined, and sometimes

flawed assumptions about present and past systems.'[27]
By combining critical thinking with a closer observation
of context and a precise description of the actual nature
of any given problem, futures literacy helps us orient
our learning processes towards the third horizon. The
questions that then become important are: What is the
desired result, and what is stopping us from achieving
it? And why is it stopping us?

'A futures literate person has acquired the skills
needed to decide why and how to use their imagination
to introduce the non-existent future into the present,'
writes Riel Miller, head of Futures Literacy at
UNESCO.[28]

We already do that without thinking. We picture
how things might develop, imagine what we might
think about that development, and consider how likely
it is to come about and what others might think about
it. Those imagined ideas affect not only our decisions,
but also the options we take into consideration in our
decision-making in the first place. That's why it is
important to be fully aware of the selection mechanisms
at play when we write possible futures, and to use them
more consciously.

The super-fit start-ups in Silicon Valley have
already realised this, and tell us of the fantastic results
their products will bring. 'Fake it till you make it' is
their maxim when competing to attract investment
from venture capitalists. Well-sold, imagined future

cashflows can mobilise the investment funds necessary in the present to make the future a reality. But I believe we must democratise the issue of what kind of future becomes reality. It should not simply result from the force of money or be reduced to projected financial yields. How can we continue to grow our garden in a meaningful and nutrimental way when the only crop in the garden is money?

Social innovative learning therefore also opens up the issue of who makes decisions about the third horizon. After all, start-up valleys and gleaming financial towers are not the only places in the world where visions of the future are forged.

Do you know, for example, what the United Nations enshrined in Point 1 of the final statement after its first international conference on the environment in Stockholm in 1972? 'Man is both creature and moulder of his environment, which gives him physical sustenance and affords him the opportunity for intellectual, moral, social and spiritual growth.'[29] The document goes on to say that that creative potential should be further developed in international cooperation.

Fifteen years later, a United Nations commission chaired by the former Norwegian prime minister Gro Harlem Brundtland laid out a vision of what such international cooperation might look like: 'Humanity has the ability to make development sustainable to ensure that it meets the needs of the present without compromising the ability of future generations to meet their own needs.'[30] The title given to the report was *Our Common Future*.

And today?

Today, it takes a pandemic or a war for our elected representatives to even dare to include terms such as 'solidarity' and 'common destiny' in their political messages. And we are not making any real headway in achieving our common goals, ranging from environmental protection to social justice. This is perhaps due to the fact that individualisation and far-reaching financialisation have led to a situation in which, despite everything, we continue to privatise the future. 'Social goals have become personal ambitions,' as the Jacobs Foundation stated in its study.[31]

Are we going to allow our future to be privatised by the few, while the many can only do their best to get by in that future? Or would it be preferable for as many people as possible to convey to the world the answers to the questions of how to shape desirable futures?

The good news is that many of the necessary skills for this are already part of various education concepts.[32] There are many places where they overlap: curiosity and critical thinking, self-efficacy, multi-perspectivity, cooperativeness, cultural sensitivity, digital resilience, and communication skills.[33]

If enough of its members are educated in this way, the transformability of a society increases. A group of researchers led by the Canadian professor of social innovation, Frances Westley, described transformability as 'the capacity to create untried beginnings from which to evolve a fundamentally new way of living when existing ecological, economic, and social conditions make the current system untenable'.[34]

The guiding principle for transformability, therefore, is that defending one's worldview, come hell or high water, is not proof of the power or superiority of that view. On the contrary, transformability is a repeated invitation to enter different worlds and to be both bemused and inspired by them. Social learning is not restricted to educational institutions. It takes place everywhere and every day in our regular lives as effectors.

Knowledge, will, and action, according to the Jacobs Foundation, are what make up the responsibility with which everyone of us can participate in shaping the future. Knowledge means being able to describe the current state of things and how it came about. Will means being able to identify the target condition; being able to say what a desirable future should look like and what can help us achieve it. And, finally, action refers to the social and personal skills required to set out as a proactive traveller on this journey that begins with the first step towards a new world. Letting go of the

old is part of that renewal. When the time has come
and a system has run its course, supporting its removal
is a sign of greatness. And then untried approaches
will develop into a new normality all the faster. As one
world sinks out of existence, another arises. If we are to
master the great transformation of our time successfully,
we will need to be a midwife and palliative care nurse
all in one.

System trap: seeking the wrong goal

*The behaviour of a system can be influenced most efficiently
via its purpose. That is true of both societies and their
educational canon. If the purpose does not clearly determine
what we want to achieve, the system cannot possibly
produce the desired result. If, for example, we measure a
system primarily by who or what is most successful in it, we
will chiefly be maintaining the status quo. That leads to a
lack of flexibility and innovation. If we want to enable as
many people as possible to shape and take responsibility for
a desirable future, we must update the system purposes of
education, science, research, and learning.*

7

Wealth: growing better

'But in contemplating any progressive movement, not in its nature unlimited, the mind is not satisfied with merely tracing the laws of the movement; it cannot but ask the further question, to what goal? Towards what ultimate point is society tending by its industrial progress? When the progress ceases, in what condition are we to expect that it will leave mankind?'

JOHN STUART MILL, PHILOSOPHER AND ECONOMIST[1]

Goldman Sachs is not just any investment bank. It is the epitome of investment banks. Of course, there are other companies on Wall Street, such as insurance companies and investment funds, that manage the capital of big investors, organise takeovers for multinationals, or help states to borrow money on the financial markets. But few were as brutally successful and simultaneously admired, feared, and sometimes even hated, up until the banking crisis of 2008, as Goldman Sachs, or 'Goldmine Sachs', as it is known admiringly within the industry.

When signs of the impending crash appeared in 2007, and its competitors were already having to lay off staff, Goldman Sachs paid its bankers a record 145 bonuses, to the value of $20 billion. The boss at the time, Lloyd Blankfein, received a payment of almost $70 billion on top of his salary.[2] It was the highest bonus ever paid on Wall Street; meanwhile, all over America, people were losing their homes and their jobs, and states were having to take on debt to rescue failing banks, and the global economy was sliding into crisis. Despite all that, Blankfein sounded like a man with a clear conscience when he later tried to justify his work and that bonus.

'We help companies to grow by helping them to raise capital,' he told a reporter at the London *Times*. 'Companies that grow create wealth. This, in turn, allows people to have jobs that create more growth and more wealth. It's a virtuous cycle.' If the financial markets collapse, Blankfein went on, everybody's business collapses, so banks 'have a social purpose'. And no matter how much he was hated for it, he was just a banker 'doing God's work'.[3]

What exactly is it about statements such as this that is so galling?

The narrative that Blankfein is repeating here is what is commonly and succinctly expressed as 'Growth means wealth. Growth maintains jobs. Growth makes innovation possible — and vice versa. Growth keeps the system stable.' Most bankers, CEOs, and heads of government would have said exactly the same. This is what is taught in university economics courses, printed in the business sections of newspapers, and featured in the policies of almost all political parties. It is not just the personal opinion of a banker who clearly thinks he's both infallible and untouchable. These are the words of someone who knows that people in positions such as his are difficult to hold to account because they are protected so efficiently by the growth narrative.[4] Lloyd Blankfein may no longer be the head of Goldman Sachs, but the bank is still one of those considered too big to fail. The state will always bail them out in an emergency, even if their pursuit of growth is the cause of that emergency in the first place.

We have built our entire system on this growth narrative. It is the only story that connects us across all nations, religions, genders, and identities. Anthropologists see this as the cultural driving force behind our successful subjugation of all other species on the planet.[5] Breaking out of that system is not easy. We said 'yes' to the growth narrative, and now we are forced to say 'yes' to everything it produces.

So where is change supposed to come from?

The first part of this book gave the answer: from structural upheavals and courageous people.

In February 2021, a group of young first-year bankers at Goldman Sachs sent their bosses a PowerPoint presentation that, at first glance, looked like a typical presentation produced by the bank when it performed an analysis of a company's business.[6] The only difference was that the presentation was not about another company. It was about Goldman Sachs itself. The young financial analysts had carried out a survey among themselves to ascertain their level of satisfaction with Goldman Sachs as an employer — and the results were devastating, as was the public impact when they were published.

Nearly every young banker was working 100 hours a week or more, and sleeping just five hours a night, and yet they were unable to complete the work assigned to them. Every one of them found the deadlines they were expected to meet unrealistic. They rated their own physical and mental health to have been around nine on a scale of one to ten, corresponding to 'very good', when they started their jobs. By the time the survey was taken, that assessment had plummeted to well below three points. The bankers rated their satisfaction with their personal life at just one point out of ten, corresponding to 'very dissatisfied'. Many of the analysts said they were likely to leave Goldman Sachs within six months if their working conditions did not improve.

'There was a point where I was not eating, showering, or doing anything else other than working from morning until after midnight,' one of them is quoted in the publicly available survey. 'Being unemployed is less frightening to me than what my body might succumb to if I keep up this lifestyle,' said another.[7]

A job at Goldman Sachs is typically seen as a ticket to a dazzling career. Applicants usually come from among the top graduates of America's elite colleges, and, if successful, they enter the even-more elite world of investment banking. It is a place where they can not only earn a lot of money, but also make invaluable contacts. Hardly another bank is as networked with the world of politics as Goldman Sachs. Three of the last ten US Treasury secretaries came from there, as well as the later head of the European Central Bank, Mario Draghi. José Manuel Barroso went in the other direction, joining Goldman Sachs International in London after serving two terms as president of the EU Commission. That was two weeks after the Brexit referendum. Speaking to the *Financial Times*, he said he would do what he could 'to mitigate the negative effects of the Brexit decision [on Goldman Sachs]'.[8]

Young people who take a job with Goldman Sachs know all that. They also know that the competition is harsh and fierce. But for the young analysts who presented that survey, the price seems to have become too high at some point. They were no longer willing to trade health for wealth. Their preferences had changed. They had made it through the doors of the cathedral of big money—presumably to do 'God's work'—and had then lost their faith.

When we speak critically of growth today, we often have in mind only its present or future negative effects on our environment. Almost as if we will only start to feel those effects when sea levels rise, droughts break out, and forest fires or tornados devastate the country. What we like to call wealth creation is largely proportional to the damage we inflict on the natural system with our economic behaviour. But we can already feel at first hand the consequences of a system in which economic growth takes precedence over all else. This is not just in the form of health hazards such as high nitrate levels in our drinking water, exhaust fumes in our lungs, and microplastics in our bodies. Today, we describe psychological phenomena such as burnout, depression, panic attacks, and anxiety about the future with terms like 'overload' or 'overwhelm'. They have long since become as much a part of life in the supposedly successful, wealthy industrialised nations as obesity, diabetes, or cardiovascular disease, which we call 'lifestyle diseases' without giving the phrase a second thought—as if that phrase weren't indication enough that something has gone wrong somewhere.[9]

We also know about a metric called 'marginal utility'—describing, in this instance, the point at which increased ownership of property no longer translates into an increase in life satisfaction, while things such as health, sleep, the quality of our personal relationships, and a certain amount of control over our own lives in every situation become important.[10] When people in Germany are asked how much leisure time they would ideally like to have, their answer is between three and four hours a day.[11] Of course, this is assuming that some prerequisites are fulfilled, including having all our material needs sufficiently met and a safe roof over our heads. But particularly in rich societies, it is not the *absolute* standard of living that most affects feelings of wellbeing, but the *relative* standard of living—in other words, what we have in comparison to others. In rich countries, whether or not we have enough of something is not necessarily judged by objective criteria, but by social ones. Nonetheless, we rarely talk about the connection between human wellbeing and the way we live our lives, engage in economic activity, and behave as consumers.[12] It's as if we are shying away from asking the obvious question: What is this all-encompassing compulsion for growth actually doing to us?

When I give a talk, this is the stage at which I sometimes ask the audience to close their eyes for a moment and imagine what a desirable future would feel like for them. Yes, what it would *feel* like. Surprisingly, although we have quite different concepts of what a desirable future might look like in real terms, we our ideas do not diverge much when it comes to the quality of our interactions with each other, our everyday life experience, and our place in the world. Try it for yourself.

I then ask listeners to visualise one or two icons of economic growth — men such as Tesla's Elon Musk, Meta's Mark Zuckerberg, or Amazon's Jeff Bezos. I then get them to think about figures whose achievements could never be measured in terms of share prices — Mahatma Gandhi, for example, or Nelson Mandela, or Mother Teresa — and then I ask them to discuss with their neighbour which of all those people they would prefer to have running the country. And to think about how each of the possible futures feels to them.

This experiment produces an almost physical feeling for how much pressure would be taken off societies if we were not all obsessed with always running faster, and rebuilding and accumulating more and more. Doing or supporting things although we know they will not make us rich, or indeed for no money at all, is also part of the story of human progress. It is also a source of satisfaction. Our nature is not only to be selfish. We can also be selfless, we can care for, appreciate, and share things, and feel a sense of responsibility and solidarity. I am often left speechless by the way we consciously ignore so many aspects of our existence in order to prop up the narrative that ever-faster growth is a synonym for progress, prosperity, or is part of the natural course of human history.

Of course, the question of what the actual purpose of economic activity is, is not new. The art of the 'good life' has occupied the minds of influential thinkers since the start of the Industrial Revolution 250 years ago, and it still informs our economic concepts today. One of those thinkers was the English jurist and philosopher Jeremy Bentham. He saw human behaviour as being controlled principally by two feelings — pleasure and pain — which rule over people like two sovereign masters. Everything people think, do, or want, they think, do, and want — according to Bentham — in order to feel more pleasure or less pain. 'On the one hand the standard of right and wrong, on the other the chain of causes and effects, are fastened to their throne,' writes Bentham.[13]

Bentham believed that the motive of maximising happiness and minimising unhappiness was both the driving force and the goal of human endeavour. For him, an action is judged to be either good or bad not on the basis of moral considerations, but solely on its utility. Hence the name of this school of thought: utilitarianism. It says that the net utility of an action is what dictates whether it contributes to the happiness of a society or not.

Many economic models today still work with this Greatest Happiness Principle. The preferences according to which the economic decisions simulated by those models are played out are programmed precisely along the lines of that principle.

The Neoclassical economists who came after Bentham took monetary value to be an expression of utility, and higher monetary value is consequently seen to represent greater utility; no one would be willing to pay for things if that weren't the case. Thus, for Bentham, the primary objective (he calls it *purpose*) of a utilitarian society is to achieve 'the greatest happiness for the greatest number'. Translated into monetary terms, that means the amount of money in our national economy is an indication of whether we are on the right track or not.

But a few years later, John Stuart Mill, one of the pioneers of liberalism and the father of classical economics, realised that that could not be the whole story. So, in 1948, he asked the forthright question: Why should it be seen as a sign of success when people who already have more than anyone can ever need double their fortune — especially since that growth will result in barely any benefit, save the opportunity to show that added wealth off. Even back then, on his frequent walks, Mill observed the effects of such expansive and extractive economic behaviour on nature and the countryside, which he valued highly. Mill was therefore convinced that the phase of vigorous material growth was a temporary one, and that ever-increasing material comfort would not remain the purpose of progress. 'While minds are coarse they require coarse stimuli, and let them have them. In the meantime, those who do not accept the present very early stage of human improvement as its ultimate type, may be excused for being comparatively indifferent to [this] kind of economical progress; [...] the mere increase of production and accumulation.'[14] In his view, the art of the good life would not flourish until society had reached a state of equilibrium 'in which, while no one is poor, no one desires to be richer, nor has any reason to fear being thrust back by the efforts of others to push themselves forward'.[15] Mill believed a stable population size and reduced working hours were required to open up the necessary space for humanity's deeper potential to unfold. Economic growth as Mill understood it was not an end in itself, with everyone trying to accumulate as much property as they can. It was a means by which social progress could unlock freedoms in life that lay beyond material necessities.

John Maynard Keynes, one of the twentieth century's leading economists, outlined precisely the same idea over eighty years later, in his much-quoted essay *Economic Possibilities for Our Grandchildren*.[16] In that work, Keynes writes that there will come a time, in 100 years at the latest, when humanity will be free of the burden of satisfying its basic material needs. Like Mill, he also believed a stable population size was a necessary condition for this. Keynes imagined that technological developments and financial capital would raise productivity to such a level that 'the economic problem may be solved'.[17] What Keynes meant by that was a situation in which everyone's material needs are met. And he estimated that by the year 2030, each of us would only have to work three hours a day to cover our needs for food, clothing, and shelter. Then we would be confronted with the question of how to use that extra leisure time 'to live wisely and agreeably and well'.[18]

He really uses that phrase: 'To live wisely and agreeably and well'.

When John Stuart Mill wrote his essay, the results of three to four hours of work a day were very different to today, when we have countless machines in operation. Keynes's essay was published in 1930, when the world was in the midst of the Great Depression. The problem of broad swathes of the population having to grapple with the meaning of life to avoid becoming bored by prosperity seemed a very distant one indeed. Ninety years have now passed, and Keynes's predictions about productivity and growth have turned out to be quite modest. The material standard of living in the global North is now not just eight times, but seventeen times higher.[19] People's material needs are more than covered.

According to Keynes's prediction, annual working time could have, should have, come down by two thirds. But instead, even in the global North, it fell by only about one-third, while the proportion of people in employment in those countries has risen by 10 per cent since 1960. So a larger proportion of the population in the global North are contributing to their country's GDP than nearly 100 years ago.[20] We are still very far removed from a three-hour working day.

Where is all the extra leisure time we're supposed to have gained?

Modern societies are growth machines. Compared to our grandparents' generation, we have more social contacts, own more stuff, move house more often, take shorter but more frequent holidays, and change partners and jobs more often. The information that is available to us and the amount of stored data double at ever-shorter intervals, while the half-life of products and trends also grows ever shorter. Twice as many people use air travel now than were even alive during Keynes's lifetime.[21] Our feeling for how far away somewhere is or how long something takes is constantly being updated. Algorithms have long-since replaced humans in making trading decisions on stock markets, because those are now split-second decisions. Never in human history has a single tool given us as much access to the world as the smartphone. But we still consider it normal to get a new, even faster phone every couple of years.

In her 2017 book *Fully Connected: surviving and thriving in an age of overload*, the British writer and entrepreneur Julia Hobsbawm compiles a number of terms that put a less positive spin on the miracle of exponential technological growth: information obesity, time starvation, techno-spread, network-tangle, organisational bloat, and life gridlock. Rather than marvelling at the growth in processing speed, she draws attention to something that is decreasing rather than growing: our social health. 'You cannot be productive if you are not motivated, or if you feel stuck, squashed, poorly managed, or in a dysfunctional setup. But most of our business lives and political lives are just that: deeply dysfunctional. They lack Social Health.'[22]

When someone asks how you're doing, how often have you answered with something like, 'Yeah, fine, it's all just a bit much at the moment'?

Do you really believe that will change in the next five years? Or, when you look back at this time in the future, will it seem more relaxed compared to all the things you will be doing by then?

The half-life of the definition of how much is 'a lot' is also changing at breakneck speed. But however much it is, it is never enough.

If we look at modern societies from a systems-theory point of view, we see that they are systems in a state of structural imbalance. To gain stability, they need external energy to continue to increase their activities. They grow more complex, and thus cause environmental or social upheavals, which they try to compensate for by growing even bigger, faster, and more complex. It is just like the Red Queen's explanation to Alice in *Through the Looking-glass*: 'Now, here, you see, it takes all the running you can do to keep in the same place.'[23]

As a result of this, people in modern societies can't slow down without stumbling. Acceleration and escalation become the norm. Until we escape that logic, any attempt to solve the problems caused by that escalation will be merely cosmetic, since we are basically trying in vain to run from a treadmill.

So who gets to decide what progress is? Is it humanity, or is it the exponential-growth-bound systems we live in? Who decides when we have achieved the original aim behind all the technological development: that of living a good life? Who will tell us when we can stop running?

Of course, dynamic systems are always changing, and we have to react to those changes. But, as we saw in the first part of this book, the kind of reaction that might be helpful depends on the stocks of resources that remain and on the pre-existing dynamics of the system. When people are suffering from material shortages, it

can make a lot of sense to speed up or increase some
processes. And, sometimes, to do that very quickly.
Nonetheless, it does not relieve us of the question of
what aim we are *actually* trying to achieve, and which
networked environment is affected by our activities.
When acceleration and interconnectedness reach their
limits within a system, the result is over-load. That's
when a system tries to produce more or expend more
resources than it is designed for. That is always possible
in the short term, as complex systems have such a great
capacity for buffering. But if the system is then not
allowed time to regenerate, serious damage can ensue.
That's equally true of the natural world and human
beings. There are only twenty-four hours in a day, even
for employees at Goldman Sachs.

So why do we persist?

This is the question explored by the British economist
Fred Hirsch in his 1976 book *Social Limits to Growth*.[24]
His book basically charts a search for the reasons why
there appear to be absolutely no signs of Keynes's
prediction coming true. Why do people who are already
wealthy continue to compete with each other — thereby
creating shortages for others? And why do people in
materially rich societies still experience so much
frustration — sometimes more than people in poorer
countries.

Hirsch begins with what we traditionally associate with 'growth': goods and services, and the value they have for human beings. A direct benefit is easy to understand—it arises from the consumption situation itself, as in when your central heating warms you, a sandwich fills you up, or an hour's learning increases your skills. Beyond that classical view taken by economists, Hirsch was interested in the sociological. He was interested in the academic disciplines that aim to gain a better understanding of why it is always considered better to have more and more goods and services, no matter how many are already on the market.

Hirsch concludes that the reason is the social benefit we hope to gain from them.

This kind of benefit is not primarily about the consumption of something doing me good or tasting nice; it's about the fact that others don't have what I have. Ownership of or access to those goods and services affords me a different position in society—one in which I feel better about myself, which is why Hirsch calls such goods 'positional goods'. He believes such goods are the social force that propels us into the growth dynamic. As with other drivers of growth, there is no problem with this until a dynamic of exponential increase leads us to overshoot the mark. Hirsch links positional goods to his concept of 'social scarcity'. Hirsch's theory states that the growth society is simply unable to provide the greatest happiness for the greatest number of people. Instead, it produces a lot of jostling for positions.

We witness this everywhere. On the one hand, if everyone wants more and more of everything all the time, *physical shortages* will occur in a limited environment such as one planet. Ever-increasing mobility in an ever-increasing number of cars does not lead to more freedom, but to more congestion. On the other hand, a society can never achieve a three-hour working day as long as competitiveness is part of its DNA—a good is only positional if it happens to be inaccessible to many others. But, as Hirsch points out, economic growth, and, with it, the opportunity for more people to afford previously unattainable goods, only *appears* to offer an escape—which quickly becomes apparent as soon as you take a long-term perspective. Firstly, as we orient our lives based on comparing ourselves with others, positional goods tend to take on even more significance when we are materially well satisfied. And, secondly, the benchmark by which we measure whether we feel positionally better off keeps rising. This combination leads to many kinds of *social scarcity* that thwart the big promise of achieving the greatest happiness for all.

We can take the example of lakeside plots of land to illustrate the concept of physical scarcity. There is a limited supply of such plots, and so they are valuable in two senses of the word. If they are owned by local authorities, and the authorities succumb to the temptation of gaining short-term profits by selling the plots, the shores of the lake will soon be lined with buildings and will become inaccessible to the majority of people. The plots then become increasingly expensive, and the amount of land available for public leisure shrinks. That frustrates both the less well-off and those who thought they were about to be able to afford to be lakeside landowners themselves.

As an example of social scarcity, we can take highly paid or desirable jobs. They are also in limited supply, and when more and more people achieve the academic qualifications required to get them, the competitive culture becomes even more intense. The resulting frustration could never be balanced out by yet more growth, even if we had four planets. The individual benefit of a purchase activity seen individually is clear. But, 'since the individual benefits of this kind do not add up, the connection between individual and aggregate advance is broken,' Hirsch writes in summary.[25] Social jostling trumps physical jostling, because *your* increasing fortune is always *my* relative loss.

We cannot buy our way upwards out of this prosperity paradox — if we were to try, the stakes would just go up, and the game itself would not end. To those who live in a positional society, it seems rational, or even inevitable, for them to play the game. In that way, as the pressure for growth constantly increases, the promise of freedom stumbles off the treadmill. For most of us, '*getting* what one wants is increasingly divorced from *doing* as one likes,' as Hirsch puts it.[26]

Thus, the growth society's promise of happiness and freedom cannot continue to be kept for long before we confront the phenomenon of social scarcity.

Do people need to change in order to change this?

According to Fred Hirsch, people do not need to be trained out of their natural inclination to compare themselves to others and to want to surpass them, and instead trained to engage in cooperative behaviour, to share with others and work with them. This is because humans are already capable of both — rivalry and solidarity. The questions Hirsch is more interested in answering are what makes us choose one or the other of these human patterns of behaviour in any given situation, and how we can influence that choice within our social structures?

Hirsch writes that the success of the market system in its early days can, ironically enough, be explained by the fact that it took hold in a society that was characterised by a strong pre-market social ethos. That is, it was a society that had not yet organised everything according to the principles of competition and monetary value, in which the norms of voluntary cooperation and social obligation were strong. It was not until later, argues Hirsch, that individual interests increasingly came to be considered the general behavioural norm and organisational logic, thus, to put it in systemic terms, weakening the dampening effects of the feedback loops that guaranteed and normalised a balanced repertoire of behaviours.[27] 'The benefits derive from the existence of some minimum of competition and of choice open to individuals,' writes Hirsch, 'whereas the drawbacks derive from the false prospectus of the competition—from the false signals given to individuals seeking to optimise their own position.'[28] This results in the illusion that everyone has the possibility of optimising their position, rather than just a few.

Hirsch points out that economists such as Friedrich Hayek and Edmund Burke, whom he describes as liberal-conservatives, warned of these social limits to growth. In the big picture, the whole is not necessarily the sum of its parts: 'If individual valuations do not add up, then the aggregated valuations based upon them become biased measures.'[29]

How do we get that big picture back?

Hirsch believes that changing our perspective on the interaction between individuals' striving for prosperity and a society oriented towards social goals and indicators is pivotal to achieving this.[30] He sees no way of overcoming social scarcities if societies do not engage in open and democratic debate about where limits are set and how they can be maintained. In reality, those scarcities are not even of an economic nature in rich countries, but are cultural and social challenges. Taking a different view of the big picture therefore means seeing both sides: one's own preferences and the situation of others. That then results in an ethical guide to which behaviour — rivalry or solidarity — is appropriate for which situation.

'One of the sins committed by the glorification of economic freedom has been precisely that it has tended to confuse individuals as to where the boundary between the two cases lies.'[31]

Mill and Keynes would have agreed. The latter was concerned that it would be some time before we escaped the grip of 'the old Adam' in us, who always has to do and own more and more to be satisfied. That's why it would never have occurred to him to align the systems of economic incentive and social structures primarily towards supporting such an 'old Adam' orientation. Amid all the positional jostling, at least, there can be no answer to the question of when enough is really enough.

And that only leads to the counter-question.

Which is: How much do others have?

In 2005, *National Geographic Magazine* explored the question of where the secret to longevity might lie, travelling to five parts of the world where people are known to live particularly long lives.[32] Those regions, known as Blue Zones, range across almost every continent. They are to be found in Sardinia,

Greece, Japan, Costa Rica, and California. As diverse as those cultures are, they all share a number of features. Scientists believe those commonalities may be the secret to these people's tendency to live so much longer and healthier lives than the average. In all of those cultures, family and close personal ties are given top priority. All find meaning and fulfilment in doing things for their community. For all, exercise, engaging in moderate physical activity, is an integral part of their lives. They all eat in moderation, with a mainly plant-based diet. They don't smoke, drink only the occasional glass of wine, and all have developed rituals to mitigate the effects of stress.

Is it any wonder those people are content?

No, I don't find it surprising either.

Clearly, the activities that lead to a long and healthy life are often those that lose their worth when we try to move too quickly or do too much — in other words, when we try to cram ever more into the same space of time — getting enough exercise, eating a healthy diet, engaging in positive rituals, and maintaining satisfying social contacts. That doesn't mean those long-lived societies show no development, but it's development with a better purpose. And when people in the Blue Zone engage in activities, they apparently do so for the activities' own sake, and not with the aim of improving their position compared to others. What grows out of that is a long lifespan, good health, and meaning. This has a value that cannot be expressed in the monetary terms that economists normally use. Growing better must therefore also mean using better metrics. Otherwise, the values we measure will not tell us whether the goal has been achieved, and if so, how. Even numbers tell stories. When those stories change, so do innovations, new technologies, rules, and forms of cooperation — creating a better experience of the world and of ourselves.

I am reminded here of a concept that the Hungarian American psychologist and happiness researcher Mihály Csíkszentmihályi called *flow*. Back in the nineteen-seventies, he wondered what goes on inside people when they become completely engrossed in a task. It's a state of mind we're all familiar with, which we can usually maintain only briefly, and which we strive to repeat once we've experienced it. Csíkszentmihályi called it flow,[33] to describe the way the test subjects in his study — artists, athletes, scientists — acted completely intuitively, as if they were being carried along by a flowing river. This state grows out of a harmony between the person, the task, and the situation, and is an experience that unites disciplined training and inner balance, a playful moment somewhere between control and creation. It is important that the activity take place in a space — also known as the growth zone — between 'too challenging' and 'not challenging enough', so the task should be neither too difficult nor too easy, enabling concentration, dedication, enjoyment, and a sense of accomplishment to develop.[34] Flow can occur in any activity when there is a match between the person and the task, between the demand and the ability to meet it, either individually or as part of a group. They can be activities that produce and consume goods and services, for example—just not by working 100 hours a week at Goldman Sachs. And not when health and childcare teams have to work under chronically understaffed conditions. Incidentally, both personal worries and the fear of being judged by others are excellent ways to prevent a state of flow from occurring.

Csíkszentmihályi writes elsewhere, 'There are two opposite tendencies in evolution: changes that lead toward harmony (i.e., the ability to obtain energy through cooperation, and through the utilisation of unused or wasted energy); and those that lead toward entropy (or ways of obtaining energy for one's purposes through exploiting other organisms, thereby causing conflict and disorder)'.[35]

Like Mill, Keynes, and Hirsch, Csíkszentmihályi was preoccupied with the question of how it is possible to curtail the logic of eternal increase in human societies. He found the answer in flow activities, whose defining characteristic is that they are pursued for their own sake and not with the aim of improving the actor's position within the system.[36] Flow not only produces feelings of happiness due to the activity itself—which beats jostling for pay, status, and power—but often also breeds excellence, creativity, talent development, productivity, stress resilience, and self-esteem. This adds a collective dimension to Csíkszentmihályi's seemingly individual approach. If individuals can arrive at a state of harmony with themselves about what they do, there is a chance that a society made up of many such *effectors* will run less and flow more. This is a matter of intrinsic rather than extrinsic motivation. 'This enjoyment that comes from surpassing ourselves,' writes Csíkszentmihályi, 'from mastering new obstacles, is the positive counterpart of the eternal dissatisfaction [...] so well expressed by Goethe's *Faust*.'[37]

Would we think about such moments of surpassing ourselves if someone asked us about our wealth?

We would probably think first about our bank account, savings plans, and stocks and shares, and then try to estimate the market value of the assets we own—a car, a flat, a piece of land, or a house, for example. If we were then asked whether that was everything we owned, we might talk about our projected income from working, or renting or leasing out our property. And we might argue that those financial resources allow us to secure access to the goods and services we consider important.[38] As a rule, more money equates to more personal freedom, especially in market-based societies.[39]

But would we ever think to speak of what we can contribute to the world around us? Or, conversely, how other people, public goods, and infrastructures contribute to our ability to live well? Would we even think of the services provided by nature, which we use and take for granted every day?[40]

In my view, doing so would be very helpful, since we now see that the efforts we expend in trying to consume, and own more and more, cause damage to both the natural world and the people in it, and that damage is no longer outweighed by the gains.[41]

There are now numerous approaches that attempt to expand the concept of Gross Domestic Product to better reflect social wellbeing. Not just as a momentary snapshot, but also with a view to the prerequisites for wellbeing in the future. The standard-setting Organisation for Economic Cooperation and Development (OECD), for example, now works with four different definitions of capital.[42] They are: *Economic Capital*, which includes both human-made and financial assets; *Natural Capital*, encompassing stocks of natural resources, land cover, and species biodiversity, as well as ecosystems and their services; *Human Capital*, which refers to the skills and health of individuals; and *Social Capital*, referring to the social norms, shared values, and institutional arrangements that foster cooperation. Together, they make up the assets of a society, from which information, skills, resources, and investments in the shaping of society can flow.

Introducing a better way of satisfying humanity's

needs also holds a great deal of potential for regenerating and improving the quality of those assets, rather than running them down and exhausting them.

The great value of this extended concept of wealth was highlighted most recently by a biodiversity study carried out by the British economist Sir Partha Dasgupta for the British government in 2021.[43] In a 600-page report, he and an international network of co-authors explain how inextricably our social metabolism is permeated by nature.[44] The research team distinguishes three kinds of ecosystem services: *provisioning* of materials and energy, which we make use of every day in the form of food, fresh water, biochemicals, pharmaceuticals, and genetic resources; *regulating and maintenance* services play out more in the background, and include the Earth system processes that attempt to capture concepts such as planetary boundaries, and covers such services as maintaining the carbon cycle, purifying water, decomposing waste, oxygen production, and recycling nutrients; and *cultural services* are those with non-material benefits, which are connected with recreation, inspiration, religious rituals, and spiritual experiences.

Natural, complex systems are only able to provide all these services because they are in flux—or, we might say, *flow*—and are connected by nutrient cycles and energy. In this way, they are able to provide immense wealth for human life over and over again, given time.

However, their rhythm is not dictated by humans' need for positional goods or a standard of life measurable in dollars or pounds, but by the speed at which natural organisms can pollinate, decompose, filter, purify, transport, transform, and reorder. Those who fail to see the value of these processes because there are no numerical indicators for them will also be highly unlikely to cherish them. This might explain why we are always so proud to mention the fact that global per-capita GDP doubled between the years 1992 and 2014, while ignoring the fact that the per-capita stocks of natural resources shrank by 40 per cent over the same period.

'It would look as though we are living at the best of times and the worst of times,' write the authors of the Dasgupta Study.[45]

And what are our political strategies to deal with?

Let's consider the grain shortages caused by the war against Ukraine. The current response is to suspend biodiversity-protection goals and to give that land up immediately for crop growing—but not to even contemplate reducing the number of livestock whose stomachs we in Germany, for example, fill with 60 per cent of those much-needed crops, and who we give 70 per cent of pasture and arable land over to growing feed for globally.[46] To farm one kilogram of beef, around 25 kilograms of feed—maize, soya, beets—are necessary, while 94 per cent of the protein they contain is lost as it passes through the cow and on to human beings. In terms of energy values — that is, expressed as calories — this transformation process is even less economical. Only 1.8 per cent of the calorific value of the feed remains by the time the beef ends up on our plates.[47] We could eat that grain or those vegetables ourselves instead, or export them to poorer countries. That would benefit the climate, animal welfare, and our health.

To give a meaning to the concept of wealth that is appropriate for the 21st century, we will first have to take an honest look at what can keep on growing, how it can do so, and for how long — and what emissions and pollution can be re-absorbed, where, and for how long. That's why it is so important that a rapidly increasing number of initiatives, companies, local authorities, and economists are busy gathering more detailed information on natural assets and their value.[48] And they are not only concerned with quantifying that value; they are also interested in how the complex processes behind those assets work and how their regeneration can best be supported.[49] Yes, the actual situation is alarming. But it is only when we take an honest view that we will be able to provide the solutions to rebuilding the reserves of those natural assets. This will lead to more scope for action in the future, rather than less.

The associated costs have long since been recognised as a profitable investment. Every dollar invested in forested areas, for example, can be expected to generate \$7 to \$30 of added value.[50] According to the World Economic Forum, adopting a 'nature positive' attitude—which means changing the way we exploit ecosystems economically to direct human activities towards rebuilding their reserves and reinvigorating their cycles—would generate more than \$10 trillion in added economic value by 2030.[51] It would also create 375 million new jobs in which people train their ability to understand these regenerative networks and learn to treat the other living beings with whom we share our planet more respectfully.

But what if the political world drags its feet?

Then it will need more encouragement from society. So it behoves all effectors to state clearly which assets should grow in the future and which path we need to take to make that happen. The wellbeing-economy movement is already making a convincing case for future action.[52] And it is up to all of us to demand that companies publish transparent cost-benefit figures, so that the effects of their economic activities are visible beyond their market price values—including those that don't generate money, but do create a lot of added value. This is a practice that various business representatives are now promoting.[53]

Our modern culture celebrates money and belongings as the measure of success. But here, once again, the debate over better indicators for financial markets and investors shows that making a lot of money is far from synonymous with sustainable value-creation.[54] Imagine a society in which we only celebrated solutions that clearly show they are regenerating our social, human, and environmental assets, and how they were doing that. Outside in. It would no longer stand for the ownership of something, but for the ability to make something better. Which would be a very good thing. It would be the first step on the path from Horizon 1 to Horizon 3.

And wouldn't we then have to abolish capitalism?

As much as I understand this question—I am asked it over and over again—I find it to be of secondary importance in this context.

Let's start the process of casting off the shackles of all the 'isms'. These are terms that are often no more than slogans behind which some people hide and others build, which mark boundaries but seldom act as bridges. Of course, capitalism comes in many flavours, and our market economy has changed at breakneck speed in just the past forty years. Let's leave the labels aside, as the most important thing is to understand why our modern economic system is unable to keep the promises it makes. And as long as that is the case, something must change. Identifying the central driving forces of that change is the job of science. We can label it criticism of capitalism, or we can call it an agenda for progress.[55]

I prefer the latter term, since it raises our eyes to the third horizon. The most important thing is that we progress, with a clear head, awareness, and and a mind that is constantly open to learning new thing. The future grows out of our present. It is not a state of being. It is a state of mind.

System trap: dependency

When a society tries to solve a problem by treating the symptoms but not the underlying causes, the result is a dependency on the medicine that alleviates the symptoms. It is similar to burnout: if we fail to face the troubling state of our health honestly, we will not be able to make any interventions to strengthen our ability to regain equilibrium. Any clear view of what is really at issue is clouded, and we are left unable to get to the root of the problem. We get bogged down in our efforts the treat the symptoms, further weakening society, and strengthening dependency. If we want to avoid reaching a tipping point, we must shift the focus from short-term relief to long-term restructuring.

8

Media(tion): using technology better

'A society that embraces technology needs a great inner strength to avoid becoming too greedy and distracted from its goals.'

JOSEPH WEIZENBAUM, INTERNET PIONEER[1]

In 2017, the executives at Facebook made a worrying discovery. The social-networking platform was still by far the biggest in the world, with more than two billion users worldwide, and it was still growing. But the company's statistics showed that people on the platform were no longer as engaged with it as they used to be. They were leaving fewer comments and sharing less content, and weren't logged on for as long. It seemed that spending time on Facebook was becoming boring and lame, and the bosses didn't know why. But they did know they had to do something about it. After all, Facebook does not make money by providing the world with a free social-network platform that people can take or leave as they like. It makes its money through the advertising that can be placed on the network. It offers companies that want to position targeted ads not just access to the attention of its users, but also information about their interests, opinions, and decision-making patterns.

That is Facebook's real stock-in-trade. Its business model earned the company $17 billion in profits in 2017[2] — making it one of the biggest players in an industry that is quite rightly known as the economy of attention.[3] So, when it looked as if users were losing interest in the network, the bosses were alarmed, and resolved to make changes to one of the core parts of Facebook — the algorithm.[4]

When someone signs up to the platform, they receive a list of recommended content that Facebook deems interesting or relevant to them. That list, called a newsfeed, is like a personalised journal created and constantly updated for each user by the platform. It includes photos, videos, links, and content that friends and family have commented on. Of course, that's not all the content circulating on Facebook by far. That would be far too much. It is just a selection, curated specifically for each user by a computer algorithm. On the basis of the data it collects on each user, that algorithm decides what content should be displayed prominently and what shouldn't. It decides what receives exposure and what falls by the wayside. The newsfeed algorithm is the core of Facebook's business model, and its number-one trade secret.[5] No one outside the company has an insight into how it works and the selection criteria it uses — which is not unproblematic for a tool that shapes billions of people's outlook on the world.

In 2017, the executives at the company changed the algorithm more than ever before. Their aim was to provoke users into engaging in more social interaction, so they would spend more time on the platform than if they only passively consumed the videos and news stories posted by media and branded companies. Facebook introduced emojis — little cartoon faces that express happiness, sadness, surprise, or anger — and reprogrammed its algorithm to rate content that received emoji reactions five times higher than that which only received a normal 'like' in the form of the 'thumbs up' symbol. Comments and shares were now also rated more highly by the algorithm. When a post by a user provoked a discussion, its profile in the newsfeed was now automatically raised.

'I'm changing the goal I give our product teams from focussing on helping you find relevant content to helping you have more meaningful social interactions,' wrote Facebook's CEO Mark Zuckerberg in a post at the time. 'We feel a responsibility to make sure our services aren't just fun to use, but also good for people's wellbeing.'[6]

It was not long before the change took effect. Content with emojis appeared more quickly in people's newsfeed due to its higher rating by the algorithm. At the same time, the company's data analysts noticed that many of those posts contained fake news, conspiracy theories, and hate speech. Media companies told Facebook that they were now appearing in people's newsfeeds mainly in connection with boorish, polarising content. Political parties described how the tone of their communications had become more abrasive, and their attacks on political opponents had become tougher, because that gave them more exposure on Facebook.

Although the algorithm had not been programmed to reward negative content and was only supposed to give preference to emotional content, the simple fact is that negative news has a bigger emotional impact on people than positive news. It upsets, frightens, or angers them. The more a post upset people, or the more comments it received, and the more quickly it provoked a discussion, the more highly it was rated by the algorithm. People were now spending more time on the platform, but it was often because they were determined to have the last word in arguments. Dogmatism, confrontation, and exclusion increased. Rather than bringing people closer together, as promised, Facebook magnified their differences. Instead of improving people's wellbeing, it simply increased their anger. That, too, did not go unnoticed by Facebook's data analysts.

In 2019, some of the company's employees decided to do an experiment and create two fictitious profiles on the platform. Both people were supposed to be mothers in their early forties, living in North Carolina and interested in politics. The only difference between 'Carol' and 'Karen' was that Carol was a Republican supporter who followed the accounts of Donald Trump and his wife, Melania, as well as *Fox News*, while Karen was more inclined towards the Democrats, and followed the left-wing senator Bernie Sanders.

The Facebook employees then let the algorithm do its work, and within a short space of time it was recommending content to the two women that was on the far extremes of their political views. Carol, who was politically conservative but not reactionary, was sent material from the far-right conspiracy theorists of QAnon claiming that the world was run by an elite group of paedophile Satanists led by Barack Obama. Liberal Karen, on the other hand, was recommended anti-Trump sites containing faked photos, some of which were very graphic. Within a few days, two women who were not so different at the start of the experiment were immersed in two completely opposite worlds.[7] This is an example of how Facebook can produce the same echo chambers that we are familiar with from other social networks.

The report on that experiment was one of the

documents secretly passed to the press by Frances Haugen in 2021. It gave the public an unprecedented glimpse into the workings of the company. Haugen worked at Facebook as a manager in a department officially responsible for combatting fake news and hate speech on the platform, but she had become increasingly disillusioned with the lack of staff and resources in her department compared to the size of its task, and frustrated by the company's overall lack of commitment to achieving its stated aims. When her department was disbanded following the 2020 American presidential elections, Haugen decided to go public and become a whistleblower.

'I am here today because I believe Facebook's products harm children, stoke division, and weaken our democracy,' she testified at a Senate subcommittee hearing in autumn 2021. She went on to say that the company's leadership knew how to make the platform safer, 'but won't make the necessary changes because they have put their astronomical profits before people'.[8]

It's not as if Frances Haugen was the only Facebook employee to recognise that the algorithm was helping to divide society, and that outrage had become the force driving the metrics by which Facebook measured its growth and success. Employees repeatedly sent memos and made suggestions for how this might be corrected. In the days leading up to the storming of the Capitol in Washington, D.C., by Donald Trump supporters who believed his election defeat was due to the vote having been stolen, Facebook employees sent repeated warnings internally about how rapidly the movement was growing across the platform, and demanding an intervention. After all, they reasoned, they were working inside what was perhaps the most influential communication system ever controlled by a single group of people.

They knew the sort of dynamic developments the company would be better not to accelerate if it wanted to fulfill its declared purpose, which was to help people have more meaningful social interactions on Facebook. At the same time, they also noticed that their employer was acting contrary to that aim, and that its actual, lived purpose was quite different. The only person who could take the choice to move decisively to narrow that gap was Mark Zuckerberg, Facebook's founder, CEO, and main shareholder. But he was unwilling to do anything to slow down those developments, hesitated, and only much later managed to bring himself to correct the algorithm.

'In the end, the buck stops with Mark,' said Frances Haugen at the Senate subcommittee hearing.[9]

How is it possible for a single person to end up being in a position to influence the communicative behaviour and worldview of almost three million people — the conglomerate that now calls itself 'Meta' includes not only Facebook, but also Instagram and WhatsApp—without the public (or even him) knowing precisely what he is doing and what the repercussions will be?

Is it an inevitable consequence of technological progress? Or could we do better?

Technology is now so omnipresent in our lives that we barely think twice about it. We consider it to be part of the solution, not the problem. And that is not surprising, as it is the ever-increasing opportunities to use technology to work for us and solve our problems that we have to thank for the fact that we now live wealthier, safer, and better lives than any generation before us. Technology is the most tangible aspect that separates our world from that of our parents' and grandparents'. While machines initially supplemented human physical strength and increased the speed at which humans could move about, they now multiply the amount of information that can be gathered, processed, and transmitted, and the speed at which that happens. While once we were fascinated by massive industrial complexes, it is mostly increasingly miniaturised networked devices that now captivate us.

That's why our technology expert at the German Advisory Council on Global Change (WBGU) insisted that our report on digitisation and sustainability include in the description of the current reality a section on the technosphere, 'which makes up the technical environment of humans', and which is 'generally used to describe the totality of technical systems produced by humans and the associated formative changes in nature'.[10]

If we were to trace human history along a line marking its technological achievements, the line would describe an exponential curve, starting from the hand axe made of stone and ending with the quantum computer. Humans feature in such a history as fast-learning and enormously inventive creatures working tirelessly to improve their own situation. If it is traced along a line marking its civilisational achievements, however, human history is not so easily told, since those achievements—including such things as the abolition of slavery, equal rights for women, and democracy as a form of government—appear far from secure, and indeed often seem to be endangered or even slated for revision. Social technologies such as laws, institutions, and normative rules require our constant active cooperation if they are to persist. They form a web of relationships and tasks, with roles and responsibilities, and leave room for people to step out of line if they want to. That is the difference between social and automated systems.

Perhaps that is the reason why technological achievements feel more permanent: they are made from solid materials. By contrast, humanity repeatedly forgets, for example, that war is not the most helpful means of ending conflict, despite knowing better. But for humanity to forget how to program a computer seems unthinkable. It is therefore tempting to believe that humanity's technological developments are unconnected to the achievements of civilisation. That technology is purely material and not social. That it is nothing more than a neutral tool. And that it does not itself change societies.

But is that true?

When the American philosopher of technology Albert Borgmann explored this question in the mid nineteen-eighties, many of the innovations that are commonplace today were still in the realm of science fiction. But that does not make his analysis any less pertinent to our current situation—on the contrary. As Borgmann sees it, the promise of technology is to provide humanity with prosperity and freedom. It keeps that promise by creating availability. Technological availability means something has been rendered 'instantaneous, ubiquitous, safe, and easy'. Borgmann calls the means through which technology achieves this a 'device', in contrast to what he designates a 'thing'—which cannot do the same.[11]

According to Borgmann, a central heating system would be a 'device'. Once we turn the nob, it puts out heat instantaneously in every room with a radiator, and is safe and extremely easy to use. No one needs to understand how central heating works to use it. By contrast, heating with an open fireplace involves using wood, which has to be felled, transported, and chopped. And the heat is still not produced instantaneously. The fire needs to be lit—which takes skill and knowledge—and tended and fed. The heat it produces is not ubiquitous, as a fireplace can only warm a single room.

All of that inconvenience is swept away by central heating. It detaches the use of heat from all the activities that used to be necessary to produce it. No one needs to leave the house, get up extra early, or tend the fire. Family members who would have been assigned one of those tasks can now spend the time doing something else. They no longer have to sit together to be warm, because the central heating now warms more than one room. The fireplace is no longer the central focus of the household. And that impacts the way that individuals experience the world around them—they no longer associate warmth with a particular smell, atmosphere, the crackling of logs, or the common activity of making a fire.

As Borgmann sees it, we live in a world in which the 'device paradigm' sits at the centre of all our technology narratives. Goods and services are available in a 'non-burdensome way' by removing the inner workings of the necessary processes from human view. And therefore possibly from human perception and understanding.[12] Devices always change our day-to-day lives.

So does that mean we all have to go back to sitting together by the open fire?

What it means, first of all, is that when we *do* do that—on vacation, in a holiday home, at friends' houses—we do it mostly because of precisely the things that central heating is supposed to spare us from.

The crucial difference between a 'thing' and a 'device', according to Borgmann, is that a thing connects us to our surroundings. It requires engagement, craft, skill, and the knowledge to understand the situation in which the desired benefit will result. Devices render all, or almost all, of that unnecessary. Devices separate the resources and processes necessary to achieve a goal from the actual moment of use.

That is the basis of the freedom—and the convenience—that technology promises us: we no longer have to bother about all the peripheral stuff. We do not know how our smartphone works, but we don't need to. We wouldn't be in a position to repair it anyway. We don't know the working conditions of wherever it was assembled, how many rare earths had to be dug up to make it, or how much energy is consumed by computer servers every time we access the information stored there. We open up Google and find what we're looking for without having any idea how the search results were filtered or what the company will do with the data we leave behind. We order things from Amazon, but we don't know why a particular company's products were recommended to us rather than a different company's. We accept delivery of a parcel, but we only find out how far it has travelled when a stranded container ship blocks the Suez Canal, or when distribution-centre workers go on strike for better pay. We order from universal supply companies, and are then surprised when smaller brands become unavailable and independent shops disappear from the High Street.

And for all those activities, we open up a social media app on a little product for global communication, our personal portal to the free internet, our gateway to the World Wide Web. But that little product is simply an interface to access a huge collection of networked things, and access to most of that data is now controlled by just a small number of companies. Take a moment to notice next time. Most websites have a 'buy now' button linked directly to Amazon, and you can use your Google, Facebook, or Apple profile to save you having to type one of a myriad passwords into various companies' websites. The more log-ins you associate with your profile, the more the company knows about you, and the less likely it is that you will ever delete them—after all, that would mean resubscribing to everything. This is what is called a 'network effect'.

And so, although the original vision of a free internet still lingers in some narratives, or has been rebranded as the Metaverse, access to those worlds is by no means free—it is a mediated commodity. Many individual digital product developments have come together to create a worldwide, parastate-like technosphere under the control of a few companies, which have become immeasurably rich as a result.

The internet has now become the world's biggest 'device'. We stare at our screens, but they conceal connectivity behind availability, and the way that availability feeds back to those networks and our resources. In Japan, a country that is culturally very accepting of digitisation, the effects of the 'digital curtain' on people's experience of the world and the environment they live in are seen as 'unintended side effects'.[13]

Even though Albert Borgmann wrote his book before the advent of the internet of things, he identified the device paradigm as a central feature of our modern civilisation. This shows us why we need to look behind the screens to understand whether the progress of technology and civilisation are in step with each other.

What progress are we pursuing with technology, anyway?

In 2019, the American technologist Andrew McAfee published a book in which he appeared to prove that it makes perfect sense to think of technological progress and GDP growth as coupled to each other. He argued that striving for profit maximisation would always lead to the most efficient solutions—also saving the environment in the process.[14] Taking the United

States as an example, he set up calculations to prove an old technological dream: that what is still the world's biggest economy is able to decouple economic growth from the consumption of natural resources, thanks to technological progress and a style of capitalism oriented towards constant cost reduction. The book is called *More from Less*, and, if the subtitle is to be believed, it tells 'The surprising story of how we learned to prosper using fewer resources—and what happens next'.

The examples McAfee cites are striking. It is indeed true that the US economy has continued to grow since the turn of the millennium, although its consumption of important metals such as aluminium, nickel, copper, steel, and gold has fallen. The same is true of cement, sand, stone, wood, and paper. According to the US Geological Survey, which records data on the national use of 72 natural resources, consumption of 66 of them has already peaked. It appears the rich countries are now also becoming the clean ones.

Things that used to be big, heavy, imprecise, polluting, or energy-guzzling are now smaller, lighter, more precise, and more efficient. According to McAfee, far greater public awareness, as well as far faster reactions from governments, are still needed, but otherwise, it's enough to just keep on doing as we have always done: 'We don't need to yank the steering wheel of our economies and societies in a different direction; we just need to step on the accelerator.'[15]

It sounds like a fantastic story. But there's just one catch. McAfee can only tell this story because he has adjusted his screen so that it doesn't display a significant proportion of the resources and processes necessary to prop up America's model of prosperity. That is made doubly clear, ironically, by the case of the iPhone—which he holds up as the prime example of the way that technological progress can create *More from Less*. iPhones are manufactured almost exclusively in the global South: the necessary raw materials and labour come from there. But the profits from selling the phones is recorded as part of America's GDP. And the damage caused by the mass production of the devices remain in the global South.[16] Unfortunately, the reason that so many countries in the global North appear to have such a good environmental-protection record is often because they have outsourced the dirty links in their value-added chains to poorer countries. It's a practice known as 'externalisation'.

As soon as we zoom our screens out, unlike McAfee, to take in not just one country, but the whole world, it becomes clear that humanity has not yet succeeded in decoupling natural resource consumption from economic growth.[17] The figures for raw materials extraction alone have risen by more than 50 per cent since the turn of the millennium, and are twice as high as they need to be for a sustainable use of our planet's resources.[18] Metals, non-metals, fossil

fuels, or biomass—all the consumption curves point
upwards. And the same is true of global water and
energy consumption.[19] Even several years ago, resource
consumption in the US was significantly higher, at 32
tonnes per capita, than the G20 average, three times
higher than the global average, and ten times higher
than the average in Africa.[20]

Of course, against this background, it can be
counted as a success when a country manages *not* to
increase its consumption of resources *even more*—but
that then also begs the question of how much per-
capita consumption it would be good to aim for, when
other countries aspire to do the same as America.[21]

There was a large media reaction in the US and
Europe when McAfee's book was published, which
is not surprising, given that it provided the wealthy
part of the world with a narrative to restore its self-
image as a pioneer in the accumulation of goods. That
accumulation is driven by the competition for positional
status in which social media, with their personalised
messages tailored to the current mood, undermine the
few remaining purchase barriers in real time, although
the markets are already saturated.

In 2020, global spending on digital advertising
reached $140 billion, three-quarters of which came
from ten major companies. Facebook and Google

accounted for half of all spending on online advertising in the US.[22] In this way, the digitisation brought by the technology revolution is playing a significant part in the rising level of consumption. Ultimately, we are using the efficiency gains from technology to consume even more—rather than to lessen the burden on the environment. This effect has been known for a long time under the term 'rebound'.[23] As long as our demand for supply security continues to grow year by year, that is not going to change.

This is perfectly illustrated by the much-bewailed supply shortages in rich countries: state spending and cheap loans, coupled with the rapid spending of the dollars that people saved during the lockdowns, led to a growth in the flow of goods in the US of 17 per cent in two years.[24] But most reporting about worries over the gaps in the supply chain did not even mention that fact. Media reports were more concerned with how quantum computing might be used to coordinate the movements of drivers, trucks, and containers even more efficiently, so that supply demands could continue to be met. A far simpler solution, which would, however, require more social and cultural revolutions than digital ones, was suggested by the US columnist Amanda Mull in the pithy title of her article 'Stop Shopping. America needs you to buy less junk.'[25]

'In a system where technological innovation is leveraged to expand extraction and production, it makes little sense to hope that yet more technological innovation will somehow magically do the opposite,' writes the British-based economic anthropologist Jason Hickel in a book that reads like the counter-argument to Andrew McAfee. The book is called *Less is More*, in contrast to McAfee's *More from Less*, and is based on a different definition of progress: instead of focussing on GDP, it centres on the question of what people actually need in order to be healthy, happy, and satisfied.[26]

Unless we constantly remind ourselves of the purpose technology is supposed to serve, we will never understand its form, or control its use.

Let's take our energy systems as an example once more. For a long time, we had no way of producing large amounts of electricity sustainably, except from hydroelectric power. From the late nineteen-fifties on, there were attempts to build solar modules, but they were only used to power satellites in space. That did not change until the oil crisis in the late nineteen-seventies. The US president at the time, Jimmy Carter, had solar collectors installed on the roof of the White House and, in a speech that now seems almost visionary, declared the dawning of the solar age, although the collectors were only able to provide warm water.[27] They were immediately removed by his successor, Ronald Reagan. The oil crisis was over, climate change had not yet been studied, and the pressure for structural change had dropped.

A similar fate befell wind energy. Serious attempts to harness electricity from the wind were mainly based in Denmark at the time, but they never made it beyond the test phase. The world's biggest wind turbine was built on behalf of the German Ministry for Research in the early nineteen-eighties. It was located in Schleswig-Holstein, Germany's most northerly federal state, and was so prone to faults and breakdowns that it only ran for a couple of hundred hours in total. There are very persistent rumours that the motivation of the energy companies that were supposed to operate the turbine was purely to prove that wind power had no future.

I remember drawing up a poster presentation at the World Future Council in 2016, in which we wanted to highlight the fact that renewable energy was about more than just the price of a kilowatt hour and the climate crisis. We had drawn up a long list of advantages: less transition loss, thanks to centralised power generation; lower electricity costs once the equipment was installed and there were no fuel bills to be paid; and citizen-controlled energy production, since consumers can become producers and are therefore not at the mercy of price manipulations. And not forgetting: energy security instead of dependency on resource-rich countries. Politicians no longer appeared to have any interest in such multi-solving, especially after 2010: while Germany officially declared its 'energy revolution', the most influential voice when it came to setting targets appeared to be that of the big, powerful energy providers, whose aim was to find a way to prolong Horizon 1 for as long as possible, while also making sure they remained the winners in the new system.

So what do we do when a system fails to deliver on its promises?

Are the declared purposes — for example, the energy revolution, or Zuckerberg's much-vaunted meaningful social interactions — and the real, lived purpose — the pursuit of maximum profits — really mutually compatible? And who decides whether the gap between them is too big when damage to human and social assets on an unprecedented scale is at stake? Is it wise to place control of the communicative and cooperative nervous system of our societies in the hands of just a few large companies? On profit giants with no care for the general good? Which have grown so big that we barely have the choice to turn to competitors, even if we don't like what they're offering? And which now use their immense lobbying power to make sure this situation doesn't change?

Of course, many formerly or currently active representatives of the technosphere are asking these questions. According to Google technology ethicist Tristan Harris, 'Tech addiction, polarisation, outrage-ification of culture, the rise in vanities [and] microcelebrity culture are all, in fact, symptoms of a larger disease: the race to capture human attention by tech giants. And as those giants are making technology smarter, they are indirectly making all of us dumber, meaner, and alienated from one another.' The result is what he calls 'human downgrading', which he describes as 'the climate change of culture'.[28] That sounds pretty pessimistic. Others who have left Silicon Valley giants express similar opinions.[29] And scientists who study the effects of that captured attention on our wellbeing and cooperative coexistence view this development with concern.[30]

So should we just switch all technology off?

No, of course not.

We just need to design it and use it differently.

'New technologies are constructed mentally before they are constructed physically,' writes the British economist Brian Arthur, 'and this mental process will need to be carefully looked into.'[31]

In a nutshell: when our thinking and our intentions change, our apps will also change, along with the way we connect with each other and the rest of the world. To raise awareness of this, Albert Borgmann contrasts the device paradigm with what I would call the focus paradigm: 'To focus on something or to bring it into focus is to make it central, clear, and articulate,' he writes. Like adjusting the aperture of a camera.

Many of the things that allow us to focus, in the

sense described by Borgmann, are tools, in the classical sense of the word, that we use with our human strength and flexibility, thereby connecting us physically with the situation we are in. Thus, the focus paradigm always describes interactivity, which Borgmann calls 'focal practices'. When we engage in them, we do not block out the relationship between use and production. We see it clearly before our eyes, enabling a 'unity of achievement and enjoyment, of mind, body, and the world, of myself and others'.[32] I'm not sure whether Borgmann ever discussed flow with Mihály Csíkszentmihályi, but since our digital technosphere is bound to continue growing, a balancing focus paradigm would undoubtedly be useful if we want to avoid losing sight, and awareness, of the technosphere's connection to physical reality.

Continuing that thought: devices can also make the means and processes behind the screen visible and appreciable. This kind of technological development happens everywhere, but it usually takes place outside the grand narratives of the future deployed by those competing for our attention. One example of how this can work is Triodos Bank, which has a clear and easy-to-understand website detailing where the money invested with it goes.[33] Another example is the Ecosia search engine, which plants one tree on average for every forty-five online searches, to compensate for its energy consumption.[34] Or projects such as those of the Global

Commons Alliance—a network that uses modern sensors, drones, databases, and computer modelling to learn how to gain a better understanding of ecosystems so that it can educate farmers and companies about how to preserve them, so they can get paid for doing so.[35]

Personally, I would be very interested to hear a discussion between Brian Arthur, Albert Borgmann, and Audrey Tang, who is the currently Taiwan's Minister of Digital Affairs, and who has shown impressively how social and technological progress can go hand in hand. She started programming at the age of eight, but left school at fourteen since, as a highly gifted child, she had little connection to institutional education and was bullied by schoolmates who were in competition with her for the best grades. She created her own educational spaces using online courses, learning English, reading academic journals, and engaging with experts more than twice her age. She founded her first IT company at the age of nineteen.[36] Moving to America, she worked for Apple and the Wikimedia Foundation and as an IT consultant. By the age of thirty-three, she was considering retirement.

But 2012 saw political protests in Taiwan. The mostly young protesters were angry about their government's strategy of rapprochement with mainland China, and suspicious that many of its campaigns were financed by Beijing. It all came to a head when a trade agreement with China was approved, and hundreds of students and academics stormed the parliament building and the cabinet office. Their demand was for transparency. Tang flew back to her native Taiwan 'because democracy need[ed] me', as she puts it.[37] She mixed with the protesters and lugged metres of data cables into parliament to report to the rest of the world from there. That was the birth of Taiwan's Sunflower Movement for transparency and efficient democratic decision-making. Its search for solutions always involves the use of digital technologies, starting with the question of what aims are being pursued.

'Situational applications' is the term Tang uses to describe the various platforms and initiatives: 'configurations for social interaction in the digital space'. The participants themselves dictate the character of those interactions. The applications are open source, and carry a clear declaration of support for such norms as clarity, inclusive debate, and stakeholder participation. Tang does not trust the narratives of the tech giants an inch: 'I tend to think in terms of a prosocial, civic infrastructure as opposed to an antisocial, private sector infrastructure.'[38]

She describes her vision of a life-enhancing technosphere in the form of what she calls a poem-prayer:

> When we see the 'internet of things', let's make it
> an internet of beings.
> When we see 'virtual reality', let's make it a shared
> reality.

When we see 'machine learning', let's make it collaborative learning.
When we see 'user experience', let's make it about human experience.
When we hear 'the singularity is near', let us remember: the plurality is here.[39]

Audrey Tang became Taiwan's Minister for Digital Affairs following the Democratic Progressive Party's victory in the general election of 2016.[40] But, rather than feeling she is part of the government, she sees herself as a mediator between the decision-makers, voters, and activists. As a citizen, Tang is a staunch supporter of democracy as a means of solving social problems. As a programmer, however, she is dissatisfied with the way it works. She cannot see why voters are only asked for feedback once every four years when elections come around, rather than being involved in implementing social change directly themselves. She also cannot understand why only politicians get to define what any given problem is and how it should be tackled. She believes politics should be about more than just presenting a programme that citizens can only accept or reject in an election—or refuse to cast their vote at all. Tang believes that is a waste of potential.[41]

Today, more than a quarter of Taiwanese citizens' initiatives operate on digital democratic platforms initiated by young people. They highlight social issues, and include critics directly in the search for solutions.[42] That also includes teaching both digital and democratic skills as part of the education system, although those skills should not be confused with the ability to operate personal devices or to programme them. Controversial issues can be put up for debate on one platform, while another can be used to submit petitions, and a third might be a place to report unsubstantiated or false information. It's about agenda-setting, co-creating digital social spaces, and school students taking on the *responsibility* to participate in the digital minister's policy-making.

In a democracy that is not recognised as an independent country by neighbouring China, social media are often a means of influencing public opinion, especially during elections.[43] Taiwan's answer is 'humour over rumour'. Under that slogan, even school students can help sort through suspected fake news reports using software, as part of a large group of fact-checkers, and post a satirical response within hours. 'When we roll out within a couple of hours a funny response [to toxic content], it motivates people to share something enjoyable, rather than something retaliatory or discriminatory, and then people feel much better.'[44] Again, we see the declared goal of enabling people to feel better—but with the opposite effect to Facebook's.

Tang and her initiatives are an impressive example of how the role played by citizens is changing—from passive approval-givers to active policy co-creators. But the role of parliamentarians is also changing, as the results of parliamentary votes and budgetary decisions have become publicly available. Every cabinet session, every parliamentary debate, all talks between citizens and government representatives are recorded, and the transcripts are put online. Tang makes herself available every Wednesday at her office in the Social Innovation Lab in Taipei. Citizens can spend up to forty minutes each talking to her there. The only condition is that a transcript of these conversations must also be published online. Every two weeks she is similarly available at one of the country's four service centres, which she also uses as a way of learning about the latest social innovations.[45]

And in Europe? There, the European Commission is trying to negotiate the exclusion of phone texts and direct messages from its Transparency Directive. Nowadays, such services can relay the same amount of text as emails, so someone like a commission president could arrange billion-euro deals with a vaccine manufacturer, for example, without the public having the right to know any details.[46]

According to the democracy index published by *The Economist*, Taiwan, with a population of 23.5 million, features higher than both Germany and Switzerland, while the journal *Foreign Policy* counts Audrey Tang among the leading global thinkers of our time.[47]

Does the kind of action championed by Tang sound like one of the 'meaningful social interactions' that Facebook claimed to want to encourage? I think so. When such interactions occur in real life, they result in the establishment of completely different infrastructures. Then, as Tang shows, the state sector can become far more than a lame duck, limping along behind the disruptive power wielded by the tech giants.

Perhaps the private sector simply moves too quickly to achieve the aim (the *purpose*) of the common good.[48] Long before the first dot-com bubble burst around the turn of the millennium, Donella Meadows had already realised that, for all technologies, 'it depends on who is wielding it, with what goal. [...] If corporations wield it for the purpose of generating marketable products, that is a very different goal, a very different selection mechanism.'[49]

So it is worth taking a very close look at how much focus-based thinking takes place in big companies, especially those that subscribe to the 'move fast and break things' model, with verifiably aggressive business practices.[50] And it's important to understand that such companies can only change so much so quickly because they have so much financial capital available to them—financial capital that is primarily oriented towards making money fast, rather than towards the common good, or respectful of the limited availability inherent in living systems. All that money-making means we constantly have to buy more convenience goods. And replace our devices regularly. Otherwise, share prices might go down, or companies might face hostile takeovers.

Does that sound like another vicious circle?

It isn't.

First, it is just a system trap, in which the majority of our technology is now created. It is not a law of nature. If we want to keep within our planetary boundaries, we need to have a bold debate about which technologies our limited resources should be used for. The supply problems we're currently experiencing are good practice for that, if we don't pretend that the problems are just temporary. Should computer-chip manufacturers prioritise supplying the gaming industry over the solar energy industry, just because the former is able to pay more?[51]

'Meaningful social interactions' can take many forms. So don't be intimidated by the cryptic jargon of the tech and finance industries, don't accept ridicule for not keeping up with the Metaverse and its optimised performers, if what you prefer is to take the time for caring, human interactions and pleasures, rather than striving for more speed, more packaging waste, and more multitasking. The social licence (or social licence to operate) debate is just now picking up speed with regard to tech companies.[52] The same is true of the search for alternative business models such as cooperatives, open innovation platforms or steward-ownership, as promoted by the Purpose Foundation. It sees its purpose as being to protect a company's declared purpose and the people working on achieving it from being hindered by the individual interests of those financially involved in the enterprise.

A legal structure is also a technology—a social one. The word originally comes from the Greek *tékhne*, which meant craft, skill, technique, or art. But it also meant 'cunning' or 'wile'. And—the other side of the coin—gaining a clear view. For instance, if Facebook as it exists today is the answer, what was the question? There is still plenty of room for improvement when it comes to communicating on a human-to-human level.

System trap: competition and escalation

Healthy and agile systems are made up of many subsystems that find solutions to overarching questions. However, if those subsystems are primarily geared towards the repression of others, cooperative competition descends into escalating rivalry. Once oligopolies emerge, the trend can quickly lead to extreme results and a lack of freedom to choose: even critics of Amazon have little choice but to use its platform to sell their goods, which further fuels the trend. One possible way out is through unilateral disarmament; another is an imposed re-orientation towards the overarching questions by means of better rules.

9

Behaviour: organising better

'This country will not be a permanently good place for any of us to live in unless we make it a reasonably good place for all of us to live in.'

THEODORE ROOSEVELT, 1912

Paris is the most densely populated city in Europe. More than two million people live in an area only one-eighth the size of Berlin. That's probably irrelevant to the tourists who swarm the city in their hundreds of thousands every year, as most of the city's visitors are attracted by quite different superlatives. But it has enormous implications for the people who live in and around Paris. It means that space is scarce in the city—and that makes it expensive. Anyone looking for somewhere to live in central Paris has to be able to afford rental prices of almost 30 euros per square metre, while real estate costs almost 13,000 euros per square metre to buy.[1] Very few people can afford such prices, and those who can, often don't live in the city at all, and use their apartment as a financial investment. Paris is not only the most densely populated city in Europe; it is also the second-most expensive in the world.[2]

That's why ten million of the twelve million people who live in the greater-metropolitan area live in the suburbs, the *banlieues*, high-rise estates built beyond the multi-lane orbital highway that divides the city from the surrounding area. They commute into the city every morning, and travel back in the evening after work, causing traffic congestion. They spend almost seven whole days a year stuck in traffic — another European superlative.[3] Or they take the regional train or the Metro, which are almost always so overcrowded that passengers have to squeeze themselves into the train carriages.

Métro, boulot, dodo is the phrase Parisians use to describe the triad that dictates their daily lives. It is French slang for 'Metro, work, sleep', and goes back to a nineteen-fifties poem by the French writer Pierre Béarn. It describes the seemingly inescapable monotony that results from the unalterable fact that people's workplace and home are far apart.

The original guiding model of a European city — to conveniently connect many different places of exchange within a short distance of each other — seemed to have been lost in Paris.[4] Other major cities suffered a similar fate. That's why one of the Global Agenda's seventeen sustainability goals is dedicated to creating sustainable cities. It is in these conurbations that the links between social, environmental, cultural, and economic trends are most obvious. For European cities, there is also the Leipzig Charter of 2007, updated in 2020, which provides a clear guiding model for 'integrated cities' with a focus on the common good:

> This includes general welfare, reliable public services of general interest, as well as reducing and preventing new forms of social, economic, environmental, and territorial inequalities. Our common goal is to safeguard and enhance the quality of life in all European towns and cities and their functional areas. No one should be left behind.[5]

Whether such a declared aim can become a reality depends on—you guessed it—us humans, of course. On the effectors in our world.

When the mayor of Paris, Anne Hidalgo, campaigned for re-election in 2020, she ran on an agenda she called 'the fifteen-minute city'. She wanted citizens to be able to complete any personal business or errands by travelling for no more than a quarter of an hour. That included not just shopping, visits to the doctor, attending school, and going to the cinema, theatre, or gym, but also travelling to work—all doable without a car.[6] The mayor had already begun the process of transforming Paris with this aim during her first term in office.[7] She closed the large east-west expressway along the Right Bank of the Seine, turning the road that previously carried more than 70,000 cars a day into a park for pedestrians and cyclists. It is now home to cafés, bars, and small shops. During her re-election campaign, Hidalgo promised to turn almost half of the city's public parking spaces—almost 70,000 in number—into green spaces. She also now intends to limit cars carrying only one person to a single lane on the orbital highway. The rest of the road will be open for carpools, buses, and bikes. Some of the grand avenues that criss-cross the city will be turned into cycle ways, and some of its most famous squares are to be pedestrianised. In some residential quarters, she even plans to narrow every street so that cars can no longer overtake each other. Paris already has an almost city-wide speed limit of 30 kilometres per hour.

What would happen in Germany if a politician were to run for office in such a big city with such an agenda? In Hanover, the Green Party's Belit Onay was re-elected as mayor in 2019 on a promise to ban cars from the city centre. But now, as it gets down to brass tacks, the level of acceptance for his plan is falling. Retailers claim their customers simply prefer to do their shopping by car, and, they argue, the city must welcome all-comers, no matter how they arrive.[8] But the initial aim is only to reduce the amount of through-traffic. Incidentally, it seems that people don't buy fewer goods when they shop on foot or by bike rather than by car. Studies show that they go shopping more often and buy smaller amounts each time.[9] And in Berlin? The city's government refused even to allow a referendum on making the inner city car-free. However, the plebiscite would also have included proposed legislation to ban even local residents from using their cars except with a permit for special occasions, such as going on vacation or transporting heavy belongings. The local authorities found that would be too much of an infringement on citizens' freedoms.[10]

And, just like that, we're back in Tanaland, because of over-focussing on what appears to be the most pressing problem. This 'preoccupation with immediate goals' clouds our view of the bigger picture.

Anne Hidalgo did not fall prey to that. Hidalgo realised she couldn't just take residents' cars away from them, no matter how good the reasons for doing so. She knew she had to offer them a way to manage their daily lives better without a car, in a way that would be more pleasant and less stressful. With a clear view of the third horizon, combined with effective communication, even if it might mean a little added inconvenience in the short term.

She was returned to office in 2020. In her second

term, she intends to extend the Metro by 200 kilometres to improve connections to the suburbs. The network of cycle paths will be increased to 1,000 kilometres. According to the city authorities, the number of cyclists in Paris doubled between 2019 and 2020.[11] Paris already has one of the biggest bikeshare systems in the world outside China, since introducing its '*Plan Vélo*' some years ago.[12] In the coming years, Hidalgo plans not only to build 40,000 social-housing units, but also to return 30,000 apartments to the city's housing market that are currently unavailable to Parisians because they are rented out to tourists via platforms such as Airbnb. She also intends to plant 170,000 new trees, creating small forests outside City Hall, the Opera House, and the Gare de Lyon station, for example. Although Hidalgo's critics like to claim the opposite, she is not opposed to any particular mode of transport. She simply wants to re-open the limited space in the city for the common good, and places the social, environmental, and spatial equality of all citizens at the centre of her urban planning.

The ideas that form the basis of Anne Hidalgo's policies go back to the concept of a 'living smart city' devised by the French-Colombian urbanist Carlos Moreno.[13] He observed that modern metropolises rob their citizens of their natural feeling for space and time. Space is compressed, because long distances can be covered by the many means of transport, and every part of the city can be reached relatively easily. But as soon as such transport is used, time becomes stretched, as people spend several hours a day in their cars or on public transport, although all they want to do is get to work. Moreno wants to give citizens their feeling for space and time back, with his idea that everything necessary for life in the city should be reachable within fifteen minutes on foot or by bike. He believes that the structures of the city should be oriented towards the needs of its residents, and not the other way round.

Carlos Moreno told journalists that when Anne Hidalgo called him to find out more about his urban concept, he initially thought it would just end up as a footnote at the bottom of a campaign flyer. 'But she put it at the heart of her political campaign.'[14]

Time Magazine has since named Anne Hidalgo as one of the 100 most influential people in the world,[15] and Paris is regarded internationally as one of the most interesting places when it comes to eco-social urban restructuring. The French capital is one of a group of European cities undergoing similar changes, including Copenhagen, Amsterdam, Vienna, Zurich, and Barcelona. When tourists visit those cities and admire their vibrant atmosphere, they usually say it is the city's culture that makes it so special. Few realise, though, that culture grows out of the urban structures that enable such vibrancy to develop. Conversely, infrastructures are an expression of culture. They give order to relationships and encounters, influence our perceptions, shape our social attitudes, and establish desired patterns of behaviour within the system — or, at least, make some decisions easier and some behaviours more probable than others. They make moving in one direction easier, while making it harder to move in the other.

For many years, urban infrastructure planning — for road building, traffic-light programming, and parking spaces, for example — has been geared towards the guiding principle of the car-friendly city. It influences rules such as traffic regulations, which prioritise cars by allowing them to go faster than cyclists and by coordinating the green phases of traffic lights; it also influences the authorities that issue construction permits and plan traffic and transportation routes and urban designs. All this results in a system that makes certain forms of mobility more attractive than others. And it thereby also influences the 'stocks and flows' of a mobility system — that is, the number of cars, trams, cycle paths, and parking spaces, as well as the frequency and speed at which various means of transport move. Let's just imagine for a minute that traffic lights were programmed to give pedestrians and cyclists a green light for twice as long as cars. That would have an enormous effect on congestion, travelling times, and decisions about how to get from A to B. And that, in turn, would have an enormous impact on the number of vehicles in the city.

The principle of the fifteen-minute city thus shifts the purpose of the rules and incentives—and creates a city where there is a completely different attitude. That can't be achieved overnight, of course, but it can happen over time, if the innovations from the second horizon are oriented towards the new purpose. Then the many individual actions and decisions of the effectors acting within a system gradually combine to create new solutions to the problem of how to organise efforts to achieve the overarching aim.

In short: social-innovation learning takes place.

'When systems work well, we see a kind of harmony in their functioning,' writes Donella Meadows.[16] This could be called the 'harmony of hierarchies'. It arises when the superordinate system—in this case, the municipal authorities—which is supposed to provide for the good of the whole, offers a framework within which the subordinate systems—in this case, those concerned with living, working, selling, moving around—can organise themselves freely according to their different needs. Such harmony can only develop if all activities taken together enable the purpose of the superordinate system to be met. If the guiding principle of 'car friendliness' can no longer be reconciled with environmental, social, spatial, and economic equality, then a new guiding principle is required. If that new principle becomes a real, lived purpose, the structures will follow the declared goal. Ideally, this would happen in such a way that the authority in charge of traffic no longer has to compete with the authority in charge of resource protection, or those responsible for housing construction or economic development—and, instead, all four would pool their ideas about how spaces, infrastructures, and mobility routes can be designed so that any given square metre can serve several goals.[17]

From sectoral thinking to spatial thinking.

From a zero-sum game to multi-solving.

Germany's woodlands are another good example. In our imagination, they look like the magical forests where the fairy tales of our childhood play out—ancient, wild, and mysterious, full of oak and beech trees, with trunks many metres thick. But, in reality, they have not looked that way for a long time. They are now mostly dominated by spruce trees, especially in the lower mountains of central Germany.[18] They stand in neat rows like soldiers, so close together that the forest floor barely receives any sunlight. That's no accident; it's how they are planted. The long, straight logs produced by the spruce tree have always been highly sought-after for construction timber, and spruce has always been a profitable crop. That's why it was common practice for a long time to force young saplings to grow faster under stress. After a plantation was staked out, the saplings were deliberately planted too close to each other, so that they grew fresh wood quickly in their effort not to be overshadowed by their neighbours in the competition for sunlight. This so-called crowding also results in fewer side branches, creating the less knotty timber preferred by the construction industry. When they stand apart, spruce trees are naturally conical in shape, but when crowded, they are more reminiscent of a row of fenceposts.

If you want to see how a sectoral silo mentality and an overly narrow definition of a system's purpose — in this case, increasing timber yields — are reflected in a given structure, just visit one of Germany's forests. If you want to know what happens to that structure when changes come its way, just stay there and wait.

When violent storms swept across Germany in 2018, they caused serious damage to its forests. Normally, fallen trees are cleared from the forest floor immediately after a storm, as they provide an ideal breeding ground for bark beetles — the forestry industry's worst enemy. But the damage caused by those storms was so extensive that forestry workers were unable to remove all the uprooted trees in good time. This led to a veritable bark beetle invasion over the next few years. Spruce trees have two natural mechanisms to defend themselves against such attacks. One is to grow strong lateral branches to protect their trunk from the sun. Bark beetles love warmth, so that shade offers the tree some protection. But in artificially crowded plantations, the trees have no lateral branches, so cannot protect themselves in this way. The second defence mechanism is the tree's sap, which reseals the holes drilled in its bark by the beetles. But increasing climate change means summers have become so much hotter that the spruce trees, weakened by drought, are unable to produce as much sap. Even healthy trees fell prey in this way to the bark beetle, which was additionally able to reproduce four times a year, rather than the usual twice, due to the hotter conditions.[19]

Just as with car-friendliness, the system's aim of increasing the volume of timber was too narrowly defined, artificially reducing its scope. If, for example, the aim had been to preserve the health of the forest, the woodlands would have been less crowded and more varied in terms of both species and terrain. The leaves of deciduous trees would have created a forest canopy to provide shade, and both berry bushes and moss banks would have acted as water stores, exposing the trees to less drought and making them more able to resist attacks by the bark beetle, which are in fact part of the natural life cycle of the forest, as the trees they kill provide food for insects and eventually replenish the soil as humus. But, instead, Germany saw the biggest wave of spruce die-back in its post-war history. The country is now faced with reforesting an area five times the size of Lake Constance.[20]

Systems change and are changed. Reacting to that constant dynamic and finding answers to questions that have not been asked before is achieved by progress, and by anticipating and correcting developments that are too one-sided and that prevent the system from fulfilling its overarching purpose. This is about finding the appropriate 'feed-forwards' to prevent crises, or to cushion the system against them and help it emerge from them quickly.

At the beginning of 2021, Germany was in the midst of the third wave of the Covid-19 pandemic. In an essay published in the news journal *Der Spiegel*, the German sociologist Andreas Reckwitz asked what response the state could give to these challenges.[21] The pandemic revealed how well or otherwise the state was prepared, as did the banking crisis and migration before it, and we will see it again with climate change and species extinction—and those are just the crises we know await us in the future—without even counting the unexpected crises ahead.

How should the state prepare for such a future?

Reckwitz brings the idea of resilience into play—a seemingly ubiquitous term at the moment. It was originally used by psychologists to describe a person's ability to cope with extremely traumatic experiences and to 'get back on their feet' quickly. The term comes from the Latin verb *resilire*, meaning to bounce back, which is a phrase also used by academics for the same concept. Reckwitz points out that the term has now also become common in political rhetoric, which can have both positive and negative consequences. 'There is no doubt that a paradigm shift towards a politics of resilience in the 21st century in some respect would be a smart or even wise move,' he writes, but he goes on to warn that it also has its pitfalls.[22]

A politics of resilience, writes Reckwitz further, would be different from all politics to date, insofar as it assumes a completely different future from the one we currently expect to see. In the politics of the welfare state of the nineteen-fifties and sixties, and of the competitive state since the nineteen-eighties, the future was always seen as open and full of opportunities just there for the taking, leading to more progress, freedom, and prosperity. But in the politics of resilience, the future is principally characterised by dangers that might cause repeated, serious disturbances or even wholesale collapse. Reckwitz argues that this is a fundamental change of perspective in which the narrative is turned on its head. 'From striving for the new and positive, to avoiding or enduring the negative. From the point of view of resilience, society appears less as a space for departure into a progressive future than as being in a state of elementary vulnerability. The task now is to prevent the worst.'

Reckwitz believes this creates a 'policy of negativity' that must learn 'to reckon with the losses'.[23] Although the sociologist accepts the necessity of such a political change, he is clearly also ill at ease with it, for fear it may blunt people's sensibility to the possibilities of transformational change.

Interestingly, research approaches exist that place precisely this kind of transformability—that is, 'the capacity to create untried beginnings from which to evolve a fundamentally new way of living'[24]—at the centre of the idea of resilience, rather than seeing it as an alternative to resilience. This is the approach taken by the Stockholm Resilience Centre, for example, which analyses resilience as a structural and dynamic concept: how can socio-ecological systems not only recover from crises as quickly as possible, but also evolve in a forward-looking way so as to reduce the likelihood of crises in future?[25] In short: rather than bouncing back, can such systems react by bouncing forward?

A similar approach is taken by the scholars at the Joint Research Centre (JRC), a European institution based in Ispra, on Lago Maggiore in northern Italy. Its team of researchers from a wide range of academic disciplines provides basic research for and advice to the European Commission. Set up in the nineteen-fifties as a joint atomic energy research centre, by the nineteen-eighties it was working on solar energy, leading to its researchers becoming pioneers of European environmental policy. When I visited, I saw how they used satellite images from Google Earth to observe ecosystems—for example, riverine systems—in quite some detail over time, for the early detection of the type of 'critical slowing down' phenomena observed at Peter Lake. Their focus is on crisis prevention, so they do not just observe crises as they happen and then consider what can be done. Instead, they analyse the best ways to prevent crises from occurring in the first place, while continuing to positively monitor the overarching purpose of each system.[26] In this context, they introduce an important pair of concepts, distinguishing between the output of a system and its outcome.

Let's take the concept of output first.

As a rule, we judge the functionality of a system by its output in quantitative terms. Returning to our example of the German forest, that would be the size of the timber yield. In such an approach, more is generally considered better, and the figures from the current year are taken as the benchmark for the following year. There is little that sums this up better than our understanding of supply security.

We hear at every turn that supply security must be guaranteed. However, this no longer means housing with central heating, free schooling, or basic medical care for all, regardless of income. That was back in our grandparents' generation. For us nowadays, supply security means having complete mobile network coverage, digitised government services, or access to a food-delivery service that whose couriers turn up at our front door with our order within minutes. All that, of course, is in addition to what our grandparents expected, and we expect it to be highly optimised at all times.

The European Union banned the sale of vacuum cleaners with an output of more than 900 watts from 2017, although manufacturers until then had been fitting them with motors with a capacity of up to 1,600 watts, supposedly because customers demanded were demanding vacuum cleaners with ever-more power.[27] Have homes been any less clean since then?

What we call supply security really describes nothing other than the expectation that our ever-increasing material demands will be constantly met without disruption, as if it were the most normal thing in the world. But we never ask how the supply system is supposed to achieve that. Or what level of supply or security is enough to satisfy us.

Like the researchers at the Stockholm Resilience Centre, the Joint Research Centre identified this deficit and investigated how much it influences our concept of resilience. This has led them to formulate a three-part concept to better illustrate the pillars that support our resilience management.

Their first step in developing this model was to replace the concept of output with the concept of outcome, which is the result we actually want to see from a possible output. In the case of Hidalgo's fifteen-minute city, the outcome would be a city oriented towards the general good. For society as a whole, it would be human wellbeing, or the greatest possible good for the greatest number of people. As we saw in the chapter 'Wealth', that can be achieved through a very wide variety of different strategies.[28] This broadening of the third horizon alone massively expands the space for a positive politics of resilience.

Two more pillars of resilience management identified by the researchers at the JRC consist, first, of a society's current social and environmental processes of cooperation and production, which they call 'the engine'; the second is what they call 'the assets'—natural, human, social, and built capital, the last of which describes all fully functioning constructed infrastructure.

Depending on how we organise our social operating system, all three pillars of resilience will change: the assets, the processes, and the kind of output with which we want to achieve the result—the outcome—of human wellbeing. And along the way we have quite a bit of scope for action: reducing or increasing the amount of waste and environmental degradation we produce, making learning more or less helpful, increasing or decreasing trust and cooperative skills. We can do this in our daily lives by acting as effectors for these processes. And not simply with a turbo-charged vacuum cleaner, as the purely output-based economic models would have it.

And why will that help us 'feed-forward' better?

Because we can organise those processes in such a way that the buffers in our stocks of assets are replenished. In other words, we can develop very many different strategies, not just to deflect crises with a better operating system, but also to make them less likely to occur in the first place. We have seen many examples of the way that crises often result from our failure to pay attention early enough to the fact that the assets are dwindling: when there is no longer enough space to satisfy the needs of city-dwellers, or when there are no longer sufficient balancing feedback loops in the forests. The situation becomes really unstable when there is a structurally conservative reaction to crises — that is, when everything possible is done to defend against the shocks caused by the crisis, but no transformation is sought.

A positive politics of resilience, by contrast, would mean shaping the future in a way that is structurally creative, asset-conserving, and, not least of all, timely. This strengthens the assets that feed directly into the wellbeing of society. Unspoilt nature, good health and education, and trusting and reliable relationships and institutions are not just economic factors; they describe how we live and coexist. It is also important to strengthen our capabilities, processes, and structures in good time. Transformation by design, not disaster.[29]

How can this be done?

Transformation scientists describe a permanent

learning process, typically consisting of four steps.[30]

The first step involves not only taking action in good time, but also gaining a real understanding of the problem. And, in doing so, also coming to understand the system that created it. This sounds like it should be a matter of course, but it isn't. All too often, a new boss will announce how they intend to shake up the department before even speaking to the workers. And the way a problem is understood is rarely questioned — as was the case with the irrigation canal in Tanaland. Fresh insights and a better understanding of the context and connections, however, often do not develop until all the important actors in the system have been consulted. That means listening to the needs of those who are confronted with the problem every day, and to the improvements they say they require to solve it, rather than imposing solutions from the outside that they can't see the point of. Transformation scientists call this step 'getting the whole system in the room'.

The second step is to describe the goal and develop a corresponding mission to bring about the necessary changes both in the system and with it. While the first step focusses on knowledge of the system and describing the problem adequately — in other words, describing the connections, dynamics, and possibly a range of real-life goals — the second step focusses on a generally accepted knowledge of the goal: that is, agreeing on what issue needs to be tackled and in what way or ways. For a mission to gain broad support, those involved in or affected by it must be able to connect with it. It has to be a suitable topic for the stories we tell each other at the water cooler. And it must demonstrate that the individual steps can be contextualised as part of the grand scheme of things, along with the appropriate parameters and indicators of success that keep people behaving in the right way and that represent progress.

The third step is often described as the 'portfolio'. It involves developing a repertoire of ideas to bring about the necessary changes and choreographing their implementation. This is the phase of exploration and experimentation that opens up space for a variety of different possible approaches that can interact with each other and, ideally, combine to create multiple solutions — multi-solving. Complex systems need this dance and this interaction, often above and beyond the existing divisions between different departments and institutions. What they don't need is the impassive execution of fixed plans. This step always requires both quantitative and qualitative indicators that capture an organisation's culture, or its real, lived aspect. All too often, insisting on fixed areas of responsibility puts off misfits who want to take on responsibility themselves. And, all too easily, effectiveness can be stifled by procedural rules. 'That's not how it's supposed to be', should always elicit the response, 'Why not?'

The fourth step is to spread and consolidate what

has been learned in the other three steps. The successful solutions are then fixed in the system and adjusted to its scale. This does not always mean scaling them up. Some may work only up to a certain scale, and may be better applied in different variations. It is important not to see the experimentation phase as a playground for a few annoying idealists, but as a place for the pioneering work necessary for major transformations — and to treat it as such. Only in this way can it inspire societal learning and become a permanent part of our new normality. And that requires the right attitude, as well as leaders who have the qualities of both a midwife and a palliative care nurse — in other words, who have the capacity to welcome in the new and see off the old. This then enables the development of what Donella Meadows calls 'self-organisation', which is a central feature of systems that develop along with the times in a structurally creative way.

The harmony of hierarchies in complex systems is thus not what we often imagine it to be. It evolves from the bottom up. 'The purpose of the upper layers of the hierarchy is to serve the purposes of the lower layers,' writes Donella Meadows.[31] Curating a harmony of hierarchies is an art in itself. It is comparable to the work of an architect — only, rather than dealing with buildings and cities, it deals with organisations and nations, and rather than being about physical structures, it is about social ones. And there is more sensitivity, excitement, and erraticism in those social structures than in piles of sand and brick.

I and some of my colleagues at the World Future Council instigated the Future Policy Award to honour the art of social architects. It is still awarded in cooperation with international institutions such as the United Nations. It is the only prize in the world that honours legislation, and it recognises laws that promote better living conditions for current and future generations.[32] The first winner, in 2009, was the city of Belo Horizonte in south-eastern Brazil.

It was the first planned new city in the country, which is still recognisable by the checkerboard design of the city centre. However, the metropolis long ago outgrew the limits of those urban plans, spreading into the surrounding hillsides. With more than two-and-a-half million inhabitants, Belo Horizonte is one of Brazil's biggest cities and an important business and cultural centre, whose first impression is one of broad avenues, expansive parks, and an impressive skyline. But the prosperity originating from the metal, textile, and automobile industries has not reached all the city's inhabitants. There is a high level of social inequality, as there is in many places in Brazil. In some parts of the city, the standard of living is comparable to that in Scandinavian countries, while there are also poverty-

stricken quarters, known locally as *favelas*, where the
quality of life is on a par with that in North Africa.[33]
At the beginning of the nineteen-nineties, more than
a third of families in the city were living below the
poverty line, and almost a fifth of its children were
malnourished.[34]

When Patrus Ananias became the city's mayor in
1992, he and his municipal government, in an almost
prototypical way, took precisely the abovementioned
four steps to change the situation.

They started by considering the system for supplying
citizens with food, which was the free market. The
system worked well for those who could afford the
food on sale in the city. But it failed everyone else. For
those who saw food security as a public responsibility,
as Patrus Ananias and his municipal government did,
state action was required to correct this market failure.

The city passed Municipal Law No. 6.352 on 15
July 1993, establishing regulations for food security
and giving every citizen the right to sufficient good-
quality food. In passing the law, the municipality also
gave itself the responsibility of guaranteeing that the
provisions of the law were fulfilled and enforced.

In other words, they formulated a mission.

At the same time, Patrus Ananias set up a new
authority, the Municipal Secretariat of Supply, in
which he drew together representatives from all
areas connected with the problem — from business,

academia, the churches, and various levels of the state, to the consumers themselves. He got the entire system in the room, so to speak, and at the same time created a place within his administration where all initiatives aimed at approaching a solution converged and could be coordinated.[35] The mission was given the name 'Food Dignity'. It removed the stigma associated with poor people asking for handouts, and handed over the task of ensuring that everyone was well fed to the community, getting away from the tendency to apportion blame for previous failures, and instead assuming joint responsibility for proving that food security was achievable in Belo Horizonte. This became a case study of better cooperation and the effective use of resources for the common good.

One of the most effective initiatives was free school meals, providing more than 45 million meals a year for pre-school, school, and university students. One of the most popular initiatives was the *restaurante popular*, the people's restaurant. It grew to five branches that provided subsidised meals costing less than one euro on average.[36] The ingredients were bought from small local producers, and although the meals were subsidised, anyone had the right to eat there. School and city gardens were set up, in which people came together to grow vegetables and to learn about healthy eating and cooking. A foodbank was established to process surplus groceries, and 'people's baskets', containing discounted food, were distributed by mobile sales vans in areas where there was no fresh fruit or veg in the shops. The city also issued special licences to sell food, which included a provision that the sellers could only ply their wares in the richer parts of the city if they also sold them in the poorest neighbourhoods at reduced prices. Small farmers from the local area were offered discounted stall rentals at markets so they could sell their produce directly, rather than paying expensive commissions to middlemen. Unused areas in the possession of large landowners were given over to food production. The number of ideas was enormous.

How did Patrus Ananias manage all this? It is similar to other cases where leaders with an infectious vision and coordination skills arise, who then turn followers into co-designers of various parts of their vision. From this, a portfolio emerges, which in turn leads to the creation of mutually reinforcing approaches and then to multi-solving—by recognising patterns of interconnection, and formulating an attractive mission that communicates to others what role they can play in it. This process is not just about creating new structures, but also the attitudes and ethical positions expressed within them. It is an in-depth re-scaling process that gets to the very basis of our values. And it then gains a quality of its own that reveals our will to find ways to move forward, rather than pointing to the causes of the current situation.

Ultimately, the aim of this mission in Belo Horizonte was more than just to combat hunger. It also aimed to put an end to a culture of poverty. By including the entire food-chain system, everyone involved was able to internalise everything they saw, and learned during the process. They saw that previous silos — that is, separate actors operating individually — could cooperate with each other and combine their resources and influence in new ways. Belo Horizonte shows that innovations can become permanent if they are rooted in the culture. Altered structures reflect an altered culture. What was previously seen as deviant behaviour becomes the new normal.[37]

It is clear, said Patrus Ananias on accepting the Future Policy Award, 'that the obstacle to hunger eradication is not the lack of resources, but the lack of political drive'.[38]

With the necessary drive, however, Belo Horizonte managed to improve the food-security situation palpably at a cost of less than $10 million a year — just 2 per cent of the municipal budget in 2009. Child mortality fell by 60 per cent in the space of ten years, and the proportion of malnourished children was reduced by 75 per cent.[39] The model has now been copied in countries such as Namibia and South Africa.[40] It also provided the basis for the programme with which Patrus Ananias later tried to combat poverty and hunger in the whole country when he became the minister for social development. In Belo Horizonte, citizens' participation in political organisations has not remained limited to food-supply issues. For many years now, citizens have been able to have a say in the distribution of public funds as part of a scheme called participatory budgeting.[41] A solution has left its niche and has spread, grown, and deepened.

Paris, with its mobility scheme, and Belo Horizonte, with its food-security programme, show that real change does not just involve new authorities and academic papers; it also depends on how the new relationships and learning processes are organised.

That's also true of functioning markets, as the complexity economists Eric Beinhocker and Nick Hanauer, of the Institute for New Economic Thinking in Oxford, write. The two academics ask us to think of a complex system as a 'fitness landscape'.[42] In a balanced fitness landscape, people and groups cooperate or compete to find solutions to problems. But if the landscape is not tended properly, the fitness of the entire system is reduced. If some subsystems make too much use of their advantages in order to change the landscape in such a way as to strengthen their own position, we all quickly fall into the 'success to the successful' trap, as in the game of *Monopoly*:

> Just because dandelions, like hedge funds, grow
> easily and quickly, doesn't mean we should let them

take over. Just because you can make money doing something doesn't mean it is good for the society. [...] Whether a market produces more solutions for human medical challenges or more solutions for human warfare—or whether it invents problems like bad breath for which more solutions are needed—is wholly a consequence of the construction of that market, and that construction will always be human made, either by accident or by design.[43]

In democracies, giving markets an orientation—in other words, spelling out the common good to be achieved by the imposition of political regulations—is not just an option, but a constitutionally legitimised duty. When that duty is fulfilled, the market economy functions as a tool to achieve that social objective. And, of course, not every one of a society's objectives should be organised via the markets. Public services and social security, especially, concern constitutionally derived rights, and should be available to everyone without impacting on their human dignity and without reference to the person's purchasing power.

Of course, this will inevitably involve conflict. Individual, personal interests come into play everywhere. The trick is being able to pinpoint and resolve them. This requires both transparency and cooperation, as well as fitting incentives or compensation. It requires agenda-setting power through excellent social technology. And an education system that gives us the necessary skills to achieve that.

Do you know what the beauty of good design is in this context?

It creates positive feedback loops.

They can take the form of citizens' councils, future councils, or trialogues initiated by political institutions or by civil society.[44] These can be Open Social Innovation projects such as the *Wir Gegen das Virus* (Us Against the Virus), which are collaborations between the German government and actors from all sections of society;[45] support programmes such as the *Innovative Hochschule* (Innovative University) initiative, which fund a third mission at universities alongside teaching and research, which is to communicate and embed 'knowledge creation' in society; a wide variety of regulatory sandboxes in which new solutions and rules for tackling tough problems are explored beyond the boundaries of current organisations;[46] and globally networked research and advice on the success criteria for such processes.[47]

The way of designing organisations and institutions that will lead to a harmony of the hierarchies in any given case will always vary depending on the task at hand and the cultural context. Its ultimate success is never exclusively dependent on leadership figures; it also depends on the behaviour of followers. If the push by powerful interest groups becomes too strong and self-centred, these powerful subsystems or actors should not be surprised if the harmony starts to slip.

Do you know who noticed this a long time ago? The ancient Greek philosopher, Plato. The precondition for a functioning harmony of the hierarchies—he used the term 'democracy'—is an education system that is geared towards the challenges of the day and that equips citizens to act in a proportionate way. Only then can a self-regulating system be maintained.[48] That kind of education must also teach individual resilience in the face of the temptation to use a privileged position primarily to further one's own advantage.

System trap: resistance to change

Organisations are an expression of a particular objective at a particular point in time: do we want car-friendly or human-friendly cities? Timber production or a healthy forest? Organisations perpetuate processes and ways of thinking, and keep developments on a particular course. When maintaining their own existence becomes more important to them than coevolving, the results will be unsatisfactory for everyone. If we do not want to remove this trap by means of power, it can help to define a new mission that allows actors to break out of their limited logic and to explore new paths and new patterns of cooperation.

10

Understanding: relating to each other better

'The best of these many attempts to imagine society in fresh ways grappled with the biggest consistent challenge of human history—how to organise cooperation at larger scale while sustaining some degree of freedom and fairness.'

GEOFF MULGAN, INNOVATION RESEARCHER
AND POLITICAL ADVISER[1]

More than 10,000 years ago, when humans still roamed the Earth as hunters and gatherers, each individual required about five gigajoules of energy per year to survive.[2] That figure comes from the Czech Canadian ecologist Vaclav Smil, who estimated how much meat a person back then would have needed to eat per day, and how much wood they would need in order to cook it and to keep warm at night and in winter. To make sure his estimate was as accurate as possible, the known 'numbers freak' Smil even took into consideration the fact that mammoth meat contains more energy than the flesh of gazelles or wild horses, but the maths was not very complicated. After all, food and firewood were the only two sources of energy available to humans more than 10,000 years ago. Today, we burn up those five gigajoules that every individual used to consume on average per year in a single 500-mile / 800-kilometre car journey.[3]

At first sight, describing human life purely in terms of the energy it takes to maintain it might seem to be grossly missing the point. After all, we see ourselves as more than just beings who do little more than eat, cook, and keep warm, even though, from the point of view of energy consumption, that was the case for the vast majority of time we have lived on this planet. But now we feel that our lives unfold with far more realities and possibilities. We organise ourselves into complex social constructs. We explore, plan, build, and fly. We alter the genetic structure of plants and animals. Our lives today have little in common with those of the people who lived 10,000 years ago. But whether in our past or present lifestyles, we cannot live without energy. And the more complex we make our lives, the more energy we need to consume.

By the time the process of industrialisation began, every human being consumed twenty gigajoules of energy a year, on average. That means consumption had increased by a factor of four in 10,000 years. But it took just 150 years to quadruple again. Today, average annual per-capita energy consumption has reached almost eighty gigajoules.[4] The reason for that rise is, of course, the constant increase in the number of machines we so rely on to do our work for us, or at least to make it quicker or easier. This inspired the American architect, designer, and author Richard Buckminster Fuller to come up with the concept of the 'energy slave', which he describes as 'an inorganic energy-processing device that is an externalisation of one of the internal functions of man'.[5] It gives us an idea of the extent to which we have pushed our energy throughput beyond what was originally biologically possible, according to Borgmann's device paradigm of availability. The German physicist Harald Lesch illustrates this with a simple calculation: if you produce 100 watts of energy per hour by pedalling on an exercise bike, in ten hours you will have generated just one-100th of the average amount of energy consumed per person per day in Germany. The ratio is 1:100.[6]

If we come to rely on these many extremely energy-intensive processes, we become dependent on a constant external supply of the necessary energy. And we can see in a very striking way right now what impact that has on our ecosystems. And no less striking are the resulting injustices.

Let's take the eighty gigajoules that every person

on Earth consumes on average in a year. If you happen to live in Germany, for instance, you will soon realise that eighty gigajoules won't get you very far. Some people use up that amount of energy purely with their annual car-fuel consumption—without counting food, heating, lighting, charging their phones, or any other kind of energy source requiring an infrastructure and logistics system—which, by the way, also consume energy. On a daily basis, the German population consumes twice as much energy per capita as the global average.[7] People in the US consume twice as much energy as those in Germany. And in Saudi Arabia and Canada, per-capita energy consumption is significantly higher than that. Per-capita energy consumption in almost all the countries of Africa and South America, as well as some in Asia, including India, is below the global average, and for some countries considerably so. Even in a nation such as Turkey, people consume no more than those eighty gigajoules that represent the global average. That's how variable the size of the army of energy slaves working to maintain the different standards of living in different countries can be.

In a world with inexhaustible resources, this inequality could be rectified simply by helping those whose consumption lags behind to catch up with the big consumers. That's precisely the strategy we have followed officially until now. In 2015, the UN's Global Sustainable Development Goals still included the aspiration 'to progressively achieve and sustain income growth of the bottom 40 per cent of the population at a rate higher than the national average'.[8] Nowhere was there any mention of the possibility that someone might actually have enough at some point, despite the fact that the goal was pretty bold in view of scientists' predictions about the state of the Earth and its ecosystems. More than bold, in fact: almost utopian.

But, then, what would be a realistic goal?

A team of researchers at the University of Leeds led by the ecological economist Julia Steinberger investigated that question recently with a project called 'Living Well Within Limits'. They wanted to find out what lifestyle would be good for everyone and still remain within planetary boundaries. Taking a global scenario, they calculated the minimum levels of supply, infrastructure, and equipment necessary for such a lifestyle, and how much energy would be required to meet those minimum standards.[9] Their conclusions were surprising. If their minimum standards were applied, ten billion people could live well on our planet, even with the current state of technological development and without increasing overall energy consumption. On the contrary, consumption could even fall. We would not require more energy overall than was available to us in the early nineteen-sixties.

And what would such a lifestyle look like?

Of course, in such a low-energy world, houses would still have heating and running water, and there would still be mobile phones, refrigerators, the internet, hospitals, and schools. Eating meat and travelling would still be possible. No one would be forced to live naked in a cave. Meeting people's basic needs for shelter, food, clothing, mobility, education, communication, and healthcare would still be the aim in such a world. It would probably be of no use if that weren't the case.

What makes this imaginary world so different from our own is *the way* those needs are met. For example, in this scenario, each person occupies only fifteen square metres of living space — one-third of the current average in Germany.[10] Each person can consume fifty litres of water per day — significantly less than half the amount that each person living in Germany currently uses.[11] Meat consumption by individuals is limited to fifteen kilograms a year, which is a quarter of the average amount currently eaten in Germany.[12] Mobile phones are limited to one per person; laptops to one per four-person household. Each person can buy four kilos of new clothes per year, and do eighty kilos' worth of laundry. Individuals can travel 15,000 kilometres annually, most of which will probably be covered using a highly expanded public transport network, or by bicycle, while car journeys will be less likely, and flights even less likely still.

Does that sound completely unrealistic to you?

It's true that in such a world, countries such as Canada and Saudi Arabia would have to reduce their energy needs by up to 95 per cent. A lot of their current consumption goes on heating or cooling. By contrast, in countries such as Kyrgyzstan, Uruguay, or Rwanda, per-capita energy consumption is already below the required level. And some sub-Saharan countries could even afford to add a few more energy slaves.

One of the benefits of such a transformation would be to slow down the process of global heating. The amount of renewable energy we currently produce globally would already be enough to cover half our needs under this scenario. (In the current world, that proportion is still below 20 per cent.) In such a world, there would be a significant improvement in the living conditions of many millions of people in the global South, including less poverty, better nutrition, more education, and more healthcare. For many people in the global North, it would probably result in shorter working hours, as envisaged by John Maynard Keynes and John Stuart Mill, and would free up people's minds and hands for things that currently fall by the wayside as we trudge the 'treadmills of happiness', as the Swiss economist Mathias Binswanger calls them.[13]

It would result in a world in which ten billion people all have roughly the same, without it costing us the planet. Would that be worth the effort?

You're not sure? I understand that.

I don't think we have to wait until we all have the same amount of stuff and space before we change the way we interact and live together. But that was not the intention of Steinberger and her team when they outlined this scenario. Their principal motive was to demonstrate that the Earth has enough resources to provide for a good life for all. And that we just need to start changing the way we manufacture, use, and share things. And direct our innovations towards creating a high standard of living with as small an ecological footprint as possible.

But that does not look very likely to happen.

Let's take carbon dioxide emissions. In a system that still extracts most of the energy it needs to sustain itself from fossil fuels, carbon dioxide is a good indicator of how unequal the distribution of energy use is. Applying that indicator to individual states shows that China is currently responsible for one-third of global emissions.[14] Even the United States emits only half as much as China. Europe, India, and Russia are the next biggest emitters, with Germany in sixth place. Emission figures become more revealing when a historical aspect is included and the amount of carbon dioxide emitted since the Industrial Revolution is factored in.[15] On this count, China only comes in third. The United States is the biggest all-time energy consumer, accounting for one-quarter of all historical consumption of energy from fossil fuels. Germany is the fourth-biggest — behind Russia, but ahead of Britain.

This illustrates how important the boundaries we draw are when we want to focus on a particular problem. On close inspection, then, the idea that the big consumers can continue to consume more and more, while the small consumers need to catch up faster, turns out to be a risky strategy, at the very least.

And completely unrealistic, too.

That becomes crystal clear if we apply the indicator of carbon dioxide emissions to people rather than states. The per-capita emissions of the poorer half of the world's population have risen slightly since 1990, from 1.2 to 1.6 tonnes per year, remaining about four times lower than the global average. In wealthy countries, per-capita emissions of the poorer half of the population have stagnated, while those of the richer half have risen, especially among the top 1 per cent. That group — currently 771 million people — now produces 110 tonnes of carbon dioxide per capita per year, accounting for 17 per cent of all emissions.[16]

Who can catch up with that, and at what price?

Whichever way we twist and turn it, we cannot avoid the need to strike the right balance. And who should be responsible for measuring this indicator, and why?

But do we even want to set limits?

Is that compatible with our idea of unlimited freedom?

Or will it only lead to an environmental dictatorship?

I think it's important to ask these questions; otherwise, there's a pretty good chance that's where we will end up. The environment will dictate what remains possible for the biological species *Homo sapiens*, and what doesn't. As it did in our past. Prehistoric humans just expanded further and further into unsettled areas, or drove other settlers out. Then we replaced the dwindling resources in such settlements with others that were not yet exhausted, or used technology to exploit completely new resources.[17] We cannot continue this way in a world where the number of protected areas is too small, with the population soon reaching ten billion people.[18] So I think the question about an environmental dictatorship is a little weird. The decisions about what we do with these findings, and what conclusions societies should draw from them, lie in the hands of humanity.

So, for a moment, let's engage in what in Germany is typically called a *Verbotsdiskussion*—a discussion about forbidding things, about what limitations should be placed on such things as meat, mountains of clothes, short-haul flights, plastic bags, and driving. These do not only take place on TV talk shows or in social media threads. I think all of us have had conversations with friends and acquaintances about whether, and under what conditions, it is okay to ban some things completely if not enough people are prepared to change their behaviour voluntarily. We probably all know from experience that such discussions are not easy, due to the high value given in our society to the freedom to live our lives as we see fit.

What can you say to that?

From a systemic point of view, the individual freedom we claim for ourselves is first and foremost a result of the system we call society. Humans are social animals. We learn who we are and what we want through our contact with others. It also only makes sense to speak of the freedom of loners in terms of a society from which they can distance themselves. And even loners will always have a connection to society. Whether we like it or not, there is no 'I' without 'We'. And, in the best case, many 'I's come together to form a 'We', which works in cooperation to extend the possibilities for all—leading, in other words, to collective freedom, which would not be accessible for one person alone. Most of the freedoms we take for granted today— from functioning infrastructures to the food on our plates—are of this kind.

'Individuals and communities have a right to freedom,' writes the constitutional law expert Christoph Möllers in his book *Freiheitsgrade* (*Degrees of Freedom*). 'There is no primacy of individual freedom over community freedom, if only because individuality can only be described as a social phenomenon.'[19]

Once humans become part of a society, they can no longer do completely as they please. That can sometimes be exhausting, and sometimes it is limiting. But it also enables people to do more or different things than they could do alone. This is the only way that humans can expand their cooperative structures, and broaden the scope for opportunities, products, services, and experiences. But that is only the case so long as, in exercising their individual liberty, people do not impinge on the collective freedom of society. 'The more individualised freedom is,' writes Möllers, 'the more that right depends on the existence of a certain framework, and on people's ability to rely on the fact that they will continue to have the right to use their freedoms in the future.'

Such a framework provides the direction, the purpose, of a system. In democratic states based on the rule of law, that purpose is set out in a constitution or statutory laws. In companies, it takes the form of a legal and social licence to operate. In various organisations, it resides in their statute or charter. Social systems are also always embedded in other systems, or networked with them. In this way, the purpose of the superordinate system of the constitutional state individual laws, licences, and charters. Such an example is constituted by the rules of the road, imposed by mutual agreement

because being killed or severely hurt in a traffic accident
is not a desirable outcome of driving or walking beside
a road. Another example is the provision of a public
health system intended to protect, treat, and cure
people, and which sometimes makes use of tools such
as public smoking bans, for example. A tax system in
which everyone must contribute according to their level
of wealth is an expression of the social contract. Only
when everyone contributes can actions for the common
good be organised at the superordinate level to provide
education, healthcare, public infrastructure, security,
and constitutional procedures for all. At least that is the
purpose expressed in many democratic constitutions.
And the objective of providing a permanently secure
supply of food and resources is ultimately dependent
on relatively stable, regenerative ecosystems. I believe
we should not thoughtlessly jeopardise those freedoms.

What about finding and communicating the right
balance?

In his book *Überreichtum* (*Overrich*), the Austrian
economist and psychotherapist Martin Schürz shows
that it is not enough to compile statistics on poverty
and wealth. We must also consider whether to speak
in public about those issues, and if so, in what ways.[20]
For example, in asking to what extent wealth and
poverty are connected, and why, in the debate about
inequality, terms such as envy and hate tend to be used
in connection with poor people, while rich people

are more likely to be associated with words such as generosity and compassion. Or asking why the huge amounts of money donated by the superrich hit the headlines, but no one asks how anyone was able to come by so much wealth in the first place. 'The negative consequences for the community of the concentration of wealth are less visible than the charitable acts of the superrich,' writes Schürz.

The term 'overrich', which once again goes back to Plato, includes the idea that there is a such a thing as a balanced amount of wealth. This doesn't mean that a 'criticism of over-richness based on concerns for justice' demands that everyone should have the same amount of wealth. Rather it expresses, as Schürz puts it, 'excess, a surfeit of riches'.[21]

How does such excess come about?

What's the origin of such boundlessness?

The escalation trap has struck with a vengeance when executives and company board members don't even bother to justify the fact that their pay and bonus increases are huge compared to other employees in their company by arguing that their work has generated more money to go round for all within the company, and simply point out that other companies' executives have received similar pay rises. And this once again begs the question of how the democratic common good can be achieved when the framework conditions set up to achieve it—such as tax systems, transparency, and equality—don't apply to those who can pick and choose what's best for them from several societies.[22] The sale of European citizenships—so-called golden passports—is perhaps just the most egregious example of this.[23] It never ceases to astound me that extreme wealth continues to be regarded positively, and both its origins and its consequences remain unquestioned, even when such central principles of justice are violated.

'There cannot be just a law of the individual,' Christopher Weeramantry, a former judge at the International Court of Justice, told me during a conversation we had at the World Future Council on the issue of legislative frameworks, 'There must be a law of the whole.'

In the late nineteen-eighties, the American sociologist and cultural historian Riane Eisler investigated the way that groups of individuals organise themselves into a single unit, and the systemic socio-cultural configurations at play. She noticed that we most often distinguish societies according to political, economic, or religious categories: capitalist or communist; left-wing or right-wing; agrarian, industrial, or post-industrial; Islamic, Christian, or secular. Eisler found these distinctions to be inadequate, as she believed that the individual categories only focus on any given society. They fail to show that there can be considerable differences within each category—not all countries that follow a certain religion are the same, for example. Such distinctions also fail to take into account the similarities between societies in different categories — for example, between Germany under Hitler, the Soviet Union under Stalin, and Afghanistan under the Taliban. Eisler wanted to find a more accurate and, at the same time, more comprehensive way of categorising societies. She achieved this by categorising them according to the kind of relationships that prevailed among their members, or to which their members aspired.[24]

Do groups always involve domination?

Or partnerships?

According to Eisler, people who live in a domination system are either dominant or subordinate, and the amount of control they can exercise is defined by their position in their social and cultural environment. A structurally rigid idea of hierarchy prevails in domination systems, and the emphasis is on climbing up or falling down the hierarchy ladder. Each position in the hierarchy is justified socio-culturally by the fact that every person or subsystem is either superior or inferior to every other. That means men dominating other men, men dominating women, one class dominating another, one ethnic group dominating another, one religion dominating another, humans dominating nature, and parents dominating children.

'In the domination system, there are only two alternatives for relations: dominating or being dominated. Those on top control those below them—be it in families, workplaces, or society at large,' writes Eisler.[25]

Deciding what is, or may be, accessible to each individual is a top-down process.

This both sows fear and creates an incentive for individuals to aim for 'more than the others' with regard to their position in the system, and to influence the way the system's structures are designed to achieve that aspiration. Letting go of or surrendering something then becomes tantamount to an admission of bankruptcy, of failure, or it is seen as dispossession. And that's reflected in the way we talk about it. In domination systems, such things as caring, compassion, and solidarity are suppressed, devalued, or restricted to just one group. They are seen as private issues. Or religious matters. Or women's business. Or the stuff of naive utopianism. Basic human needs such as love and appreciation, or the sense that life is meaningful, are hard to satisfy under such conditions. Having a better hand in the struggle over the distribution of wealth becomes more important—and, as a consequence, ruthless methods are seen as justified if they help maintain that good hand. Control and political influence become concentrated; flexibility and diversity are reduced. And the freedom to stop defending rapidly disappears. It becomes too risky.

In a partnership system, on the other hand, people

are seen as equal participants, and treated as such. Such a system aims to allow as many people as possible to participate and to recognise each individual's contribution towards achieving the superordinate aim. In this context, Eisler's research particularly focusses on the so-called care economy, which mostly involves the work of women. Usually unpaid and undervalued, it is the care economy that creates the conditions in families, neighbourhood relations, and voluntary organisations that are necessary to achieve the central objectives stated in the legislative frameworks upon which our societies are built. But, like the value created by ecological systems, it is blocked from view by the dominant narratives of success and progress.

Alongside her interest in *what* holds societies together, Eisler is also interested in *how* they are held together. Partnerships are found in relationships characterised by respect and trust, rather than compulsion and mistrust. In partnerships, the focus is not placed on material goods, which are often scarce for one reason only: if they were distributed more equitably, they would lose their positional and power-political effect. Instead, in a partnership system, the focus is shifted onto the full potential of each human being and its development. And to the living systems that offer freedom and security if we tend and share them well. That doesn't mean there are no hierarchies in partnership systems. But those that exist do not serve to degrade people, and instead are organised in such a way that all sides are accountable to all others, and harmony between the activities of different parts of the system is possible. As we have seen, they are structured in a bottom-up way. '[In a partnership system,] leaders […] facilitate, inspire, and empower rather than control and disempower,' writes Eisler.[26]

Admittedly, the current global political situation does not exactly look as if an increasing number of leaders were adopting such behaviour. Rather, we repeatedly find ourselves confronted with the question of how to react when a head of state such as Putin clearly has no desire to contribute to a partnership-based solution, preferring the aggressive use of war in its worst form. In my view, partnership does not mean setting no boundaries and letting others overrun you. Negotiating boundaries involves giving a firm show of support for the agreed framework and the protection of it as a whole, even when violence must be met with violence for self-protection. Individuals don't live forever, and regimes are not immutable. Certain kinds of behaviour are unacceptable, but we must take care to ascribe that behaviour to the aggressor and not to entire groups of people or nations, some of whom are also suffering under the same aggressor. There is an opportunity to forge new international alliances. And that is the only solution if we are to increase collective freedom once more.

Of course, in reality, neither domination systems nor partnership systems exist in a pure form. Eisler does not claim that. Rather, they are the two ends of a continuum in which all social groups can be arranged according to which side they tend more strongly towards. It is this tendency that we can influence by means of the decisions we make and the actions we take.

Consider the pandemic, and the way that the global community dealt with it. Only a year after the SARS-CoV-2 virus was discovered, humanity had already developed the first vaccines against it. By the following year, more than ten billion doses of the vaccine were available — more than enough to vaccinate every teenager and adult in the world at least once.[27] Prior to that, both developing and producing such a large quantity in so short a time would have been considered impossible. This shows that, with enough will and cooperation, we can outstrip ourselves. However, when it came to distributing the vaccine, we saw the resurgence of a big dose of domination. Many high-income countries secured vaccines for themselves early by investing in research carried out by private companies, in exchange for which they were able to reserve production capacities for themselves, or they placed orders with several producers at the same time, before it was even clear which company would win the race. The production of ten billion doses was planned for the first year, and before even a single one of those had left the production line, the twenty-seven countries of the European Union, along with the US, Britain, Canada, Australia, and Japan, had already secured half of them, although those states account for only 13 per cent of the world's population.[28]

Those states at the top of the money-dominated ladder of purchasing power took advantage of their position to hoard a scarce commodity—vaccines in this case, although it could have been a different resource. This was a short-term success for them on a national level.[29] While some poor countries had barely enough vaccine to protect their most vulnerable citizens, the rich nations were already offering such of their people a booster shot.[30] It soon became apparent, however, that 'vaccine nationalism' was only prolonging the pandemic. Not just because SARS-CoV-2 mutated and found its way back to the richer countries in the form of new variants, but also because those countries gained nothing from their own citizens' immunity while their trading partners were still grappling with the pandemic.

According to a study published by the International Chamber of Commerce, the unequal distribution of vaccines caused financial damage to the tune of $9.2 trillion globally in 2020, half of which fell to richer countries, precisely because they profit so much more from the fact that national economies are so globally interconnected. If those countries had invested in a different distribution system instead, they would have earned a return of $166 for each dollar invested.[31] As this shows, domination strategies do not even pay off for those at the top of the pyramid. They can just hold out for longer.

How would the distribution of vaccines have developed in a partnership system?

In fact, the World Health Organisation (WHO) proposed such a strategy very early on. The idea was that every state would pay into a joint fund from which vaccines could be bought in bulk. Covid-19 Vaccines Global Access (COVAX), as the initiative was called, established a partnership-based strategy in the face of a common danger. But many high-income countries decided to bypass the fund. They signed bilateral deals with the manufacturers, and stockpiled more vaccine than they needed while also donating far less to poorer countries than they had pledged as part of COVAX. Ultimately, rather than purchasing vaccines for all, COVAX ended up handing out alms to the needy.[32]

The advantage of a partnership-based strategy would not have been just that the global North and the global South could have launched their vaccination campaigns at the same time. It would also have given the global community a stronger position in their negotiations with pharmaceutical companies. Those companies charged 20 euros for a dose that sometimes cost them less than one-tenth of that to produce, and were not prepared to waive patent protection for the vaccines even temporarily.[33] A harmony of hierarchies at the start of the pandemic morphed into an escalation trap between subsystems, when the focus shifted from research to distribution.

That, too, could have been handled better.

When, in the nineteen-fifties, the American immunologist Jonas Salk developed a new type of vaccine against polio based on work carried out by many of his fellow scientists, US infection rates fell by 80 per cent almost immediately. He was asked in an interview at the time who owned the patent for the vaccine.

'Well, the people, I would say,' he answered. 'There is no patent. Could you patent the Sun?'[34]

Do we have enough?

Do we share enough?

And who are 'we' anyway?

Ultimately, these are always questions about limits and boundary-setting by humans. Limits on stocks of resources. Boundaries in our dealings with each other. Limits on belonging to that cooperative community. Questions of choice about what we consider morally acceptable and worthwhile doing, and therefore worth learning to do. Questions about the standards in our economic and technological systems, around defining acceptable risks when exploiting limited resources, and around agreeing what kind of added value successful companies should pursue. Questions about what spatial and temporal boundaries to set within which we show solidarity and accept responsibility.

Where those boundaries are drawn or shifted, and how and by whom, reveals the extent to which we live in a domination or partnership system. Domination and partnership are two very different strategies for boundary-setting. In one system, a portion of the group defines the boundaries for all others, who don't get a say in the process. In the other system, boundaries are negotiated in a participatory process. If we want to achieve and maintain maximum happiness and freedom for the maximum number of people, only participation can lead to an expedient solution.

This is particularly evident in the case of what we call common goods. These are assets that can be used by everyone, which no one can be excluded from consuming. They are often the product of well-functioning ecosystems that exist independently of human-made boundaries. They include benevolent climate conditions, healthy oceans, intact biodiversity, and a well-functioning water cycle. Such worldwide assets are known as the 'global commons'. The many organisms and creatures they contain that clean the air, pollinate plants, water the fields, and produce food are a free gift to humans from the world around them. Humans use and adapt them, and no single country can claim exclusive rights to them. A country can unilaterally declare the airspace above it to be part of its territory, but it cannot control the climate in that territory by acting alone. Carbon dioxide emissions float around freely, and ecosystems themselves decide where the climate damage strikes hardest.[35] It would be fair if those doing the polluting had to pay for the damage they cause, which is recognised in international agreements and legislation as an important principle. But, in practice, human institutions, financing, and boundary-setting lag lamely behind partnership systems.

Conversely, so-called global public goods emerge from human institutions, and their availability and quality are the same for everyone. They are not the product of functioning ecological systems, but of functioning social systems. These assets also cannot be produced or maintained by individuals alone. But if they are well cared for, everyone can benefit equally from them. And gaining the use of them is not associated in principle with rivalry or competition. These goods and services include many things that are provided or secured by public institutions, such as maintaining public health by controlling the spread of infectious diseases, or providing a healthcare system, energy, water, and transport infrastructures, as well as security and mechanisms for peaceful conflict-resolution, or a functioning financial system for which the state is ultimately the guarantor.

The size and quality of resource stocks develop according to the way they are used by subsystems or individuals. In this sense, freedom is also a 'global public good', and it requires that we all have sufficient respect for other people's desire for freedom — as well as a willingness to talk about setting and, if necessary, recalibrating, boundaries. Should industrialised nations and rich individuals really continue to have the right to declare they are entitled to overconsume, just because they grabbed the global commons earlier, quicker, more aggressively, and more expansively than others? It is worthwhile reopening the conversation about this if we don't want to forfeit the general rights of everyone.

For all the differences between environmental and social commons, they have something fundamentally in common: their quality suffers when there is a lack of a sufficient joint effort to maintain it. This is equally true of freedom and the climate.

The important difference between those two commons has to do with the kind of boundaries they involve. Here, a distinction must be made between *limits* and *boundaries*. 'Limits' tends to be used to express physical threshold values in connection with currently available resources or the laws of nature. 'Boundaries' is more likely to refer to social agreements. For example, we talk in terms of 'planetary boundaries' when we set budgets for resource use in order to reduce the risk of bumping up against hard limits and to learn from past shocks. Humans can't fly unaided—that's a hard limit that is not affected by the fact that we have invented aeroplanes. It also shows, however, that boundaries can be shifted—that we can change the way we deal with limiting factors. Progress is usually a result of the conscious shifting of our boundaries, ideally with a networked and forward-looking view of the expected limits to come. Successful systemic management, according to Donella Meadows, is therefore always geared towards the next anticipated limit. The sooner we identify those limits and transform them into helpful boundaries and useful alternatives, the less likely that crisis and chaos become.

In times of conflict such as those we are living through right now, this can be a very uncomfortable process. There is a great temptation to think only of ourselves and to secure our own position to ensure that we have access to resources or power for longer than others. But the more widespread and embedded that attitude becomes, the smaller our chance of replenishing depleted stocks, increasing freedoms, and transforming negative defensive policies into positive policies to increase social assets becomes.[36]

'We have to invent boundaries for clarity and sanity,'

writes Meadows, 'and boundaries can produce problems when we forget that we've artificially created them.'[37]

Where a social system begins and ends, who or what it encompasses, and who or what is excluded are not givens; they are all things that are determined by our individual or collective behaviour. In such cases, it is not really accurate to speak of boundaries running here or being there. More accurately, we should speak of such boundaries being drawn or decided upon.

For example, in her book *The Code of Capital*, the American legal expert Katharina Pistor examines and describes in detail how legislation, in particular US and English civil law, has repeatedly been used to privatise previously public assets, reallocating their utilisation rights.[38] The fact that some people, corporations, or states feel the effect of limitations less than others because they have access to seemingly inexhaustible resources, or are able to secure them more easily, does not mean that those boundaries do not exist for others. Nor does it mean that those boundaries are immutable. The configuration of the world today is not God-given.

When we redraw the boundaries on one level, they change on others, too. Our ability to shape the future lies in doing this in a conscious way. In many places, this takes place with a special view to protecting our common goods and cooperating more effectively to achieve our social aims. The Wyss Academy for Nature at the University of Bern in Switzerland places a new relationship with nature at the centre of its work. It links the protection of nature directly with human wellbeing and participation, and takes that as the basis for the development of landscape strategies.[39] Architects for Future also takes a spatial perspective to explore how the design and construction of infrastructures needs to change when we take planetary boundaries seriously. For example, we must put an end to the competition for space, and use every square metre in a more integrated way for housing, energy, biodiversity, and the conservation of resources.[40]

At the German Advisory Council on Climate Change, we explored the issue of multi-solving in land-use, and in 2020, the legal expert Cathrin Zengerling investigated the ways that trade law could be changed to focus less on exploiting natural resources and more on using them regeneratively. One important question in that context was how to get producer countries and consumer countries to assume joint responsibility for securing resource stocks.[41] A year earlier, the German government's Advisory Council on the Environment published a special report on the legitimisation of environmental policy. It made the case for interdepartmental thinking, since many issues cross multiple competencies. It also argued for an explicit consideration of the long-term consequences of the decisions we make today, which are often disregarded due to our fixation with the present. One of its suggestions in this context was to establish a council for intergenerational equity.[42]

The boundaries concerning work that is of systemic importance will also need to be renegotiated if we are to maintain the freedom we have come to take for granted. It is not only that people in those jobs must finally be paid an average wage that is equivalent to that in other branches of industry. We must also increase our appreciation of such workers — in healthcare and food production, as well as those who are required to keep working during emergencies. Their status in our society urgently needs an upgrade to correspond to the value to society of the work they do.[43]

And, finally, figures such as Abigail Disney, the granddaughter of the co-founder of the Disney Company, Roy O. Disney, together with a network of Patriotic Millionaires who style themselves 'proud traitors of their class', are advocating for fairer taxes, since they believe only pressure from members of their own class will move the rich and superrich. 'My grandfather would never have paid himself over 1,000 times what his median worker was being paid,' she commented, criticising Disney's CEO, Bob Iger, who pocketed $65 million in 2018. 'There were no laws against him doing it, it was just not an acceptable thing to do. He certainly wouldn't have been put on the cover of magazines and told he was a genius.'[44] So, in this case, too, boundaries have shifted, and that means they can do so again.

There is no doubt that this is a balancing act between individual and collective freedom, and it will always remain so. Each of us has the opportunity to learn and improve at all times in this regard. It is a continuing learning process in which we can expect to run up against our own limitations again and again. Consciously expecting this is central to the image developed by the International Futures Forum thinktank of the way we can deal with processes of transformative innovation.[45] It consists of a figure-of-eight shape made up of two touching loops — the fear loop and the love loop.[46] In essence, these are two of the feedback loops we encountered earlier, and effectors trigger reactions in others around them by reacting to those feedback loops within networked systems. The two loops play out those effects on the basis of two very deep-rooted human emotions, to demonstrate that 'love and fear are not simply ways of *being* in the world but also ways of *knowing* it'.[47]

In the fear loop, we attempt to find security through control in a complex world, which is why it is also called the control loop. In it, we see the world as a collection of objects that we quickly attempt to standardise and categorise without perceiving their respective individuality. We assume we already know what we are dealing with, and resort to formulaic answers that often ignore any nuance. The problem is that human beings, in particular, but also many situations, defy objective classification. We are often taken by surprise by people's behaviour, or it makes us feel alienated, which only serves to increase our need for control. The result is a feedback loop of tension, fear, and insecurity. We can easily observe this today in debates on social media: a person is labelled either an opponent of vaccination or a vaccination supporter, a meat-eater or a meat-hater, a petrol head or a cycle freak, a capitalist or a communist.

In the love loop, we attempt to experience the complexity of the world by embracing and participating in it, and thereby gathering knowledge and experience. So it is also called the participation loop. Instead of rapidly abstracting and categorising things, we accept surprises and ignorance as an integral part of our world. We value diversity, and recognise the individual qualities of any given situation. We see ourselves as participants, which motivates us to strive to bring about the best possible result. In this way, our feelings of belonging and trust become stronger. We are able to grow because not only do we see what we already believe, but we also begin to believe what we see. If we take the control loop to its logical conclusion, it will only lead to disappointment and withdrawal, and relations that closely resemble those in Riane Eisler's domination system. Taking the participation loop to its logical conclusion leads to a more playful and hopeful quality of interaction that tends towards Eisler's partnership system. We will all recognise this as having happened to us in certain situations in our lives, and remember being caught in one of the two loops, as well as the effect that had on the way we perceive the world.

The two feedback loops show not only the way that attitudes can become established as entire systems, but also how those systems can be changed.

Thus includes the realisation that yesterday's solutions may often be the cause of today's problems. And that we must have the humility to admit that today's solutions will often be the cause of the day-after-tomorrow's problems. By taking our own potential for learning seriously, breaking outdated patterns, and trying out new ones, and developing new skills and communicating with each other about them, we can turn a system around. If we put our need for control aside for a moment, every moment gives us the opportunity to consciously explore our boundaries — those connected with removing the old and adding the new. We can move from one loop to the other.

'Between stimulus and response lies a space,' begins a quote that is often ascribed to the German psychoanalyst Viktor Frankl. 'In that space lies our freedom and power to choose a response. In our response lies our growth and our happiness.'[48]

That is the space in which we decide who we want to be.

System trap: the tragedy of the commons

In a system where everyone depends on certain assets that cannot be manufactured or maintained by one person alone, competition develops for access to them. That competition will destroy them. There are three ways of preventing this: education and self-restriction; distribution such that the consequences of overuse are also felt by the overusers; or commonly agreed rules for use, which apply to everyone and are enforced. If this is done in a partnership-oriented way, the focus can be placed on preserving stocks of those resources, and everyone benefits.

Part III
Who are 'We'?

'"[M]aybe" has always been the best odds the world has offered to those who alter its course — to find a new land across the sea, to end slavery, to enable women to vote, to walk on the moon, to bring down the Berlin Wall. "Maybe" is not a cautious word. It is a defiant claim of possibility in the face of a status quo we are unwilling to accept.'

ERIC YOUNG, ECONOMIST[1]

11

Heads together

'When I said that the good life consists of love guided by knowledge, the desire which prompted me was the desire to live such a life as far as possible, and to see others living it; and the logical content of the statement is that, in a community where men live in this way, more desires will be satisfied than in one where there is less love or less knowledge.'

BERTRAND RUSSELL, PHILOSOPHER[1]

One of the most popular attractions at Leipzig Zoo is Pongoland. It is a huge compound, covering more than three hectares, which houses all four (non-human) species of great ape — chimpanzees, gorillas, orangutans, and bonobos. They roam in small groups through the artificial jungle in their open-air enclosure, where there is a landscape of rocks, water, and climbing trees, while visitors watch them from platforms or through thick panes of glass. Of course, the Leipzig enclosure is only a recreation of their habitat in the wild, but at least it is considerably bigger than many other zoos can offer. Even twenty years after it was built, Leipzig's great ape enclosure is still one of the biggest and most modern in Europe. It is also unique in the world as a place of scientific study.[2]

Ever since Pongoland's inauguration, researchers from the Max Planck Institute for Evolutionary Anthropology have been studying the cognitive abilities of great apes there. As well as observing how they behave in groups, the scientists also carry out experiments away from the visitors' view, in which the apes solve playful tasks individually, in pairs, or together with the researchers themselves. It might be extracting a peanut from a tube that is too narrow to fit an ape's hand, or it might be a kind of game in which they compete with other apes for a prize of grapes. Despite the huge range of scientific interests among the researchers who devise these experiments, what they all have in common is that they study apes ultimately to learn more about us humans.[3]

Genetically, there is very little difference between humans and apes. Even our most distant relatives within the great apes, the orangutans, share nearly 90 per cent of their genetic makeup with us, while we share nearly 99 per cent of our DNA with our closer cousins, the chimpanzees.[4] Apes are our closest living relatives in the animal world. We have about the same degree of relatedness as zebras and horses, or rats and mice.[5] Nevertheless, their world could hardly be more different from ours. While they still live in the jungle, we have conquered the entire planet and flown to the Moon, but have also built weapons that can destroy everything and everybody on Earth. It is we who study apes, and not the other way around.

How did this enormous difference come about?

What can we do that apes can't?

Or, in the words of the American anthropologist Michael Tomasello, the director of the Max Planck Institute for Evolutionary Anthropology for twenty years, 'What makes us human?'[6]

To answer that question, Tomasello and his team carried out countless similarly playful tests, not just with apes but also with human children, and then compared the results.[7] Their results showed that chimpanzees and orangutans are as good as, or even better than, two-and-a-half-year-old human children at simple physical tests. The apes were sometimes quicker than the children at identifying which cup a treat was hidden beneath, they made targeted use of tools more often, and they were better at adding small numbers together. But the crucial difference between apes and humans was not revealed until the subjects were tested on their ability to recognise what others mean when they point at things. Unlike apes, which can follow someone's gaze or hand gesture, we humans are also able to process such cues as supporting information, even when we can't see directly how they are intended to help us. On a meta level, we can understand that there is an intention behind the pointing. We grasp the fact that the other person is not only pointing to help us, but they also want us to understand their intention. So we look under the cup they're pointing to, even if we don't expect to find anything there. Apes are unable to put themselves in another's place mentally in this way—but it is precisely that which is the basis of learning and cooperation through communicative instruction.

Human children start pointing at the age of one to draw adults' attention to a particular object. It is then the job of the parents to figure out exactly what the child means. It might be an object the child wants but can't reach, such as an ice-cream in their parent's hand, for instance. Another example occurs often while 'reading' a picture book with a parent: the child imitates the sound of the animal they see in the picture, then looks up to check that their parent has also seen the animal or understood the 'woof woof'. Pointing opens up a space in which 'I' and 'You' can explore a situation and its meaning together. The result is a 'We' and an interpretation of what needs to be done and by whom, which everyone shares.[8] Michael Tomasello and his team observed the same behaviour in countless experiments.

When adults suddenly stopped playing with a toddler to test their reaction as part of the experiment, the children encouraged the grown-ups to continue playing. They even demonstrated to the adult how to hold the toy in question so that the game could continue. When children decided they would prefer to play with a different adult, rather than just getting up and leaving, they offered an excuse for wanting to leave the game, showing they felt connected to the joint 'we'. By contrast, when an ape was given a task to complete with an adult human who suddenly stopped cooperating, the ape would either attempt to achieve the goal alone or lose interest in the task. Also, the cooperation ended as soon as the ape received the reward. It would immediately make off with the treat. People, on the other hand, develop a feeling for whether the results of cooperation are fair or not. When two children were placed in front of a kind of play table with two balls on it, arranged in such a way that they had to work together for either of them to get hold of a ball, the toddlers would continue to cooperate with each other until each had a ball to play with. When there is a prize to share, children divide it fairly among themselves.

For Michael Tomasello, that 'we' which develops in the space of shared interest is what makes us human. He calls it 'joint intentionality'.[9] It is unique to the human species. Only humans are able to 'put their heads together', as he describes it.

This ability, not only to act together, but also to

learn, is the reason for the rapid, and rapidly increasing, rise of the human species. It enables us to share our emotions and our knowledge with others, and to combine our brain power to solve problems that can't be tackled by one person alone—which results in a huge explosion of creativity. But it also enables us to pass what we have learned on to others in a systematic way, and so to accumulate knowledge and insights down the generations. Every new-born human gains access to the collected wealth of human experience through learning from others, and is in a sense brought up to date by them. The 'rachet effect' is the term that Tomasello uses for this phenomenon, which makes it possible for each generation to stand on the shoulders of previous generations.[10] We don't need to keep reinventing the wheel, because people in Mesopotamia invented it 6,000 years ago, and that knowledge has been passed down through the ages as what we call culture. Culture is both a prerequisite for and a result of our cooperation.

'Fish are born expecting water,' says Michael Tomasello. 'They've got fins, they've got gills … And humans are born expecting culture.'[11]

And what does all this mean for the world we live in?

The ability to pass on information not just through genes, but also through culture, opens up the door to human progress, and to a kind of development in which humans can learn proactively, rather than just reactively, and avoid crashing blindly into limits. Humans can think ahead and construct 'feed forwards'. But with that ability comes a greater responsibility for its effects. What we adopt as part of our culture and what we don't, which paths we choose to take, what insights we investigate and what conclusions we draw from those investigations — these are all small decisions in the totality of human memory and the wealth of narratives it contains, from which everyone can draw to make their decisions in turn and pass those narratives on. From this perspective, all of us are both receivers of the culture of our ancestors and shapers of the culture of our descendants. Our contributions to that culture are what make its continued development possible.

The question *What makes us human?* is at its core no different from the question *Who do we want to be?*

12

Heroes

'Not Man but men inhabit this planet. Plurality is the law of the earth.'

HANNAH ARENDT[1]

From the middle of 2020, the offices of several hundred non-profit organisations in America began receiving unexpected emails saying they were to get significant financial donations.[2] Most were small and little-known organisations that were not normally on the big philanthropists' donation lists. They focussed on women's rights, racial equality, and LGBTQ rights, distributing food and medication to the poor, and tackling the structural inequalities in American society. Since most of them were active at the local level, they went mostly ignored by politicians, business, and the media.

The organisations were at a loss to explain why someone wanted to transfer money to them without them even asking. They didn't recognise the name of the sender: Lost Horse, a Delaware-based company seemingly with an anonymous benefactor behind it. At some of the organisations, the mail ended up in their spam folders.[3] Others received an unexpected phone call.

Francesca Rattray is the CEO of the women's rights organisation the Young Women's Christian Association (YWCA) in San Antonio, Texas. When she received such a phone call, the man at the other end of the line explained that a certain MacKenzie Scott wanted to donate a considerable sum to her organisation.[4] Rattray had never heard of MacKenzie Scott, so, as you do, she quickly googled the name while the man went through a few final questions with her — and that's when she realised this wasn't a prank call.

MacKenzie Scott is the ex-wife of Amazon CEO Jeff Bezos. She had become the fourth-richest woman in the world when the couple divorced.[5]

'I literally clung to my desk and braced myself for the impact,' said Rattray later, as she told a reporter about the phone call.[6] Then the man revealed how big the donation was: $1 million, with no conditions attached. All he wanted from the organisation was its bank details to transfer the money.

'When they told me the amount, I just crumpled over in tears,' recalls Rattray.

Similar scenes played out all over America in late 2020. Food banks, Covid-relief organisations, gender-equality activists, lesbian, gay and trans organisations, family associations, historically Black or Native American colleges, women's educational institutions, facilities for people with disabilities, a lender for minority-run businesses, and even a European climate foundation—MacKenzie Scott and her team selected more than 500 mostly small, charitable organisations.[7] Most were underfunded and unnoticed by society as they carried out their work, and were now to receive $1 million, $3 million, or $50 million after a single email or phone call. In the space of just four months, MacKenzie Scott gave away almost $6 billion in this way, catapulting her to second place on the list of America's biggest private charitable donors for that year.[8] But that was just the beginning.

By spring 2022, she had given a total of $12 billion to more than 1,250 organisations in the space of less than two years.[9] Few other people have ever donated so much money in their lifetimes, and certainly never in such short a space of time.

So what was it all about?

Soon after her divorce in 2019, MacKenzie Scott, as she now called herself, joined the Giving Pledge initiative. It has been established by a group of international entrepreneurs and heirs that only accepts billionaires who pledge to donate at least half their fortune to charity. It was set up in 2010 by the founder of Microsoft, Bill Gates, and the investor Warren

Buffett, and it now has more than 230 members from twenty-eight countries.[10] After joining, many members, including MacKenzie Scott, published open letters explaining their motivation.

'We each come by the gifts we have to offer by an infinite series of influences and lucky breaks we can never fully understand,' writes Scott in her letter. 'In addition to whatever assets life has nurtured in me, I have a disproportionate amount of money to share. My approach to philanthropy will continue to be thoughtful. It will take time and effort and care. But I won't wait. And I will keep at it until the safe is empty.'[11]

Her announcement attracted media attention, mainly of the amount of money involved. But it soon became apparent that Scott planned to set new standards, not only for the amount of money donated, but also for how it was given away and to whom. From a systemic point of view, that is the aspect I find most interesting. It begs the question of what kind of role models and heroes will help us navigate the 21st century successfully.

Are they people who are working to improve the system? Or are they working to protect their own position in the system?

Let's take the so-called new philanthropists in the US. Of course, there's nothing new about people who have come into great wealth supporting charitable work for the good of the community. The tradition goes back to Andrew Carnegie and John D. Rockefeller, who made their fortunes in steel and oil, and were considered the richest men of their time—as well as great philanthropists. Carnegie set up several foundations and, among other things, dedicated himself to supporting and building hundreds of public libraries—much more than the concert venue Carnegie Hall in New York that bears his name. Rockefeller set up just one foundation, whose mission is nothing less than to 'promote the well-being of humanity throughout the world', and which is still involved today in everything from education and culture to science, healthcare, and even food production.[12] All of which are, in principle, so-called public goods.

However, in the US, the boundaries are set very differently when it comes to the question of who should produce those goods and who is allowed access to them. It is described as a 'night-watchman' state, which means it is only supposed to intervene when the markets fail to regulate something—as shown by the prolonged debate over public healthcare. In the US, nobody finds anything wrong with private individuals filling the gaps in the state supply-and-support network. Still, even in America, the question eventually must arise of how those gaps came about in the first place.

Charity in the US is now principally handled by private foundations. Between 2005 and 2019, the number of such foundations rose by almost 70 per cent, and their assets more than doubled to $1.2 trillion,[13] which is approximately equivalent to the annual economic output of a country such as Spain. However, rather than supporting existing charitable organisations, many of these foundations define the aims they want to achieve with their money. That might be eradicating diseases such as polio or malaria, campaigning against smoking or obesity, developing technologies to combat climate change, or promoting research into human biology. Many of these foundations no longer restrict their activities to the country where those who monitors their aims are based, setting up transnational programmes and financing partner organisations in other countries.

Unlike elected governments, these foundations are not obliged to inform the public about who they give to, or how much. And, unlike governments, foundations can't be voted out by the public if people are not satisfied with their work. In view of the huge amounts of money these foundations are able to lay out, such arguments are often dismissed as nit-picking over the minutiae of democratic theory. And, of course, the use of private wealth for good causes rather than simply hoarding it is an act of generosity. But anyone who reads beyond the press releases about which tech billionaires want to save which parts of the world with their foundation will soon realise that such philanthropy also has a side benefit.

The American state grants extensive tax breaks to such foundations, to gain which they only have to spend a small portion of their wealth on charitable causes, while the rest can be invested in the stock market, for example, so as to increase the foundation's endowment capital. That is lost tax revenue for the state, which should be used for the common good, as stipulated in the Constitution. The money remains tied up in institutions that decide in private what it should be used for. And their founders are able to pay even less tax than they already do on their profitable business activities.[14] According to calculations by the Institute for Policy Studies thinktank, if the 100 American members of the Giving Pledge initiative were to keep their promise to donate half their fortune—that is, almost $500 billion— the American state would lose around $360 billion in tax revenues.[15]

In other words, this kind of philanthropy creates an opportunity that is only available to the few, but is subsidised by the many. And the fact, which has been repeatedly confirmed in studies, that the people with the lowest income donate the most money in relation to that income is completely drowned out by the media's interest in the huge sums donated by certain individuals.[16]

'Putting large donors at the centre of stories on social progress is a distortion of their role,' writes MacKenzie Scott in one of the short texts she publishes twice a year to announce which organisations will receive money from her. 'We are attempting to give away a fortune that was enabled by systems in need of change. My team's efforts are governed by a humbling belief that it would be better if disproportionate wealth were not concentrated in a small number of hands, and that the solutions are best designed and implemented by others.'[17]

It is those same systems that enabled the sixty American billionaires who joined The Giving Pledge in 2010 to almost double their fortune when they had actually promised to donate half of it. Fifty of them even tripled their wealth, and a few increased their riches by a factor of ten.[18] Between March and July 2020 alone, as the pandemic was hitting the world with full force, the collective wealth of the 100 US billionaires in the Giving Pledge initiative grew by more than a quarter. The wealth of the new philanthropists is increasing faster than they can give it away.

The former head of the United Nations World Food Programme (WFP), the American David Beasley, took the pandemic year of 2021 as an opportunity to address the world's billionaires publicly,[19] and called on them to make a one-off donation of $6.6 billion so that his organisation could feed 42 million people, who were in acute danger of starving, for a year.[20] He got no reaction for a long time. Then Elon Musk, currently the richest person in the world, responded publicly to him on Twitter.[21]

'If WFP can describe on this Twitter thread exactly how $6B will solve world hunger, I will sell Tesla stock right now and do it,' wrote Musk. 'Please publish your current and proposed spending in detail so people can see exactly where the money goes. Sunlight is a wonderful thing.'[22]

When Beasley pointed out to Musk that, contrary to what he seemed to have understood, $6.6 billion was nowhere near enough money to eradicate hunger from the world forever, but would be enough to save 42 million people from starvation for a year, Musk did not respond. As requested, the UN's Beasley sent Musk the charts he requested, showing how the donations would be spent, assured him of total transparency in the distribution process, and asked Musk to at least meet him in person. He added that Musk could throw him out of their meeting if he didn't like what Beasley had to say. But Musk, who received almost $5 billion in public funding to build his empire,[23] did not accept his 'challenge'—as they like to call it in Silicon Valley.[24]

And what are the side effects of this?

The institution trying to make public goods available feels powerless. And the impression that the saviours are to be found where the money is hoarded is reinforced.

Does this fit with a modern idea of heroism?

The philosopher Dieter Thomä dedicated an entire book to this question. His conclusion is that, '... the great cause that far more heroes should be fighting for is not one [made up] of individual challenges, but the continued existence of a functioning democracy'.[25]

Having established that, Thomä derives two types of hero. The first he calls 'heroes of the constitution'.[26] They stand up not only for the rules that the community imposes on itself, but also for the purpose those rules aim to serve. They defend the rights of third parties or of the whole community, even when it brings no benefit for themselves or when they are challenged by others for doing so. From a systemic point of view, they are people who intervene when the declared aim—the maintenance of democracy—and the actual situation no longer coincide. They don't question the aim or the framework, but they do question whether the path taken will lead to achieving the aim. And whether certain developments, such as excessive bureaucracy or extreme wealth, are impediments to achieving the aim.

'Heroes of movement', on the other hand, are in the realm of misfits, because they question the status quo.[27] They are not concerned with whether the path taken leads to achieving the aim; they consider the aim itself to be inadequate. Systemically speaking, they want to *update the purpose*. At first, they seem to be fighting a losing battle, and are opposed or underestimated as they push the limits of what is possible. When enough people start to follow such misfits—for example, in their commitment to a healthy climate—they can succeed in triggering social tipping points and turning entire systems around.

These two kinds of hero are not mutually exclusive. On the contrary, they complement each other. One type draws our attention to the values we want to preserve. The other makes us aware of which values we might need to change. The interplay of both is what leads to social progress. Democracy 'has a constitution — and lives as a movement', Thomä writes in summary. 'That is precisely what makes it great.'[28]

And what about the greatness of these heroes?

Many of them were neither particularly well known nor rich and powerful before they began advocating for change and throwing all their weight behind their cause. They had an understanding of what is necessary now, and so are willing to take risks, without knowing what the outcome will be.

They are doing something for a 'we' that does not make everything the same, but it does enable everything to be equal. They inspire us to join in because they 'are *doing* something' without aggrandising themselves, and 'because they are doing *something*'.[29] I am sure that you have often met such people. Perhaps even when you look in the mirror in the morning.

13

You matter

'My mission in life is not merely to survive, but to thrive; and to do so with some passion, some compassion, some humour and some style.'

MAYA ANGELOU, CIVIL RIGHTS ACTIVIST[1]

Romanesco is an eye-catcher in any vegetable aisle. It is simply a very beautiful member of the cabbage family. Its soft green colour often leads people to think that it's a cross between broccoli and cauliflower, but its real beauty lies in its unusual form. The entire vegetable seems to be made up of one basic geometrical shape—a tiny cone. From its simplest buds to the finely chiselled turrets and spires, the shape repeats itself over and over again, coming together into great spirals and forming a pattern that is the same at every scale. It's a real marvel of nature.

The next time you see some Romanesco while out

shopping, have a good look at it. My daughters think it is absolutely beautiful.

Romanesco is an example of a structure in which the individual parts resemble the whole and are self-repeating. Such structures are called fractals. They exist in geometry, where they emerge as graphic representations of complex computations. They also feature in digital art, where they can be used as graphic elements to create astounding effects. But they also appear everywhere in nature: in corals, sponges, honeycombs, snowflakes, the fronds of ferns, and the eyes of dragonflies. And in blood vessels that branch into ever-smaller capillaries. What all those structures have in common is that they result from an ever-repeating design principle. From the smallest scale to the biggest dimensions, they follow the same instructions, so to speak. That's why, when presented with a picture of a section of them, it is often impossible to tell whether the image was taken from very close up or very far away. The self-similarity of fractals can also tell us something about social change.

'Although often considered no more than a metaphor,' writes the American human geographer Karen O'Brien, 'social fractals are real in that as they can transform relationships and generate new patterns and structures in society.'[2]

Karen O'Brien began her career as a geographer, and has collaborated on several reports for the IPCC, which received the Nobel Peace Prize in 2007 for its work. In the course of that work, she became increasingly interested in the ways that societies cause and deal with the consequences of changes to the natural world—that is, in the human dimension of global change. In her book *You Matter More Than You Think*, she views that global change from the bottom up. Her ideas progress from the scale of the individual to the whole, and deal with questions that are usually held up as arguments against this perspective.

Aren't the systems that appear to be near a tipping point far too large and hefty to actually flip? And aren't individuals far too small and insignificant to do anything about it anyway?

And isn't that precisely the reason why our hearts sometimes sink when we think about those challenges?

O'Brien's response to this is to explain how we are always embedded in society in small, manageable systems in which we can make a change. And she explains that those systems in which we do have a part to play are embedded in larger systems, which in turn are embedded in yet larger systems in which they have a part to play as subsystems. That is the core of the idea that small-scale social change drives large-scale transformation. It is precisely like the image of a fractal.

'If our actions are consistent with values that apply to the whole and resonate through language, meaning-making, and values,' writes Karen O'Brien, 'they will replicate, generating new patterns that will reflect these qualities at all scales.'[3]

In a fractal structure, certain principles are repeated on different levels, multiplying them and making them part of our lived normality. If a principle is altered, a change is triggered that can spread and continue through different levels. In this sense, collective and individual changes are in constant interaction: neither top-down nor bottom-up change ever happens in isolation, nor does change between different organisations on any given level.

But that doesn't mean that everyone always has to be saying the same things.

That's not what is meant by self-similarity.

Karen O'Brien is not concerned with making everybody's opinions *about* the world the same; she's more concerned with attitudes *to* the world. When individuals value openness, for example, their behaviour will underpin that value in society, and when society values openness, individuals' behaviour will be influenced correspondingly. This does not prescribe what anyone should think or say about any given issue, but it does put structures in place for how they should think about it.

For example, there should always be a spirit of openness to the idea that others have a different opinion from our own. In this way, the diverse potential that is rooted in all of us can be activated and perpetuated culturally. That activation and continuation is reliant on the multiplicity of individuals. They listen to, recount, repeat, and change the narratives we use to interpret and organise the world around us, and to form our understanding of ourselves and others. As a result of this process, the many individuals become precisely those effectors who formulate the values that shape our understanding and behaviour as a whole.

'Institutions may change over time, and structures may be reformed, updated, or repackaged to appear new and more progressive,' says O'Brien. 'but when their underlying values do not embody or promote thriving for all, at some scale they will generate fragments rather than fractal patterns.'[4]

Fractals are examples of individual parts self-organising to create a whole, while fragments are unembedded individual parts—which are more likely to lead to imbalance than equilibrium.

So what can bring us more balance? How can we find a way to take effective action that fits into our daily life, and that does not cause us to lose sight of ourselves or of the whole?

Let me describe the possibilities we have to make an impact according to the categories of 'head', 'hands', and 'heart'.

Let's begin with the head. The ability to put our heads together to solve problems is one of the things that sets us apart from other species on the planet.

For that to succeed, however, we must reach as close an agreement as possible on how we see the world. As everyone probably knows from discussions at home or in the workplace, opinions often differ widely about why things don't work, or what solution would be appropriate for a given problem, or even sometimes over trivialities.

The American ecologist Garrett Hardin shows how the key to reaching a common understanding is the way we describe the world, and how we quickly find ourselves talking at cross purposes when our ways of describing the world differ.[5] Hardin — in his role as a scholar, before his personal views and political activities later led him to being labelled a white nationalist — takes us into the world of science to illustrate his point. He distinguishes between two typical ways of thinking and speaking about reality: the vocabulary of numbers, and the vocabulary of words. Numbers are suitable for quantitative measurements and describing ratios. Words are useful for qualitative descriptions and descriptions of contexts. Each way of speaking is able to capture some concepts better than others. But both are required to describe the world in its entirety. This is the argument made by Hardin in his 1985 book, *Filters Against Folly*.

The pandemic showed us that numbers can give a very different impression of a situation than words when we looked to the daily infection figures for an indication of how the virus was spreading, even if we ourselves had not yet been infected. The statistics could not show what such an infection might mean for an individual. For that, we relied on reports from intensive-care units in hospitals. And situations also change over time, as the pandemic also showed us. The long-term consequences of a problem must also be considered, rather than just its immediate effects; otherwise, we risk losing sight of the importance of reacting in a timely manner before the situation starts to look serious. And it is only by being aware that the solutions of today may become the problems of tomorrow that we can continue to be in constant learning mode.

What are the appropriate words?

What are the appropriate numbers?

And what then?[6]

Hardin believes that we can avoid many unnecessary misunderstandings and conflicts by always bearing these three questions in mind. It is not about a competition between words and numbers. Rather, it is about combining them in a way that is appropriate to each situation. These filters force us to examine whether the words or numbers we use to describe a problem really do express what we mean. For example, we often only enumerate things we can measure, but not everything can be measured or counted in numerical terms. And if, on the other hand, we construct our image of the world entirely without regard to numbers and measurements, we may overlook proportions, dynamics, and accumulating trends.

In this way, Hardin's filters enable us not only to describe problems more precisely, but also to test the solutions we find for them. This is central to 'futures literacy', the ability to read and write the future. Only when we are able to communicate with each other about the current situation can we reach agreement about what the future should look like and how we can help to bring it about.

That brings us to my 'hands' category. By that, I mean our actions — what we *do*. After we have described a problem and perhaps even come up with a good solution, we still need to act upon it. Many things can only be achieved one step at a time.

But which step do we start with?

One possible answer to that question is provided by the American biologist Stuart Kauffman. He investigates how developments unfold in nature. Of course, if we take the evolution of single-celled animals to human beings, there was no one sitting around thinking about what the most practical first developmental step might be. But that doesn't mean there never was such a first step. Kauffman's theory of 'the adjacent possible' is an attempt to explain the way nature regulates this. At its core, his model says that nature creates new possibilities by constantly sounding out what is directly adjacent to the currently possible.

'Biospheres,' writes Kauffman, 'on average may enter their adjacent possible as rapidly as they can sustain.'[7]

When applied to us humans, it does not mean that we shouldn't plan ahead or strive to achieve any far-reaching goals in order to transform our systems. What it does mean, however, is that we can only approach those goals step by step if we don't want the process of change to be too disruptive — that is, if we don't want to spark real crises or confrontations over dominance. The hands that want to act must always be the hands we hold out to others to offer cooperation in partnership-based strategies. And that means we must be open and flexible towards those we reach out to. Forging new alliances between people who are used to a different worldview in the subsystem they inhabit, or whose behaviour follows a different logic, requires that everyone first agree on what the problem is. The sociologist Armin Nassehi derives from this a categorical imperative of 'pragmatic opportunities of association'— everyone must be given a chance to join in, regardless of their, or your, opinions on the matter at hand.

'Act in such a way that others can join you, precisely because that is not in your control,' he writes.[8]

By always taking the step that is possible for those involved at a given time, we can bring about the kind of change that is more permanently reflected in our systems, in our real-life experience, and in self-organising processes. We must not sit back and rest for too long after each step, and instead keep moving. Then a practical dynamism will result, in which we constantly adapt to uncertainties, change our routines, repackage our institutions, and embrace a new normal. That normality then takes root because as many people as possible join in with it. And we must always keep the third horizon in mind so as not to lose sight of the direction we are heading in. As we take those steps, we can still adjust the size of our stride to each given situation.

But what if that takes too long?

This is where the heart comes into play. It shows us the attitude we can adopt to help us master this process successfully. The only real power we have to act, and to develop a meaningful sense of self-efficacy, comes from our relationship with ourselves. We can inspire others and encourage them to make changes — and sometimes call on them to move faster, if the time for such comments is right. The way we do that is, of course, important, both because of its effect on others and because of the way it affects us ourselves. On the one hand, no one can be totally dependent on the way others behave. On the other hand, everyone needs other people in order to bring about the kind of change that is culturally rooted rather than imposed from outside.

The ancient Greek Stoics had a term that can help us understand this apparent contradiction. *Arete* can be translated as 'virtue' or 'personal excellence'. The American author Jonas Salzgeber has a translation of *arete* that is a good guiding principle for our personal lives: 'Always be[ing] the best version of yourself.'[9] He describes it as an attitude that helps us to align our actions with our intentions. It is those intentions that we are responsible for—whether our actions produce the intended effect depends on many other parameters, especially on the other people involved in or affected by those actions.

It means asking ourselves every day whether and where we explored the adjacent possible in an attempt to move close to the desired goal.

If we keep that question in mind when we apply ourselves, we can set a lot in motion. And if you talk to others about it, I'm sure you will realise: we can do better.

Acknowledgements

This will be my last book. That's a promise I made to myself and to my two daughters. And I was always so touched when they so fervently wished me lots of energy for the task of writing a book. The same goes for my parents. Those wishes would be sent from a distance, or while they were busy keeping everything up and running. And Jan – no one could love my intensity so gallantly and generously as you do. What a blessing that is.

In general, I feel richly blessed to be surrounded by so many astonishing people in my private and professional life, with whom I have laughed and cried, danced and raved, lived it up and knuckled down, argued and searched for solutions, expanded ideas and advocated for our species to surpass itself. My Sissi and my girls near and far, compassionate residents, the NaSen-Plus as a tireless energy field, the motley

Göpel-Meschede crew, super-editors and crazily clever colleagues, great role models and exciting encounters: I am, only because we are.

Until her maternity leave, Sophie Bunge was always an amazing multi-talent at my side, who went through thick and thin with me. And that was a lot over the past eighteen months. This book is also a collaborative work, which grew out of intensive discussions and countless text loops. Along with me, Markus Jauer and Tanja Ruzicska have irrevocably become system thinkers, and I again had the opportunity to learn a great deal about the flow of reading in non-fiction books. Once again, Tanja deserves a gold medal for her positive and motivational process management and her amazing perseverance. Her linguistic precision put me through quite a number of learning loops.

My thanks go out to Detlev Buck for giving his permission to use the title – wonderful!

Notes

Prologue: Humanity's greatest adventure

1   Rebecca Solnit, *Hope in the Dark: untold histories, wild possibilities*, Haymarket Books, Chicago 2016, p. xiv.

2   Erich Fromm: *The Sane Society*, Routledge, London 2008, p. 266.

Part I: Our Operating System

1   Frances Westley, Brenda Zimmerman, Michael Quinn Patton: *Getting to Maybe: how the world is changed*, Vintage Canada, Toronto 2009, p. 7.

Chapter One: The story of Tanaland

1   Hans-Peter Dürr: 'Teilhaben an einer unteilbaren Welt. Das ganzheitliche Weltbild der Quantenphysik' ('Participating in an indivisible world: the total worldview of quantum physics'), in: Gerald Hüther, Christa Spannbauer (Eds.): *Connectedness. Warum wir ein neues Weltbild brauchen* (*Connectedness: why we need a new world view*), Hogrefe, Bern 2012, pp. 15–28, this quote p. 27.

2   For a description of the events in Tanaland, see: Dietrich Dörner, *The Logic of Failure: why things go wrong and what we can do to make them right*, Metropolitan Books, New York 1996.

3   'Überall Tanaland' ('Tanaland is Everywhere'), in: *Der Spiegel*, 21/1975, pp. 135 ff., www.spiegel.de/kultur/ueberall-tanaland-a-fb5c 21cc-0002-0001-0000-000041496567 (last retrieved: 1 June 2022).

4   Dörner: *The Logic of Failure*, Chapter Nine.

5   A very accessible book on complex systems—since they are the issue here—has been published by the head of the Research on Complex

Systems working group at the Berlin's Humboldt University. See
Dirk Brockmann: *Im Wald vor lauter Bäumen. Unsere komplexe Welt
besser verstehen* (*Seeing the Wood for the Trees: understanding our
complex world better*), dtv Munich.

6   Donella Meadows, *Thinking in Systems: a primer*, Earthscan, London
2009, p. 188. My italics.

7   Op. cit.

8   Those who want to have some fun exploring the way things
are interconnected in systems should try the *Systems Thinking
Playbook* by Linda Booth Sweeney, Dennis Meadows, and Gillian
Martin Mehers: www.klimamediathek.de/wp-content/uploads/
giz2011-0588en-playbook-climate-change.pdf. For a sustainability-
specialised cooperation partner for simulation games like the
Tanaland simulation, as well as simulation games that also include a
role-playing element (social simulations), see the Centre for Systems
Solutions (CRS): systemssolutions.org/ (last retrieved: 1 June 2022).

9   See, for example, Ian Goldin and Chris Kutarna: *The Age of Discovery:
navigating the storms of our second Renaissance*, Bloomsbury, London
2016.

10 Meadows: *Thinking in Systems*, pp. 169–70. Further recommended
reading: Gilbert Probst and Andrea M. Bassi: *Tackling Complexity:
a systemic approach for decision makers*, Greenleaf, London 2017; John
Gribbin: *Deep Simplicity: chaos, complexity and the emergence of life*,
Penguin Books, London 2004; Graham Leicester: *Transformative
Innovation: a guide to practice and policy*, Triarchy Press, Axminster
2016. For an introduction to systems analysis and strategies, as well
as further sources on this topic, see also the System Innovation
Handbook published by the Wuppertal Institute and the Centre for
Social Investment (CSI): www.soz.uni-heidelberg.de/wp-content/
uploads/2019/02/SysInnoLab_2016_Handbook.pdf (last retrieved:
1 June 2022).

11 See, for example, Ian Goldin and Chris Kutarna: *Age of Discovery:
navigating the storms of our second renaissance* (rev edn) Bloomsbury,
London 2017; Karl Polanyi: *The Great Transformation: the political
and economic origins of our time*, Beacon Press, Boston 2001;
Wilhelm Rotthaus: *Wir können und müssen uns neu erfinden. Am
Ende des Zeitalters des Individuums—Aufbruch in die Zukunft* (*We
Can and Must Reinvent Ourselves: heading towards the future at
the end of the age of the individual*), Carl-Auer, Heidelberg 2021;
Klaus Schwab and Thierry Malleret: *Covid-19: the great reset*,

Forum Publishing, Cologny/Geneva 2020; German Advisory Council on Climate Change (WBGU): *World in Transition: a social contract for sustainability*, Flagship Report, Berlin 2011; Ernst Ulrich von Weizsäcker and Anders Wijkman (Eds.) *Come On!: Capitalism, Short-termism, Population and the Destruction of the Planet*, Springer 2018; and the 2015 United Nations publication *Transforming our World: the 2030 Agenda for Sustainable Development*, sustainabledevelopment.un.org/post2015/transformingourworld/publication (last retrieved: 1 June 2022).

Chapter Two: Networked: everything is connected

1   Ugo Bardi, *The Seneca Effect: why growth is slow but collapse is rapid*, Springer 2017, p. 166.

2   Those interested in the precise location of these two lakes can enter the following coordinates into any online map service: 46°15'07.3"N 89°30'14.1"W.

3   For a description of the experiment and an analysis of the results, see: Stephen Carpenter et al.: 'Early warnings of regime shifts: evaluation of spatial indicators from a whole-ecosystem experiment', in: *Ecosphere*, August 2014, vol. 5, no. 8, esajournals.onlinelibrary.wiley.com/doi/full/10.1890/ES13-00398.1 (last retrieved: 1 June 2022).

4   Hans-Peter Dürr explains this message in an accessible way all the way down to the level of quantum mechanics in his essay 'Teilhaben an einer unteilbaren Welt' ('Participating in an Indivisible World').

5   Dürr, 'Teilhaben an einer unteilbaren Welt', p. 18.

6   See the webinar held by the United Nations Environment Programme in January 2021: Advancing the One Health Response to Antimicrobial Resistance (AMR): unep.org/events/webinar/advancing-one-health-response-antimicrobial-resistance-amr; the YouTube link to the webinar recording is: www.youtube.com/watch?v=eRg7XMDSHlM. See also UNEP's 2017 report on antimicrobial resistance: www.unep.org/resources/frontiers-2017-emerging-issues-environmental-concern (last retrieved: 1 June 2022).

7   See Natalie Wolchover's article, 'Nature's Critical Warning System', in: *Quantamagazine*, November 2015, www.quantamagazine.org/natures-critical-warning-system-20151118/ (last retrieved: 1 June 2022).

8   Antonio Gramsci, *Selections from the Prison Notebooks*, ElecBook, London 1971, p. 556.

9   Critical slowing down patterns are now used to predict tipping points in the analytical study of many different biological systems,

for example in medicine. See for example: Ingrid A. van de Leemput et al.: 'Critical slowing down as early warning for the onset and termination of depression', 9 December 2013, www.pnas.org/doi/10.1073/pnas.1312114110; and Matias I. Maturana et al.: 'Critical slowing down as a biomarker for seizure susceptibility', 1 May 2020, www.nature.com/articles/s41467-020-15908-3 (last retrieved: 1 June 2022).

10 See Johan Rockström et al.: 'A safe operating space for humanity', in: *Nature*, 461, 2009, pp. 472–9, www.nature.com/articles/461472a. For a critical discussion of this approach and various reactions from the natural and social sciences, including recommendations for further development, see Frank Biermann and Rakhyun E. Kim: 'The Boundaries of the Planetary Boundary Framework: a critical appraisal of approaches to define a 'Safe Operating Space' for Humanity', in: *Annual Review of Environment and Resources*, October 2020, vol. 45, pp. 497–521, www.annualreviews.org/doi/10.1146/annurev-environ-012320-080337 (last retrieved: 1 June 2022). Here the concept is used because it succeeded in doing exactly what even critical authors admit: it provides a symbol and a reference point which relates to a wide variety of different research and enables discourse. Incidentally, of studies that criticise the details of the measurements or regional variations in the planetary boundaries framework, none challenge the general message that it is high time we put a stop to destructive trends.

11 See the article on the United Nations webpage: news.un.org/en/story/2021/04/1090242 (last retrieved: 1 June 2022).

12 For more, see the findings published in January 2022 by the Stockholm Resilience Centre: www.stockholmresilience.org/research/research-news/2022-01-18-safe-planetary-boundary-for-pollutants-including-plastics-exceeded-say-researchers.html (last retrieved: 1 June 2022).

13 Dörner, *The Logic of Failure*, p. 87.

14 Cf. the informative paper by Stefan Gössling of Lund University: observatoriodabicicleta.org.br/uploads/2021/03/SocialCostAutomobilityEuropeSGet.pdf).

15 The Ariadne Research Project, as part of the German government's Copernicus Consortium, calculated in 2021 that environmental damage costs Germany 13 to 19 per cent of its GDP, which is not reflected in state financial calculations. See the article from 3 June 2021 in the *Zeitung für kommunale Wirtschaft*: www.zfk.de/politik/

deutschland/umweltsteuern-koennten-bis-zu-564-mrd-euro-mobilisieren (last retrieved: 1 June 2022).

16 Multisolving is a concept used by sustainability scientists, in particular with regard to studies that work with different scenarios and possible development paths. Examples can be found in the German Advisory Council on Climate Change's 2020 publication *Rethinking Land in the Anthropocene: from separation to integration*, where the phrase 'multiple benefit strategies' is used: www.wbgu.de/fileadmin/user_upload/wbgu/publikationen/hauptgutachten/hg2020/pdf/WBGU_HG2020_en.pdf. Further examples can be found in many research projects, including those investigating how to combine adapting to a changing climate with social and environmental aims and how they can be made economically viable—for example, Benedict Bueb et al.: *Towards Sustainable Adaptation Pathways: a concept for integrative actions to achieve the 2030 Agenda, Paris Agreement and Sendai Framework*, the German Environment Agency, Dessau-Rosslau 2021: www.umweltbundesamt.de/publikationen/towards-sustainable-adaptation-pathways. The newly founded Multisolving Institute in the USA also offers a detailed insight into this approach: www.multisolving.org (last retrieved: 1 June 2022).

Chapter Three: Dynamics: how little things grow big

1 Robert Folger in an interview with Lars Fischer: 'Die Welt wird wieder untergehen' ('The World Will End Again'), in: *Spektrum*, 6 May 2021, www.spektrum.de/news/apokalypse-die-welt-wird-wieder-untergehen/1869820 (last retrieved: 1 June 2022).

2 The video has now been viewed more than 23 million times: www.youtube.com/watch?v=GA8z7f7a2Pk (last retrieved: 1 June 2022).

3 For more on this understanding of leadership, see the TED Talk of the American author, entrepreneur, and former musician Derek Sivers, in which he uses the video to illustrate his point: www.ted.com/talks/derek_sivers_how_to_start_a_movement/transcript (last retrieved: 1 June 2022).

4 For a summary of the differences between social and ecological systems, the progress of research into tipping points in socio-ecological systems, and what commonalities can be identified, see: Manjana Milkoreit et al.: 'Defining tipping points for social-ecological systems scholarships—an interdisciplinary literature review', iopscience.iop.org/article/10.1088/1748-9326/aaaa75 (last retrieved: 1 June 2022); four conditions have been set

out for distinguishing between categories of structural change:
1. Multiple stable states (they imply a certain amount of change
and a reconfiguration of the system); 2. Abruptness (also called
non-linearity or disproportionality of cause and effect); 3. Feedback
mechanisms (as system-internal drivers of change between two
system states and as stabilisers of state); 4. Irreversibility. The
significance of the fourth condition must be reduced somewhat
in view of the fact that limited reversibility (hysteresis) and
irreversibility on a timescale relevant to human societies is sufficient
to fulfil this condition.

5   Cf. Thomas Schelling: 'Dynamic Models of Segregation', in: *Journal of Mathematical Sociology*, 1971, vol. 1, pp. 143–86. Available online at: www.stat.berkeley.edu/~aldous/157/Papers/Schelling_Seg_Models.pdf (last retrieved: 1 June 2022).

6   Malcolm Gladwell: *The Tipping Point: how little things can make a big difference*, Abacus, London 2001.

7   The paper published by Hans Joachim Schellnhuber and other climatologists subsequently became one of the most-cited scientific articles ever. Cf. Timothy M. Lenton, Hermann Held, Elmar Kriegler, Jim W. Hall, Wolfgang Lucht, Stefan Rahmstorf, and Hans Joachim Schellnhuber: 'Tipping elements in the Earth's climate system', in: *PNAS*, February 2008: www.pnas.org/content/105/6/1786 (last retrieved: 1 June 2022).

8   One scientific definition is: 'Tipping points in general can be defined as the point or threshold at which small quantitative changes in the system trigger a non-linear change process that is driven by system-internal feedback mechanisms and inevitably leads to a qualitatively different state of the system, which is often irreversible. This new state can be distinguished from the original by its fundamentally altered (positive and negative) state-stabilising feedbacks.' Cf. Manjana Milkoreit et al.: 'Defining tipping points for social-ecological systems scholarship—an interdisciplinary literature review', op. cit.

9   See Niklas Boers and Martin Rypdal: 'Critical slowing down suggests that the western Greenland Ice Sheet is close to a tipping point', in: *Proceedings of the National Academy of Sciences (PNAS)*, 17 May 2021, www.pnas.org/doi/full/10.1073/pnas.2024192118 (last retrieved: 1 June 2022).

10 Cf. The 'Albedo' article on the Encyclopaedia Britannica's page: www.britannica.com/science/albedo, or the UK Met Office's page: www.

metoffice.gov.uk/weather/learn-about/weather/atmosphere/albedo.

11 For more, see the very revealing results of this study by an
    interdisciplinary research group: Michaela D. King et al.: 'Dynamic
    ice loss from the Greenland Ice Sheet driven by sustained glacier
    retreat' in: *Communications Earth & Environment* 1, 2020, www.
    nature.com/articles/s43247-020-0001-2 (last retrieved: 1 June 2022).

12 Severn Cullis-Suzuki's speech is available to watch here: www.
    youtube.com/watch?v=oJJGuIZVfLM. The full text of her
    speech is available here: www.americanrhetoric.com/speeches/
    severnsuzukiunearthsummit.htm (last retrieved: 25 May 2023).

13 In 2021, the International Energy Agency (IEA) issued a report that
    included a calculation of energy use scenarios to achieve net zero. It
    concludes that an immediate stop to the exploration of new oil, coal
    and gas deposits would be necessary to achieve this: www.iea.org/
    reports/world-energy-outlook-2021 (last retrieved: 1 June 2022).

14 See the World Economic Forum's comprehensive report, 'Readiness
    for the Future of Production 2018', which describes and analyses
    the future production readiness of one hundred countries: www3.
    weforum.org/docs/FOP_Readiness_Report_2018.pdf (last retrieved:
    1 June 2022).

15 See the 2011 paper by Frances Westley et al. at the Royal Swedish
    Academy of Science, published in *Ambio*: 'Tipping toward
    Sustainability: Emerging Pathways of Transformation', pp. 762–80.
    It focusses on the question of what conditions are necessary to
    escape the current lock-in: http://homerdixon.com/wp-content/
    uploads/2017/05/Tipping-Toward-Sustainability-Emerging-
    Pathways.pdf (last retrieved: 1 June 2022).

16 See Paul Hawken's inaugural speech at the University of Portland
    2009: files.eric.ed.gov/fulltext/EJ1078017.pdf (last retrieved:
    1 June 2022).

Chapter Four: Purpose: the *actual* concern

1 Tim Jackson: *Post Growth: life after capitalism*, Polity Press,
   Cambridge 2021.

2 See for example *Newsweek*, 20 June 2022: www.newsweek.com/zero-
   star-hotel-founder-interview-1723393 (last retrieved: 27 May 2023).

3 Hans-Dietrich Reckhaus: *Fliegen lassen. Wie man radikal und
   konsequent neu wirtschaftet* (*Let it fly: how to do business radically and
   consistently in a new way*), Murman Publishers, Hamburg 2020,
   pp. 19 f.

4   See Fabian Schmidt's article for *Deutsche Welle*, of 30 October 2019:
    www.dw.com/en/munich-study-confirms-severe-decline-in-insect-
    populations-in-germany/a-51052955 (last retrieved: 27 May 2023).

5   See Milton Friedman's 1970 essay in *The New York Times Magazine*,
    'The Social Responsibility of Business is to Increase its Profits':
    http://websites.umich.edu/~thecore/doc/Friedman.pdf (last
    retrieved: 1 June 2022).

6   Hans-Dietrich Reckhaus: *Insect Respect. Das Gütezeichen für einen
    weltweit neuen Umgang mit Insekten* (*Insect Respect: the quality seal for
    a global new treatment of insects)*, 11th, extended edition, Reckhaus,
    Bielefeld 2021, p. 202. This passage does not appear in earlier
    editions.

7   Cf. Thomas Dyllick-Brenzinger and Katrin Muff: 'Clarifying the
    meaning of sustainable business: Introducing a typology from
    business-as-usual to true business sustainability', in: *Organization
    and Environment*, 2015, pp. 1–19: www.bsl-lausanne.ch/wp-content/
    uploads/2015/04/Dyllick-Muff-Clarifying-Publ-Online.full_.pdf
    (last retrieved: 1 June 2022). This article gives a very good overview
    of the practical and academic developments in sustainable business
    practice, as well as past and present flaws and trends. Its perhaps
    most sobering statement for a researcher—although it is not too
    surprising after several years of policy advice from academia—is that
    most conceptual management research neither reaches nor resonates
    with management practice.

8   Meadows, *Thinking in Systems*, p. 161.

9   One very interesting area of research in this field focusses on
    anticipation. It examines the role played by the present in our
    ability to envisage different futures. See the Fourth International
    Conference on Anticipation, hosted by Arizona State University in
    2022: http://anticipationconference.org/series/ (last retrieved:
    1 June 2022). Futures Literacy is the name given to a practice-based
    version of the findings from such research. Professors at several
    universities have teamed up with UNESCO to work globally
    on the issue. Riel Miller has published an academic, open access
    book on the topic: *Transforming the Future. Anticipation in the 21st
    Century*, Routledge, London 2018, www.taylorfrancis.com/books/
    oa-edit/10.4324/9781351048002/transforming-future-riel-miller
    (last retrieved: 1 June 2022).

10 Samira El Ouassil and Friedemann Karig: *Erzählende Affen. Mythen,
    Lügen, Utopien—wie Geschichten unser Leben bestimmen* (*Story-telling*

Apes: myths, lies, utopias — how stories shape our lives), Ullstein, Berlin 2021, p. 15. For a more academic consideration of the subject, see the book based on Annick Hedlung-deWitt's PhD thesis: 'Worldviews and the transformation to sustainable societies. An exploration of the cultural and psychological dimensions of our global environmental challenges', Amsterdam 2013. David Korten places the focus on our economic system in his book: *Change the Story, Change the Future: a living economy for a living Earth*, Berrett-Koehler Publishers, Oakland 2015.

11 Cf. the figures published by the German Airports Association (ADV): www.adv.aero/service/downloadbibliothek/#vz (last retrieved: 1 June 2022).

12 See, for example, the work of the German non-profit organisation Atmosfair. Although it does work with carbon offsetting, it only ever uses it as a way of reducing the damage caused by unavoidable carbon emissions: www.atmosfair.de (last retrieved: 1 June 2022).

13 For more on synthetic fuels, see Jan Rosenow und Richard Lowes' article: 'Will blue hydrogen lock us into fossil fuels forever?', in: *One Earth*, vol. 4, Issue 11, November 2021, pp. 1527–9; or the information provided by the Institute for Energy and Environmental Research Heidelberg (IFEU): www.ifeu.de/ service/nachrichtenarchiv/ifeu-studie-warnt-vor-nebenwirkungen-synthetischer-ptx-brennstoffe/; the *Scientists for Future* podcast has an informative episode on synthetic fuels: episode 13, 'Synthetische Treibstoffe' ('Synthetic Fuels)': s4f-podcast.de/ as does the *Nebelhorn* podcast, episode 4, 'Warum synthetische Kraftstoffe nicht die Lösung sind' ('Why Synthetic Fuels Are Not the Solution'): s4f-hamburg.de/2020/12/21/synthetische-kraftstoffe/ (last retrieved 1 June 2022). For more on synthetic fuels' effect on the water balance, see: Klaus Stratmann: 'Schattenseite des Hoffnungsträgers: Produktion von Wasserstoff könnte Ressourcen gefährden' ('The Dark Side of the Great Hope: hydrogen production could endanger resources'), www.handelsblatt.com/politik/deutschland/ klimaneutralitaet-schattenseite-des-hoffnungstraegers-produktion-von-wasserstoff-koennte-ressourcen-gefaehrden/27063644.html. (last retrieved: 1 June 2022).

14 Attribution science is the study of this issue. It has seen the publication of new calculations in recent years, as can be seen at news.climate.columbia.edu/2021/10/04/ attribution-science-linking-climate-change-to-extreme-weather/.

15 Cf. 'Netherlands court orders oil giant to cut emissions': www.bbc.com/news/world-europe-57257982.

16 For more on regenerative business models, see the report by John Elkington and Richard Roberts, 'Tomorrow's Capitalism.: the 2020s leadership agenda', volans.com/wp-content/uploads/2019/11/TC-2020s-Leadership-Agenda.pdf (last retrieved: 1 June 2022); examples of central company valuation networks include the Value Balancing Alliance and the Capitals Coalition.

17 Thomas Schelling: 'Dynamic Models of Segregation', p. 146. Available online at: www.stat.berkeley.edu/~aldous/157/Papers/Schelling_Seg_Models.pdf (last retrieved: 1 June 2022).

18 Cf. Felix Creutzig et al.: 'Demand-side solutions to climate change mitigation consistent with high levels of well-being', in: *Nature Climate Change*, Issue 12, 2022, pp. 36–46, www.nature.com/articles/s41558-021-01219-y (last retrieved: 1 June 2022).

19 F. Geels, A. McMeekin, J. Mylan, and D Southerton: 'A critical appraisal of Sustainable Consumption and Production research: the reformist, revolutionary and reconfiguration positions', in: *Global Environmental Change*, vol. 34, 2015, pp. 1–12; this quote p. 2.

20 Cf. here and in the following, Bjørn Thomassen: *Liminality and the Modern: living through the in-between*, Ashgate Publishing, Farnham 2014, pp. 113–41.

21 Cf. Robert Folger's interview with Lars Fischer: 'Die Welt wird wieder untergehen', Lars Fischer: 'Die Welt wird wieder untergehen' ('The World Will End Again'), op. cit.

Part II: Changing the Operation

1 Meadows: *Thinking in Systems*, p. 4.

Chapter Five: What *Monopoly* teaches us about the rules of the game

1 Riane Eisler, *The Real Wealth of Nations: creating a caring economics*, Berrett-Koehler Publishers, Oakland 2007, p. 216.

2 For more details, see www.landlord-games.com, which has extensive information on the historical development of the game—as well as the text of the patent application, landlordsgame.info/rules/lg-1904p_patent.html (last retrieved: 1 June 2022).

3 Henry George, *Progress and Poverty*, Kegan, Paul, Trench & Co., London 1886, p. 241. Available online: www.google.de/books/edition/Progress_and_poverty/lnVbAAAAQAAJ?hl=en&gbpv=0.

4 Quoted in Mary Pilon, *The Monopolists*, which tells the story of the invention of the game of Monopoly. Cf. Mary Pilon: 'Monopoly was designed to teach the 99% about income inequality', in: *Smithsonian Magazine*, January 2015, www.smithsonianmag.com/arts-culture/monopoly-was-designed-teach-99-about-income-in-equality-180953630/ (last retrieved: 1 June 2022).

5 Quoted in the 1906 version of the rules, in the section entitled 'The Monarch of the World': landlordsgame.info/games/lg-1906/lg-1906_egc-rules.htmlhttps://landlordsgame.info/games/lg-1906/lg-1906_egc-rules.html (last retrieved: 1 June 2022).

6 Meadows: *Thinking in Systems*, p. 127.

7 Ibid. p. 111 ff.

8 Ibid. p. 112.

9 Cf. the 1906 version of Elizabeth Magie's game: landlordsgame.info/games/lg-1906/lg-1906_egc-rules.html (last retrieved: 1 June 2022).

10 The story of how *The Landlord's Game* became *Monopoly* can be found widely online, as at: www.theguardian.com/lifeandstyle/2015/apr/11/secret-history-monopoly-capitalist-game-leftwing-origins.

11 Cf. ibid, p. 47.

12 Cf. Mary Pilon: 'Monopoly Was Designed to Teach the 99% About Income Equality', www.smithsonianmag.com/arts-culture/monopoly-was-designed-teach-99-about-income-inequality-180953630/ (last retrieved: 1 June 2022).

Chapter Six: Responsibility: learning better

1 Aurelio Peccei, Foreword in James W. Botkin, Mahdi Elmandjra, and Mircea Malitza: *No Limits to Learning: bridging the human gap. A Report to the Club of Rome*, Pergamon Press, Oxford 1979, p. xiii.

2 Cf, for example, the analysis in Klaus Busch, Christoph Hermann, Karl Hinrichs, and Thorsten Schulten, 'Euro Crisis, Austerity Policy and the European Social Model', Friedrich Ebert Foundation, Berlin 2012: file://C:/Users/Acer/Downloads/FES_ENGL.pdf (last retrieved: 1 June 2022).

3 See the European Commission memo 'Youth on the Move' of 15 September 2010, ec.europa.eu/commission/presscorner/detail/en/MEMO_10_408 (last retrieved: 1 June 2022).

4 Stephen Hawking's 'Millennium Interview' in: *San Jose Mercury News*, 23 January 2000.

5 Paul Raskin et al.: *Great Transition: the promise and lure of the times ahead*, Stockholm Environment Institute, Boston 2003,

greattransition.org/documents/Great_Transition.pdf, p. 7, (last retrieved: 1 June 2022).

6 Cf. John Schwartz, 'Paul Crutzen, Nobel Laureate Who Fought Climate Change, Dies at 87', in *The New York Times*, 4 February 2021 (last retrieved: 12 June 2023).

7 Cf. the Nobel Prize Summit's 'Urgent Call for Action': www. nationalacademies.org/news/2021/04/nobel-prize-laureates-and-other-experts-issue-urgent-call-for-action-after-our-planet-our-future-summit (last retrieved: 1 June 2022).

8 Jakub Samochowiec: *Future Skills: four Ssenarios for the world of tomorrow*. Gottlieb Duttweiler Institute, Rüschlikon 2020, commissioned by the Jacobs Foundation, Zurich 2020 jacobsfoundation.org/wp-content/uploads/2023/06/2020_EN_Future-Skills_JacobsFoundation.pdf (last retrieved: 1 June 2022).

9 Anticipation studies is a relatively new field of research that is explicitly interested in the way people use their ideas about the future when making decisions in the present. For more, see the *Anticipation 2022* conference series: http://anticipationconference. org/about-2022/; also the book series, the first volume of which is by the UNESCO Chair in Anticipatory Systems, Roberto Poli: *Introduction to Anticipation Studies*, Springer International, Cham 2017 (last retrieved: 1 June 2022).

10 Bill Sharpe: *Three Horizons: the patterning of hope*, Triarchy Press, Axminster 2020.

11 Ibid. p. 5.

12 Cf. the wonderfully succinct summary by the International Futures Forum (IFF), to which I refer closely in this section: www. internationalfuturesforum.com/three-horizons (last retrieved: 1 June 2022).

13 See this definition of futurology by Rolf Kreibich: *Zukunftsforschung*. Arbeitsbericht no. 23/2006, IZT (*Future Research*. Work Report no. 23/2006, Institute for Futures (sic!) Studies and Technology Assessment), Berlin 2006, p. 3. For an overview, see also *Grundlagen und Methoden der Zukunftsforschung. Szenarien (Basic Principles and Methods of Future Research. Scenarios*, Delphi, Technikvorschau. Gelsenkirchen 1997, www.prozukunft.org/buecher/18008 (last retrieved: 1 June 2022).

14 Since I am so astonished at the vehemence with which economists in particular claim that the Club of Rome scenarios are based on calculations bearing no relation to reality, I present here two

sources in which the calculations were repeated using current data: limits2growth.org.uk/wp-content/uploads/Jackson-and-Webster-2016-Limits-Revisited.pdf; and advisory.kpmg.us/articles/2021/limits-to-growth.html (last retrieved: 1 June 2022). Furthermore, this model never aimed to give a precise numerical prognosis of resource depletion. Rather, its aim was to highlight the degenerative interplay of different trends, from industrialisation and resource use to population growth, pollution and the availability of land for food production.

15 Those interested in this approach to analysing complex systems should see Dirk Brockmann's book *Im Wald vor lauter Bäumen* (*Seeing the Wood for the Trees*), which includes many anecdotes and impressive illustrations.

16 Aurelio Peccei: *The Human Quality*, Pergamon Press, Oxford/New York 1977, p. 95.

17 James W. Botkin, Mahdi Elmandjra, and Mircea Malitza: *No Limits to Learning: bridging the human gap. A report to the Club of Rome*, Pergamon Press, Oxford 1979.

18 Cf. James W. Botkin et al.: *No Limits to Learning*, pp. 43–4.

19 Cf. Jamila Haider et al.: 'The undisciplinary journey: early-career perspectives in sustainability science', www.ncbi.nlm.nih.gov/pmc/articles/PMC6086269/ (last retrieved: 1 June 2022).

20 The doctoral students' initiative has since grown into a network of initiatives investigating how science can be conducted in accordance with the way the changes recommended by systemic research take place. See, for example, the Care Operative: i2insights.org/author-tag/the-care-operative/ and O. Care: 'Creating leadership collectives for sustainability transformations', in *Sustainability Science*, 4 March 2021, link.springer.com/article/10.1007/s11625-021-00909-y (last retrieved: 1 June 2022).

21 In a podcast on transformative education, Birgit Brenner of the EPIZ Centre for Global Citizenship Learning repeatedly stresses the importance of unlearning: ich-wir-alle.com/alle-folgen/details/111-folge-podcast-birgit-brenner-transformative-bildung (last retrieved: 1 June 2022).

22 This is also the view taken in the OECD's *Learning Compass 2030*, an OECD project funded by a range of foundations in Germany, called *Future of Education and Skills: a series of concept notes*. For me, perhaps the document's most impactful statement is: 'Some education experts have noted that most 21st-century students are still

being taught by teachers using 20th-century pedagogical practices in 19th-century school organisations.' See p. 9. The table on page 12 provides a wonderful summary: www.oecd.org/education/2030-project/teaching-and-learning/learning/learning-compass-2030/OECD_Learning_Compass_2030_Concept_Note_Series.pdf (last retrieved: 1 June 2022).

23 Jürgen Renn, *The Evolution of Knowledge: rethinking science for the Anthropocene*, Princeton University Press, Princeton 2020, p. xvi.

24 Ibid. p. 13.

25 The German sociologist Armin Nassehi has described this constitutive effect on reality of (scientific) theories, concepts, and methods as a certain 'entanglement' of them and their object: 'What we see depends greatly on the categories, distinctions, and concepts we use. That is true of all cognitive information and data processing—and it is particularly true of the kind of scientific operations which decide what their object should be in the first place.' See Armin Nassehi, *Unbehagen. Theorie der überforderten Gesellschaft (Discomfort: theory of the overwhelmed society)*, C. H. Beck, Munich 2021, p. 23.

26 Geoff Mulgan: 'The imaginary crisis—and how we might quicken social and public imagination', 8 April 2020, www.geoffmulgan.com/post/social-imagination (last retrieved: 1 June 2022)

27 International Social Science Council, ISSC/UNESCO (Ed.): *World Social Science Report: changing global environments*, Paris 2013, p. 69, unesdoc.unesco.org/ark:/48223/pf0000224677 (last retrieved: 1 June 2022).

28 Riel Miller: *Transforming the Future: anticipation in the 21st Century*, UNESCO, Paris 2018, p. 15. Cf. idem: 'Futures literacy: A hybrid strategic scenario method', in *Futures* 39 (2007), pp. 341–62. A good introduction is provided by UNESCO's Futures Literacy website: en.unesco.org/futuresliteracy/about (last retrieved: 1 June 2022).

29 See 'Declaration of the United Nations Conference on the Human Environment', 1972, Point 1, http://www.un-documents.net/unchedec.htm (last retrieved: 1 June 2022).

30 Cf. the 1987 publication: *Report of the World Commission on Environment and Development: our common future*, http://www.un-documents.net/our-common-future.pdf (last retrieved: 1 June 2022).

31 Samochowiec: *Future Skills*, p. 4.

32 To name just a few of these concepts and programmes: global citizenship education, education for sustainable development, future skills and digital intelligence.

33 See the flagship report of the German Advisory Council on Climate
    Change (WBGU): *Towards Our Common Digital Future*, Berlin
    2019. It names such skills as: systemic thinking, creativity, flexibility,
    and the capacity to solve complex problems, emotional intelligence,
    reflexivity, visions of the future, technical knowledge, and media
    education. A summary of the concepts and their implementation
    is published by Annekathrin Grüneberg, Arndt Pechstein, Peter
    Spiegel, and Anabel Ternès von Hattburg in a volume of 69 articles:
    Future Skills. Das Praxisbuch für Zukunftsgestalter (*Future Skills: a
    practical handbook for future shapers*), Munich 2021.

34 Westley et al.: 'Tipping toward Sustainability', p. 763.

Chapter Seven: Wealth: growing better

1   John Stuart Mill, *The Collected Works of John Stuart Mill, Volume III,
    Principles of Political Economy, Part II*, University of Toronto Press,
    Toronto 1848. Here 'Chapter VI, Of the Stationary State, § 1'.

2   Cf. David Ellis, 'Goldman's Blankfein collects $68M bonus' in *CNN
    Money*, 21 December 2007, money.cnn.com/2007/12/21/news/
    newsmakers/blankfein_bonus/ (last retrieved: 1 June 2022).

3   Cf. 'Blankfein Says He's Just Doing 'God's Work" in *The New York
    Times*, 9 November 2009: dealbook.nytimes.com/2009/11/09/
    goldman-chief-says-he-is-just-doing-gods-work/ (last retrieved: 1
    June 2022).

4   A striking example of how this superficial story is constantly
    repeated as a patronising truism, thereby not only ignoring but
    also discrediting any more sophisticated debate in international
    institutions, thinktanks, and business circles, can be found here:
    m.faz.net/aktuell/wirtschaft/bundesregierung-will-wohlstand-
    anders-messen-mehr-wachstum-wagen-17744202.html. Those
    interested in a more sophisticated debate should see: newforum.
    org/en/beyond-growth-toward-a-new-economic-approach/ (last
    retrieved: 1 June 2022).

5   Cf. Johannes Krause and Thomas Trappe, *Hybris. Die Reise der
    Menschheit: zwischen Aufbruch und Scheitern* (*Hubris: humanity's
    journey between departure and failure)*, Propyläen, Berlin 2021. After
    an almost 300-page gallop through the genetic, climatological, and
    epidemiological influences on our development, the two authors
    come to a sobering conclusion: 'The biology of a creature that owes
    its unique success solely to an incredibly competitive organ between
    its ears (p. 291) is, unfortunately, what prevents a just distribution

and regeneration of the limited resources. Since our culture, whose 'higher, further, better' logic (p. 292) was not just a result of our genetic development, but a prerequisite for it, human civilisation will—and how could it be otherwise?—be saved by a cultural effort; one our descendants may acclaim just as reverently as we do the first cave paintings created by Stone Age humans.' (p. 298).

6   The presentation is available online at: assets.bwbx.io/documents/ users/iqj%20WHBF%20dfx%20IU%20/rim9z3X.NpYk/ (last retrieved: 1 June 2022).

7   Ibid.

8   See www.ft.com/content/04103d89-2cc3-3a60-96fe-d9a71881f41a.

9   Of course, there is also the valid argument that we now live longer than we used to and with better monitoring of our health. Nonetheless, there are studies that clearly show the consequences of an unhealthy diet and a lack of exercise, just as we debate whether companies that sell fast food or convenience food should be held responsible for those consequences, or whether people even have a choice. Such debates should also take into account research on market power, price dumping, and marketing. The German government's Advisory Council on Climate Change summarised the debate in 2021 in a four-page discussion paper: www.wbgu.de/ en/publications/publication/discussionpaper-health. In December 2019, the medical journal *The Lancet* published a good summary of the debate on health and nutrition from a systemic point of view: 'The Double Burden of Malnutrition' www.thelancet.com/series/ double-burden-malnutrition (last retrieved: 1 June 2022).

10 See, for example, Tim Jackson, 'The 'diminishing marginal utility' of goods (indeed of income itself) reflects the fact that having more of something usually provides less additional satisfaction' cf. Tim Jackson, *Prosperity without Growth*, Earthscan, London 2009, p. 38; or Tim Jebb et al., 'Happiness, income satiation and turning points around the world', in *Nature Human Behaviour*, vol. 2, January 2018, pp. 33–8, nature.com/ articles/s41562-017-0277-0 (last retrieved: 1 June 2022).

11 These findings were reached by the sociologist Martin Schröder and his team, who analysed survey data gathered by the Socioeconomic Panel of the German Institute for Economic Research (DIW) from the middle of the nineteen-eighties to the present: *Wann sind wir wirklich zufrieden?* Überraschende Erkenntnisse zu Arbeit, Freizeit, Liebe, Kindern, Geld (*When Are We Really Satisfied? Surprising*

findings on work, leisure, love, children, money), Munich 2020. The datasets include questions on work, leisure, income, relationships, and moral values, and are unique on an international level in their scale. The web page www.leben-in-deutschland.de/?lang=en includes analyses of the results, arranged by topic. Background information on methods and processing is available on the DIW's website: www. diw.de/en/diw_01.c.615551.en/research_infrastructure__socio-economic_panel__soep.htmlvvvv (last retrieved: 1 June 2022).

12 Depression is influenced by many factors, of course, and is not limited to rich countries. An explanation of symptoms and country rankings for depression rates can be found at: worldpopulationreview.com/country-rankings/depression-rates-by-country. It is noticeable that rates are increasing in rich countries in particular, where better healthcare and material security means the opposite should be expected. This may be due in part to better diagnosis. However, burnout as a diagnosis of excessive stress is directly linked to social and cultural demands, or to work overload. According to a study by the Development Dimensions International organisation, nearly 60 per cent of executives experienced these symptoms during the pandemic. See Forbes, www.forbes.com/sites/edwardsegal/2021/02/17/leaders-and-employees-are-burning-out-at-record-rates-new-survey/?sh=62842f964999. It is interesting to note that the executives were most concerned about burnout's negative impact on their 'ability to compete and succeed' (last retrieved: 1 June 2022).

13 Jeremy Bentham, *An Introduction to the Principles of Morals and Legislation*, The Clarendon Press, Oxford 1876, p. 1.

14 Mill, *Principles*, Chapter IV, Of the Stationary State, §2.

15 Ibid.

16 Available at: http://www.econ.yale.edu/smith/econ116a/keynes1.pdf.

17 Ibid. p. 4.

18 Ibid. p. 5.

19 Fabrizio Zilibotti, 'Economic Possibilities for our Grandchildren. 75 years After: a global perspective', in Lorenzo Pecchi and Gastavo Piva (Eds.), *Revisiting Keynes: economic possibilities for our grandchildren*, The MIT Press, Cambridge 2010, p. 28.

20 According to *Our World in Data*, people in Germany worked a total of 2,128 hours in the year 1929, compared to only 1,354 hours worked in 2017. That is the lowest value in the developed world. In the United Kingdom, the same metric fell from 2,257 to 1,670 hours

worked, and from 2,316 to 1,757 in the USA. See: ourworldindata.
org/working-more-than-ever (last retrieved: 1 June 2022).

21 According to World Bank figures, a total of 4.5 billion passengers
    were transported by aviation in 2019. See: data.world-bank.org/
    indicator/IS.AIR.PSGR. The world's population stood at 2.1 billion
    in 1930. See: ourworldindata.org/world-population-growth#how-
    has-world-population-growth-changed-over-time (last retrieved:
    1 June 2022).

22 Julia Hobsbawm, *Fully Connected: surviving and thriving in an age of
    overload*, Bloomsbury, London 2017, p. 18.

23 Lewis Carroll, *Alice's Adventures in Wonderland*, Wordsworth Editions
    1992, p. 124.

24 Fred Hirsch, *Social Limits to Growth*, Harvard University Press,
    Cambridge (Mass.) 1976.

25 Hirsch, *Social Limits*, p. 7. Hirsch takes a bit of swipe at our modern
    economy, stating that in a positional society it is often not the
    best, but the best-positioned, who hold sway: 'The products of the
    economics numbers factory enjoy a brisk demand; and the economic
    inducement to cater to effective demand is not suspended for
    economics itself. Nor are economists immune from the instinct of
    trade unionists; they too judge the social worth of their performance
    by the prosperity and prestige it brings to their craft.' Ibid.

26 Ibid. p. 10. My italics. Here it is important to bear in mind that
    Hirsch wrote his book before the advent of globalised financial
    capitalism. At the time he was writing, it was not common to earn
    millions, or even billions, with one product or one song in the space
    of just a few years.

27 Karl Polanyi places the same observation at the centre of his
    often-cited 1944 book *The Great Transformation*. Markets have
    always existed in various forms and been embedded in the overriding
    principles of society. He considers the utopian idea of organising
    entire societies as markets to be a basic paradigm according to which
    traditional social structures were reorganised so that humans, nature,
    and money are perceived and treated as goods.

28 Hirsch, *Social Limits*, p. 183.

29 Cf. ibid. p. 188 (on Hayek and Burke), p. 8 (on individual valuations).

30 Ibid. p. 8, p. 190.

31 Here Hirsch quotes the American economist William Vickrey. Cf.
    Hirsch, *Social Limits*, p. 189.

32 Dan Buettner, who wrote that title story for *National Geographic*,

later expanded on those findings and the research into the issue, publishing several books and setting up his own institute under the name *Blue Zones*. An extensive consideration of the similarities shared by the five regions can be found here: Dan Buettner, 'Power 9. Reverse Engineering Longevity' www.bluezones.com/2016/11/power-9/ (last retrieved: 1 June 2022).

33 Mihály Csíkszentmihályi, *The Evolving Self*. Harper Perennial, New York 1994, Introduction.

34 Ibid. Chapter Seven. It is interesting that the researcher reached this conclusion although his original idea was not to investigate individual wellbeing. Instead, he wanted to take an evolutionary view of modern societies in the 21st century. He observed parallels between the pressure to compete and distinguish oneself in human societies and the evolutionary pressures on organisms to secure as much energy intake as possible for themselves. If the pressure is not counteracted by limiting activities—balancing feedback loops—environmental collapse can result. According to Csíkszentmihályi, the activities that boost a sense of harmony and happiness in humans are often connected to experiences of flow.

35 Ibid. Chapter Six.

36 Csíkszentmihályi adds '… ordinarily people would not continue undertaking a certain activity unless it provided flow—or unless external rewards or punishments prompted them to undertake it,' ibid. Chapter Seven.

37 Ibid.

38 For more on this thought experiment, see the report published by the wealth management company IIFL Wealth, *IIFL Wealth Management Wealth Index 2018*, www.iiflwealth.com/wealth-x-2018 (last retrieved: 1 June 2022).

39 It would be different in the jungle, the desert, or in cultures or places that use time banks. For more on the idea of local time banks as 'the fourth pillar of old-age provision', see vzfbe.org/projekte/timebanks/zeitbank-modelle-in-deutschland/; for a list of time banks in Germany, Austria, and Switzerland, see www.hourworld.org/index.htm.

40 This thought experiment is similar to that described in the Foreword to the UN's 2018 *Inclusive Wealth Report*, p. 4, wedocs.unep.org/bitstream/handle/20.500.11822/26776/Inclusive_Wealth_ES.pdf?sequence=1&isAllowed=y (last retrieved: 1 June 2022).

41 Cf. Andrew T. Jebb et al., 'Happiness, income satiation and turning

points around the world', in *Nature Human Behaviour*, vol. 2, January 2018, p. 33, www.nature.com/articles/s41562-017-0277-0 (last retrieved: 1 June 2022).

42   Cf. The OECD's Initiative for a Better Life and its working programme on measuring wellbeing and progress, www.oecd.org/sdd/OECD-Better-Life-Initiative.pdf (last retrieved: 1 June 2022), p. 3.

43   Sir Partha Dasgupta, *The Economics of Biodiversity*, 2021, www.gov.uk/government/publications/final-report-the-economics-of-biodiversity-the-dasgupta-review (last retrieved: 1 June 2022).

44   This approach has been criticised as anthropocentric, since other living things are mostly only considered if they are important to humans. The authors of the Dasgupta Study recognise that that view is limited and provide an annex describing other views in which nature is assigned its own value and rights. They take an anthropocentric view for pragmatic reasons, which I agree with. If we manage to make people aware of this value for human beings, and to protect it, we will also be able to protect and better negotiate other values for various cultures and communities.

45   Ibid. p. 33.

46   Cf. Nils Klawitter and Maria Marquart, 'Kriegswirtschaft statt Klimaschutz' ('Wartime Economy Instead of Climate Protection'), in *Spiegel*, 13, 2022, 26 March 2022. Those who want to find out more about the meat production system and the further environmental costs such as water use, carbon dioxide consumption, and the risks from overuse of medication, will find extensive information in the 2021 *Meat Atlas* produced by the Heinrich Böll Foundation — including information on alternatives, eu.boell.org/sites/default/files/2021-09/MeatAtlas2021_final_web.pdf (last retrieved: 28 June 2023). The land use figures are on p. 34.

47   See the figures for 'Meat and Dairy Production' on the *Our World in Data* website, ourworldindata.org/meat-production#productivity-yield-per-animal (last retrieved: 1 June 2022).

48   As well as the examples in the first part of the book, see also in particular the System of Environmental Economic Accounting (SEEA, seea.un.org/) promoted by the United Nations. The *Green Economy Coalition* is the world's largest network of different groups of actors supporting and evaluating concepts and political processes, and recording criticism of the economisation of natural processes, www.greeneconomycoalition.org/. The *Capitals Coalition*

is particularly interesting for companies (capitalscoalition.
org/). It has published a protocol for including natural capital in
financial accounts. For information on the state of research into
macroeconomic modelling, see Peter A. Victor and Tim Jackson,
'Overview of Macroeconomic Modelling. A research agenda for
ecological macroeconomics', in Robert Costanza et al., *Sustainable
Wellbeing Futures*, Edward Elgar Publishing, Cheltenham 2020, in
particular p. 36.

49 On the links among ecosystems and the connections between
   ecological and human health and their fragility, see, for example,
   the IPCC report *Climate Change 2022: impacts, adaptation and
   vulnerability*, www.ipcc.ch/report/sixth-assessment-report-working-
   group-ii/ (last retrieved: 1 June 2022).

50 See: Science Task Force of the International Union for the
   Conservation of Nature (IUCN), *Science-based ecosystem restoration
   for the 2020s and beyond*. IUCN, Gland, Switzerland 2021, p. 26.

51 See the World Economic Forum's *New Nature Report II*, www.
   weforum.org/reports/new-nature-economy-report-ii-the-future-of-
   nature-and-business (last retrieved: 1 June 2022).

52 See, for example, the publication by the Wellbeing Economy
   Alliance, *Measuring the Wellbeing Economy* wellbeingeconomy.
   org/wp-content/uploads/WeAll-BRIEFINGS-Measuring-the-
   Wellbeing-economy-v6.pdf (last retrieved: 1 June 2022).

53 There are various initiatives pushing for ecological and social assets to
   be reflected in accounting, see, for example, Capitalcoalition, Richtig
   Rechnen, Quarta Vista, BCorporations, Gemeinwohlökonomie or
   the UN's principles for responsible investment. As well as better
   numerical values, the question of the right regulatory framework
   for company reporting and business activities are also important,
   as the German Council for Sustainable Development published
   in an official statement, www.nachhaltigkeitsrat.de/wp-content/
   uploads/2022/04/20220331_RNE-Statement_Sustainability-
   Reporting.pdf. In Britain, the debate currently takes the form of
   the campaign for the 'Better Business Act', better-businessact.org/
   about/#theact. It wants to extend the fiduciary duty of businesses
   as a way of shifting the focus away from shareholders and profits,
   and supporting companies' actual purpose. *The Financial Times*
   published a summary of these developments, www.ft.com/
   future-company?utm_source=Economic+Change+Unit&utm_
   campaign=947603310b-Biden_COPY

_01&utm_medium=email&utm_term=0_6101fe9ecd-947603310b-239339002&mc_cid=947603310b&mceid=9b9b80c5a1 (last retrieved: 1 June 2022).

54 Cf. The UN's Principles for Responsible investment, www.unpri.org/about-us/what-are-the-principles-for-responsible-investment (last retrieved: 1 June 2022).

55 An example of a nicely differentiated and easily comprehensible description of the characteristics of modern capitalism which the author considers incompatible with sustainable futures can be found in, among others, Ulrich Brand et al., 'From planetary to societal boundaries: an argument for collectively defined self-limitation', in *Sustainability: science, practice and policy*, vol. 17, no. 1, July 2021, pp. 265–92, www.tandfonline.com/doi/full/10.1080/15487733.2021.1940754 (last retrieved: 1 June 2022).

Chapter Eight: Media(tion): using technology better

1   This statement is attributed to Joseph Weizenbaum, cf. the Weizenbaum Institute, Annual Report 2018/2019, www.weizenbaum-institut.de/media/Publikationen/Jahresberichte/Jahresbericht_EN_final.pdf (last retrieved: 1 June 2022).

2   Cf. Meta's annual report: investor.fb.com/investor-news/press-release-details/2018/Facebook-Reports-Fourth-Quarter-and-Full-Year-2017-Results/default.aspx (last retrieved: 1 June 2022).

3   This term was coined by the urban planner Georg Franck in his 1998 book, *Ökonomie der Aufmerksamkeit* (*The Economy of Attention*).

4   *The Wall Street Journal* was the first outlet to report on the changes to Facebook's algorithm, on the basis of documents it received from the whistleblower Frances Haugen. She later passed internal material containing information about Facebook to other media. www.wsj.com/articles/facebook-algorithm-change-zuckerberg-11631654215?mod=article_inline (last retrieved: 1 June 2022).

5   Cf. Philipp Gollmer and Ruth Fulterer, 'Facebook ändert seinen Namen, doch die Grundprobleme seines Algorithmus bleiben. Wir zeigen, welche das sind und was man dagegen tun könnte', in *Neue Zürcher Zeitung*, 19 October 2021, www.nzz.ch/technologie/wieso-der-facebook-algorithmus-hass-und-falschinformationen-verbreitet-und-wie-angestellte-versuchten-das-zu-aendern-ld.1652201 ('Facebook is changing its name, but the basic problems with its algorithm remain. We show what they are and what to do about it.') (last retrieved: 1 June 2022).

6   Mark Zuckerberg announced the change in a Facebook post which received widespread media attention. See, for example, a *Forbes* article from 11 January 2018: www.forbes.com/sites/ kathleenchaykowski/2018/01/11/facebook-focuses-news-feed- on-friends-and-family-curbing-the-reach-of-brands-and- media/?sh=586692265b69 (last retrieved: 1 June 2022).

7   The results of the experiment were summarised by the employees in a report with the title *Carol's Journey to QAnon*: www.nbcnews.com/ tech/tech-news/facebook-knew-radicalized-users-rcna3581 (last retrieved: 1 June 2022).

8   A transcript of Frances Haugen's statement to the Senate Subcommittee on Consumer Protection, Product Safety, and Data Security of 5 October 2021 is available at www.commerce.senate. gov/services/files/FC8A558E-824E-4914-BEDB-3A7B1190BD49 (last retrieved: 1 June 2022).

9   Sheera Frenkel, 'A highlight: Frances Haugen's inside knowledge makes this hearing different', in *The New York Times*, 5 October 2021, www.nytimes.com/2021/10/05/technology/facebook-frances- haugen-testimony.html (last retrieved: 1 June 2022).

10 German Advisory Council on Global Change (WBGU), *Towards Our Common Digital Future*, Berlin 2019, p. 102. Cf. also Friedrich Rapp, *Analytical Philosophy of Technology*, D. Riedel Publishing Company, Dordrecht 1981; Jan Zalasiewicz et al., 'Scale and diversity of the physical technosphere: a geological perspective', in *The Anthropocene Review*, 2017, vol. 4, Issue 1, pp. 9–22.

11 Cf. Albert Borgmann: *Technology and the Character of Contemporary Life: a philosophical inquiry*, University of Chicago Press, Chicago 1984, pp. 40 ff.

12 Ibid. p. 44. For a description of Borgmann's thinking and concepts, see the wonderful blog by Jonathan Lipps, which is organised in chapters: blog.jlipps.com/2011/05/blogging-borgmann-overview- technology-and-the-character-of-contemporary-life/ (last retrieved: 1 June 2022).

13 Masahiro Sugiyama, Hiroshi Deguchi et al., 'Unintended Side Effects of Digital Transition: Perspectives of Japanese Experts', in *Sustainability*, vol. 9, no. 12, November 2017, p. 6, www.mdpi. com/2071-1050/9/12/2193 (last retrieved: 1 June 2022).

14 Andrew McAfee, *More from Less: the surprising story of how we learned to prosper using fewer resources — and what happens next*, Scribner, New York 2019.

15 Ibid. p. 4.

16 Cf. this hotly debated tweet by Jason Hickel, the author of *Less is More: how degrowth will change the world*: twitter.com/jasonhickel/status/1405090430367248396 (last retrieved: 1 June 2022).

17 An overview from a systemic point of view, discussing the ecological necessity of an absolute reduction in material consumption, and the lack of success of relative reduction strategies without comprehensive sociocultural and institutional change, can be found here: Lewis Akenji et al., 'Ossified materialism: introduction to the special volume on absolute reductions in materials throughput and emissions', in *Journal of Cleaner Production*, Special Issue, 20 September 2016, pp. 1–12.

18 All figures are taken from the report 'Decoupling Debunked' published by the European Environmental Bureau (EEB) in 2019. The EEB is an umbrella association covering 160 environmental organisations from 35 European countries, eeb.org/wp-content/uploads/2019/07/Decoupling-Debunked.pdf; the statistics presented by the 'Materialflows' project at the Vienna University of Economics and Business are also very informative: www.materialflows.net (last retrieved: 1 June 2022).

19 Global freshwater consumption rose from 3.8 trillion cubic metres in the year 2002 to four trillion in 2014. (See: ourworldindata.org/water-use-stress#global-freshwater-use.) Global energy consumption rose from 123 TWh in 2000 to 174 TWh in 2019. (See: ourworldindata.org/energy-production-consumption#how-much-energy-does-the-world-consume.)

20 See the report by the United Nations Environment Programme (UNEP), *Global Material Flows and Resource Productivity: assessment report for the UNEP International Resource Panel*, 2016, pp. 6–7, www.resourcepanel.org/reports/global-material-flows-and-resource-productivity-database-link. Cf. also the UNEP report, *The Use of Natural Resources in the Economy A Global Manual on Economy Wide Material Flow Accounting*. Nairobi, Kenya 2011. For more on distinguishing the different indicators and the questions they help to answer, see pp. 117 ff., the diagram on p. 122 in particular illustrates the way estimates are affected by the choice of indicator. Short explanatory videos and a database on the material flows of different countries can be found at www.resourcepanel.org (last retrieved: 1 June 2022).

21 For more on Germany's resource consumption, see the report

by the Federal Environment Agency (UBA) for 2018: www.
umweltbundesamt.de/en/publikationen/the-use-of-natural-
resources-report-for-germany. The UBA, which set up a resources
commission in May 2021, has also published a discussion of the
ecological and social tensions connected to resource extraction: www.
umweltbundesamt.de/en/topics/waste-resources (last retrieved:
1 June 2022).

22 See Megan Graham, 'Digital ad spend grew 12% in 2020 despite
hit from pandemic', *CNN*, 4 July 2021, www.cnbc.com/2021/04/07/
digital-ad-spend-grew-12percent-in-2020-despite-hit-from-
pandemic.html (last retrieved: 1 June 2022).

23 For more on the rebound effect, see the German Environment
Agency (UBA), www.umweltbundesamt.de/en/topics/waste-
resources/economic-legal-dimensions-of-resource-conservation/
rebound-effects, or the wide-ranging book on the subject by
Tilman Santarius: *Der Rebound-Effekt. Ökonomische, psychische und
soziale Herausforderungen der Entkopplung von Energieverbrauch
und Wirtschaftswachstum* (*The Rebound Effect: the economic, mental,
and social challenges of uncoupling energy consumption from economic
growth*), Metropolis, Berlin 2015.

24 See Amanda Mull, 'Stop Shopping. America needs you to buy
less junk', in *The Atlantic*, October 2021, www.theatlantic.com/
technology/archive/2021/10/stop-shopping-global-supply-chain-
shipping-delays/620465/ (last retrieved: 1 June 2022).

25 Cf. ibid.

26 Jason Hickel, *Less is More: how degrowth will save the world*, Random
House, New York 2020, p. 156.

27 'President Jimmy Carter's Remarks at White House Solar Panel
Dedication Ceremony, 1979', energyhistory.yale.edu/president-
jimmy-carters-remarks-at-white-house-solar-panel-dedication-
ceremony-1979/.

28 Cf. his comments on the *Recode Decode* podcast with the journalist
Kara Swisher, www.vox.com/recode/2019/5/6/18530860/tristan-
harris-human-downgrading-time-well-spent-kara-swisher-recode-
decode-podcast-interview (last retrieved: 1 June 2022).

29 The Centre for Human Technology has drawn up a list of the harm
and the costs generated by the technology giants' competition for our
attention, ledger.humanetech.com/ (last retrieved: 1 June 2022).

30 Johann Hari, "Heutzutage kann man kein normales Gehirn
besitzen'—der moderne Mensch leidet an einem kollektiven

Nzz

Aufmerksamkeitsdefizit. Wie gewinnen wir unser Denken zurück?', in *NZZ*, 26 January 2022, www.nzz.ch/feuilleton/aufmerksamkeit-die-moderne-welt-ist-gift-fuers-hirn-was-tun-ld.1666054?utmsource=pocket-newtab-global-de-DE (last retrieved: 1 June 2022).

31 Cf. Brian Arthur, *The Nature of Technology: what it is and how it evolves*, Allen Lane, London 2011, p. 23.

32 Borgmann, *Technology and the character of temporary life*, pp. 197, 219.

33 See the company's web presence: www.triodos.com/know-where-your-money-goes (last retrieved: 1 June 2022).

34 An example of a German network operating in the space between the protagonists of digitisation and sustainable development is Bits & Bäume, berlin.bits-und-baeume.org (last retrieved: 1 June 2022).

35 See the network's web presence: www.globalcommonsalliance.org (last retrieved: 1 June 2022).

36 For more on Audrey Tang's biography see Iris Chiu, 'Digital Minister Audrey Tang: Taiwan's 'Genius' and her Unique Past', on the website of The Nippon Foundation, 4 October 2020, www.nippon.com/en/japan-topics/g00837/digital-minister-audrey-tang-taiwan%E2%80%99s-genius-and-her-unique-past.html (last retrieved: 1 June 2022).

37 See the conversation with Audrey Tang on the website of the art platform *Framer Framed*, framerframed.nl/en/dossier/audrey-tang-we-have-to-keep-defining-what-is-the-inter-in-internet/ (last retrieved: 1 June 2022).

38 See Jonas Glatthard and Bruno Kaufmann, 'Humour over Rumour: Lessons from Taiwan in Digital Democracy', *Swissinfo*, 7 May 2011: www.swissinfo.ch/eng/politics/freedom-of-expression-humour-over-rumour---lessons-from-taiwan-in-digital-democracy/46592080 (last retrieved: 1 June 2022).

39 See the conversation with Audrey Tang on the website of the art platform *Framer Framed*: framerframed.nl/en/dossier/audrey-tang-we-have-to-keep-defining-what-is-the-inter-in-internet/ (last retrieved: 1 June 2022).

40 Cf. Iris Chiu, 'Digital Minister Audrey Tang: Taiwan's 'Genius' and her Unique Past', on the website of The Nippon Foundation, 4 October 2020, www.nippon.com/en/japan-topics/g00837/digital-minister-audrey-tang-taiwan%E2%80%99s-genius-and-her-unique-past.html (last retrieved: 1 June 2022).

41 Ibid.

42 See the Centre for Human Technology's podcast *Your Undivided Attention* with Audrey Tang and Tristan Harris, 23 July 2021, www. humanetech.com/podcast/23-digital-democracy-is-within-reach (last retrieved: 1 June 2022).

43 For example, pro-China companies bought up Taiwanese media outlets which were then used to spread propaganda from the People's Republic; also, false information is spread across social media via hundreds of thousands of fake user accounts, which resulted in pro-China candidates gaining massive support in the 2020 elections. See Frédéric Krumbein, 'Taiwan's Threatened Democracy Stays on Course', German Institute for International and Security Affairs, www.swp-berlin.org/en/publication/taiwans-threatened-democracy-stays-on-course (last retrieved: 1 June 2022).

44 Jonas Glatthard and Bruno Kaufmann, 'Humour over Rumour: lessons from Taiwan in digital democracy', *Swissinfo*, 7 May 2011: www.swissinfo.ch/eng/politics/freedom-of-expression-humour-over-rumour---lessons-from-taiwan-in-digital-democracy/46592080, or on the Centre for Human Technology's podcast *Your Undivided Attention* with Audrey Tang and Tristan Harris, 23 July 2021, www. humanetech.com/podcast/23-digital-democracy-is-within-reach (last retrieved: 1 June 2022).

45 Cf. Audrey Tang, 'Social Innovation in Taiwan', in *medium*, 11 December 2018, medium.com/@audrey.tang/social-enterprise-in-taiwan-3eb96d4dc8a7 (last retrieved: 1 June 2022).

46 See Alexander Fanta, 'Blöd der Lobbyist, der jetzt noch E-Mails schreibt', *netzpolitik*, 18 January 2022, netzpolitik.org/2022/eu-informationsfreiheit-bloed-der-lobbyist-der-jetzt-noch-e-mails-schreibt/?utm_source=pocket-newtab-global-de-DE(last retrieved: 1 June 2022).

47 Taiwan placed 11th on the *Economist* global list of most stable democracies, with Switzerland and Germany placing 12th and 14th respectively. Cf. 'Democracy Index 2020. In sickness and in health', The Economist Intelligence Unit, London 2021, p. 29. For the list of global thinkers chosen by the American journal *Foreign Policy*, cf. foreignpolicy.com/2019-global-thinkers/ (last retrieved: 1 June 2022).

48 For more on this topic and the often-overlooked connection between cultural narratives, exponentially oriented financial capital, and technological developments, see the book by the cognitive psychologist and digitisation expert Christian Stöcker, *Das Experiment sind wir. Unsere Welt verändert sich so atemberaubend*

schnell, dass wir von Krise zu Krise taumeln. Wir müssen lernen, diese enorme Beschleunigung zu lenken (*We Are the Experiment: our world is changing at such breakneck speed that we can only stagger from crisis to crisis. We must learn to control this enormous acceleration*), Blessing, Munich 2020.

49 Meadows, *Thinking in Systems*, p. 161.

50 See Lauren Joseph, 'It moved fast and broke things, now Silicon Valley must rebuild trust', World Economic Forum, 29 November 2018, www.weforum.org/agenda/2018/11/why-move-fast-and-break-things-doesn-t-cut-it-anymore/ (last retrieved: 1 June 2022).

51 Cf. Brian Eckhouse, 'Chip Shortage Hits Solar Sector With Enphase Citing Constraints', *BNN Bloomberg*, 9 February 2021, www.bnnbloomberg.ca/chip-shortage-hits-solar-sector-with-enphase-citing-constraints-1.1561491. In the automotive industry, the large, expensive luxury models were prioritised: motortrend.com/news/automotive-car-industry-semiconductor-chip-shortage-reasons-solution/ (last retrieved: 1 June 2022).

52 The concept of the social licence to operate originated in the mining and raw materials extraction industry, as a protest against the risks to the environment and the health of local populations, and/or their displacement. It includes fairness in procedures and distribution, as well as trust in the management of a company, and can influence a company's level of public acceptance. The European Union's working definition can be found at rmis.jrc.ec.europa.eu/?page=social-licence-to-operate-b86e6d. A similar debate has arisen with regard to Silicon Valley companies, especially those in the platform economy, but with reference to 'social resources', that is, the human system they draw from. In the rapidly growing area of ESG reporting (increased disclosure of environmental, social, and corporate governance impacts of a given business model), the challenge for the technology sector is predominantly in the latter two areas. For example, Meta (Facebook) received an ESG rating of only 11 and 10 for those areas from Standard & Poors Global; Apple received a social rating of just 10 points, while Twitter was the worst-performing of the big companies, with just 7 points: www.spglobal.com/marketintelligence/en/news-insights/latest-news-headlines/big-tech-navigates-operating-social-pressures-amid-russia-ukraine-conflict-69208478 (last retrieved: 1 June 2022).

Chapter Nine: Behaviour: organising better

1   According to the Property Index published by Deloitte, the average purchase price for residential property in Paris in 2021 was 12,917 euros per square metre, and the average rent was 28.60 euros per square metre, making it the most expensive capital city in Europe. Cf. www2.deloitte.com/content/dam/Deloitte/de/Documents/real-estate/Deloitte_Property%20Index%202021.pdf, pp. 20 and 28 (last retrieved: 1 June 2022).

2   Cf. The Economist Intelligence Unit, *Worldwide Cost of Living 2021*, London 2021, files.static-nzz.ch/2021/12/01/5fef9ee8-c25d-4291-8c5f-7c266524f809.pdf (last retrieved: 1 June 2022).

3   According to the *INRIX* traffic information service, Rome and Paris were the congestion capitals of Europe. Parisian drivers spent 165 hours in congestion in 2019. Cf. inrix.com/press-releases/2019-traffic-scorecard-uk/ (last retrieved: 1 June 2022).

4   Cf. E. Brunotte et al., *Lexikon der Geographie* (*Dictionary of Geography*), four volumes, Spektrum Akademischer, Heidelberg 2002. The concept of a guiding model in urban development is defined there as follows: 'The guiding concept in the field of spatial planning formulates a desired future state as a goal to be reached by appropriate action. The time frame remains open, all measures are to be coordinated and geared towards the formulated guiding concept.' For more on the historical and cultural variations on guiding models for urban planning, see the German Advisory Council on Global Change (WBGU) Flagship Report for 2016 on urbanity, www.wbgu.de/en/publications/publication/humanity-on-the -move-unlocking-the-transformative-power-of-cities, pp. 56–65 (last retrieved: 1 June 2022). The focus on suburbanisation, segmentation by use, and often car-oriented infrastructure planning did not begin until the middle of the twentieth century, driven by trends from the US, cf. pp. 61 and 64 of the report.

5   The National Urban Development Policy, *The New Leipzig Charter*, p. 1.

6   Cf. Aitor Hernandez-Morales, 'The Promise of the 15-Minute City': www.politico.eu/article/what-the-city-of-the-future-borrows-from-the-past/ (last retrieved: 1 June 2022).

7   There are many reports about Paris's traffic revolution and Mayor Anne Hidalgo's concept of the 15-minute city. In addition to the sources already cited, the following are particularly nuanced and balanced: www.politico.eu/article/

anne-hidalgo-paris-mayor-urban-revolution/ and www.bauwelt.de/
dl/1700606/artikel.pdf (last retrieved: 1 June 2022).

8   Cf. Claas Tatje, 'Der Verkehrswender', in *Zeit*, 3 January 2022,
www.zeit.de/2022/01/belit-onay-verkehrswende-hannover-auto-
verkehrspolitik (last retrieved: 1 June 2022).

9   Cf. Emil Nefzger, 'Sein Traum von einer autofreien Stadt', in
Spiegel, 24 June 2020, www.spiegel.de/auto/hannover-autofrei-
oberbuergermeister-belit-onay-stoesst-auf-widerstand-a-7121a95e-
6424-4207-8f16-49764a8dd3fa (last retrieved: 1 June 2022).

10   Cf. Sören Götz, 'Man muss Autofahren ja nicht gleich verbieten', in
Zeit, 18 May 2022, www.zeit.de/mobilitaet/2022-05/berlin-autofrei-
innenstadt-volksentscheid-senat (last retrieved: 1 June 2022).

11   Cf. Clea Caulcutt, 'Anne Hidalgo's Sack of Paris', in *Politico*,
15 December 2021, www.politico.eu/article/anne-hidalgo-paris-
mayor-urban-revolution/ (last retrieved: 1 June 2022).

12   Cf. 'Paris: The 15-minute city makes timely progress', in *smart
transport*, www.smarttransport.org.uk/case-studies/europe/paris-the-
15-minute-city-makes-timely-progress (last retrieved: 1 June 2022).

13   Cf. C. Moreno et al., 'Introducing the "15-Minute City":
sustainability, resilience and place identity in future post-pandemic
cities', in *smart cities*, 8 January 2021, www.mdpi.com/2624-
6511/4/1/6 (last retrieved: 1 June 2022).

14   Kim Willsher, 'Paris mayor unveils '15-Minute City' plan in
re-election campaign', in *The Guardian*, 7 February 2020, www.
theguardian.com/world/2020/feb/07/paris-mayor-unveils-15-
minute-city-plan-in-re-election-campaign (last retrieved: 1 June
2022).

15   When *Time Magazine* placed Anne Hidalgo on its list of the
world's most influential people in 2020, the climate activist and
former US Vice President Al Gore wrote the accompanying article
explaining why. Cf. time.com/collection/100-most-influential-
people-2020/5888321/anne-hidalgo/ (last retrieved: 1 June 2022).

16   Meadows, *Thinking in Systems*, p. 75.

17   The spatial approach is currently attracting a great deal of attention
in various areas of innovation where multifunctional spaces are
key. For rural areas — and for the relation between the city and the
countryside — landscape ecology aims to serve a range of needs
in an integrated way and thus reverse the recent trend towards
urbanisation and the simplification and segregated intensification of
land use. The 2000 European Landscape Convention (ELC) defines

a landscape as 'an area, as perceived by people, whose character is the result of the action and interaction of natural and/or human factors'. For a summary of such approaches and research networks, see, for example, Marc Antrop et al., 'How landscape ecology can promote the development of sustainable landscapes in Europe: the role of the European Association for Landscape Ecology (IALE - Europe) in the twenty-first century', in *Landscape Ecol*, 18 October 2013, issue 28, pp. 1641–7, dspace.uevora.pt/rdpc/bitstream/10174/10255/1/Antrop%20et%20al%202013.pdf (last retrieved: 1 June 2022).

18 Spruce has been the most commonly planted tree in Germany's forests since the end of the Second World War, and is the most important crop for the country's forestry industry. See the information on the forestry ministry's website: www.bundeswaldinventur.de/en/third-national-forest-inventory/the-forest-habitat-more-biological-diversity-in-the-forests/spruce-pine-beech-oak-the-most-common-tree-species.

19 See information provided by this internet portal for foresters, forestry companies, and forest owners: www.umweltbundesamt.de/en/topics/climate-energy/climate-impacts-adaptation/impacts-of-climate-change/monitoring-report-2019/indicators-of-climate-change-impacts-adaptation/cluster-woodland-forestry/fw-i-5-extent-of-timber-infested-spruce-bark-beetle#fw-i-5-extent-of-timber-infested-by-spruce-bark-beetle-case-study (last retrieved: 1 June 2022).

20 The German Food and Agriculture Ministry puts the area to be reforested at around 5,000 square kilometres. Lake Constance has a surface area of 536 square kilometres. Cf. www.bmel.de/DE/themen/wald/wald-in-deutschland/wald-trockenheit-klimawandel.html (last retrieved: 1 June 2022).

21 Cf. Andreas Reckwitz, 'Die Politik der Resilienz und ihre vier Probleme' ('The Politics of Resilience and Four Problems With It'), in *Spiegel*, 5 March 2021, www.spiegel.de/psychologie/corona-und-politische-resilienz-was-wir-aus-der-krise-lernen-sollten-a-3cea4d87-0002-0001-0000-000176138623 (last retrieved: 1 June 2022).

22 Ibid.

23 Ibid.

24 Westley et al., 'Tipping toward Sustainability', p. 763.

25 Cf. Jamila Haider et al., 'Rethinking resilience and development: a coevolutionary perspective', in *Ambio*, vol. 50, 10 February 2021,

pp. 1304–12, link.springer.com/article/10.1007/s13280-020-01485-8 (last retrieved: 1 June 2022).

26 Cf. a report published by the EU: Anna Rita Manca, Peter Benczur, and Enrico Giovannini, *Building a scientific narrative towards a more resilient EU society. Part 1a: a conceptual framework*, Luxembourg 2017, publications.jrc.ec.europa.eu/repository/handle/JRC106265 (last retrieved: 1 June 2022).

27 Cf. the European Union's ecodesign directive, No. 666/2013, eur-lex. europa.eu/legal-content/EN/TXT/PDF/?uri=CELEX:32013R0666 (last retrieved: 1 June 2022).

28 The OECD has defined the economy of wellbeing according to the following four points: 1. It expands the opportunities available to people for upward social mobility and for improving their lives along the dimensions that matter most to them; 2. It ensures that these opportunities translate into wellbeing outcomes for all segments of the population; 3. It reduces inequalities; and 4. It fosters environmental and social sustainability. Cf. OECD Working Paper 102, 'The Economy of Wellbeing. Creating Opportunities for People's Wellbeing and Growth', 2019, p. 8, one.oecd.org/document/ SDD/DOC(2019)2/En/pdf (last retrieved: 1 June 2022).

29 This phrase is inspired by the title of a book by the British economist and environmental researcher Peter Victor: *Managing without Growth: slower by design, not disaster*, Edward Elgar Publishing, Cheltenham, 2019.

30 For more in-depth information on the four steps, see, among others, Frances Westley et al., 'Tipping toward Sustainability'; or Derk Loorbach's 'Transition Management for Sustainable Development: A Prescriptive, Complexity-Based Governance Framework', 2009, in *Governance*, vol. 23, issue 1, 23 December 2009, pp. 161–83. For a more practice-oriented description, see, for example, Dominic Hofstetter of the European Knowledge Innovation Centre—Climate (Climate-KIC): www.climate-kic.org/opinion/ innovating-in-complexity/. The Wuppertal Institute has produced a handbook for its System Innovation Lab: Maja Göpel et al., *System Innovation Lab*, www.maja-goepel.de/wp-content/uploads/2020/03/ SysInnoLab_2016_Handbook.pdf. For more on strategies for systemic innovation around the four steps, see also David Peter Stroh, *System Thinking for Social Change: a practical guide to solving complex problems, avoiding unintended consequences and achieving lasting results*, Chelsea Green, Vermont 2015.

31 Meadows, *Thinking in Systems*, p. 190.

32 For information on the World Future Council (WFC) and its work, see www.worldfuturecouncil.org/de/future-policy-award/ (last retrieved: 1 June 2022).

33 See the grid portal for Belo Horizonte: belohorizontegrid.com/de/info#Food_security (last retrieved: 1 June 2022).

34 Cf. Anita Makri, 'Fighting hunger locally, from the ground up', in *Nature*, 24 September 2021, media.nature.com/original/magazine-assets/d41586-021-02412-x/d41586-021-02412-x.pdf (last retrieved: 1 June 2022).

35 Philipp Stierand, *Speiseräume. Die Ernährungswende beginnt in der Stadt*, oekom, Munich 2014, p. 154, www.oekom.de/_files_media/titel/leseproben/9783865816702.pdf (last retrieved: 20 September 2023).

36 Ibid.

37 For a list of the selection criteria for the Future Policy Award and information on the other winners in the food security category in 2009, and what they have in common, see www.worldfuturecouncil.org/de/p/2009-nahrungssicherheit-2/ (last retrieved: 1 June 2022).

38 See www.worldfuturecouncil.org/future-policy-award-celebrated-first-time/.

39 See the World Future Council (WFC), *Celebrating the Belo Horizonte Food Security Programme*, Hamburg 2009, epub.sub.uni-hamburg.de/epub/volltexte/2014/26950/pdf/Future_Policy_Award_brochure.pdf (last retrieved: 1 June 2022).

40 Anita Makri, 'Fighting hunger locally, from the ground up', in *Nature*, 24 September 2021, media.nature.com/original/magazine-assets/d41586-021-02412-x/d41586-021-02412-x.pdf (last retrieved: 1 June 2022).

41 See the brochure published by the Bertelsmann Foundation, www.bertelsmann-stiftung.de/fileadmin/files/BSt/Presse/imported/downloads/xcms_bst_dms_32411_33370_2.pdf (last retrieved: 1 June 2022).

42 See the presentation by Eric Liu and Nick Hanauer, *Complexity Economics Shows Us Why Laissez-Faire Economics Always Fails*, https://evonomics.com/complexity-economics-shows-us-that-laissez-faire-fail-nickhanauer/ (last retrieved: 13 July 2022).

43 Ibid.

44 Patrizia Nanz, Charles Taylor, and Madeleine Beaubien Taylor have published a short book about such experiences: *Reconstructing*

Democracy: how citizens are building from the ground up, Harvard University Press, 2020. In her book on globalisation, Gesine Schwan summarises her many decades of work on democracy and also stresses the importance of the local level; see Gesine Schwan, *Politik trotz Globalisierung* (*Politics Despite Globalisation*), Darmstadt 2021. The Berlin Institute for Participation explains various formats such as trialogues, www.bipar.de/trialog/ (last retrieved: 1 June 2022).

45 For more on the German government's *Wir gegen das Virus* hackathon, see the evaluation report on it drawn up by Johanna Mair and Thomas Gegenhuber of the Hertie School of Governance, at www.hertie-school.org/en/news/detail/content/new-policy-brief-evaluates-how-open-social-innovation-can-expedite-solutions-to-urgent-public-policy-problems.

46 See for example, the federal and state initiative *Innovative Hochschule* www.innovative-hochschule.de/pdf, as well as the German Federal Ministry for Economic Affairs and Climate Action's regulatory sandboxes strategy, www.bmwk.de/Redaktion/DE/Dossier/reallabore-testraeume-fuer-innovation-und-regulierung.html, and pacscenter.stanford.edu/a-few-thoughts-on-regulatory-sandboxes/.

47 transitionsnetwork.org, transformationscommunity.org/ or nachhaltigeswirtschaften-soef.de/synthese-reallabore for research-driven initiatives. The following websites include analyses and design recommendations: thegovlab.org, nesta.org.uk/feature/innovation-methods/public-and-social-labs/, nesta.org.uk/toolkit/innovation-teams-and-labs-a-practice-guide/, systemsinnovation.io/ (last retrieved: 1 June 2022).

48 The Consilience Project, which studies issues of global risk mitigation and governance design, has applied this perspective to modern-day America and the role of education and the media in a deliberative democracy: consilienceproject.org/democracy-and-the-epistemic-commons/ (last retrieved: 1 June 2022).

Chapter Ten: Understanding: relating to each other

1 Geoff Mulgan, *The Imaginary Crisis (and how we might quicken social and public imagination)*, UCL Science, London 2020, p. 14.

2 Cf. Vaclav Smil, *Energy and Civilization: a history*, MIT Press, Cambridge (Mass.) 2017, p. 27.

3 The calorific value of commercial diesel is around 35 megajoules per litre. Two 70-litre tanks of diesel contain the 5 gigajoules of energy

that hunters and gatherers are estimated to have consumed annually
over ten thousand years ago.

4   Cf. *Our Finite World*, 'World Per Capita Energy Consumption',
    ourfiniteworld.com/2012/03/12/world-energy-consumption-since-
    1820-in-charts/ (last retrieved: 1 June 2022).

5   The idea is to calculate how many people would actually be required
    to perform the work necessary to maintain our modern lifestyle,
    based on the number of kilojoules one person can expend per
    day. For an initial consideration and definition of the idea, see
    Buckminster Fuller, *The World Game: integrative resource utilisation
    planning tool*, World Resources Inventory, Carbondale (Illinois) 1961,
    p. 99.

6   Cf. Harald Lesch, Karlheinz A. Geissler, and Jonas Geissler, *Alles eine
    Frage der Zeit. Warum die Zeit-ist-Geld-Logik Mensch und Natur teuer
    zu stehen kommt (All a Question of Time: why the time-is-money logic
    costs humans and nature do dear)*, oekom, Munich 2021, pp. 12 f.

7   All figures are taken from the online information on per capita
    energy consumption at *Our World in Data*, a statistics project at
    Oxford University, ourworldindata.org/per-capita-energy (last
    retrieved: 1 June 2022).

8   See sdgs.un.org/2030agenda (last retrieved: 13 July 2023).

9   See the project's website, lili.leeds.ac.uk, and a paper by Joel
    Millward-Hopkins and Julia K. Steinberger, 'Providing decent living
    with minimum energy: A global scenario', in *Global Environmental
    Change*, November 2020, www.sciencedirect.com/science/article/pii/
    S0959378020307512 (last retrieved: 1 June 2022).

10 The average living space per person in Germany in 2020 was
    47.4 square metres. Cf. German Environment Agency, www.
    umweltbundesamt.de/daten/private-haushalte-konsum/wohnen/
    wohnflaeche#zahl-der-wohnungen-gestiegen (last retrieved: 1 June
    2022).

11 Average water consumption in Germany in 2019 was 128 litres
    per person per day. Cf. German Environment Agency, www.
    umweltbundesamt.de/daten/private-haushalte-konsum/wohnen/
    wassernutzung-privater-haushalte#deutschlands-wasserfussabdruck
    (last retrieved: 1 June 2022).

12 Per-capita meat consumption in Germany stood at 57.4 kilos in
    2020. Cf. German Ministry of Food and Agriculture, www.bmel-
    statistik.de/ernaehrung-fischerei/versorgungsbilanzen/fleisch (last
    retrieved: 1 June 2022).

13 Mathias Binswanger, *Die Tretmühlen des Glücks. Wir haben immer mehr und werden nicht glücklicher. Was können wir tun?* (*The Treadmills of Happiness: we own ever more but aren't getting happier. What can we do about it?*), Herder, Freiburg 2006.

14 See data on the rise in global carbon dioxide emissions at *Our World in Data*, ourworldindata.org/co2-emissions (last retrieved: 1 June 2022).

15 See data on carbon dioxide emissions since the middle of the 18th century at *Our World in Data*, ourworldindata.org/contributed-most-global-co2 (last retrieved: 1 June 2022).

16 See *Global Warming and the Global Inequality of Carbon Emissions 1990–2020* by the World Inequality Lab, which brings together more than 100 social scientists from around the world at the Ecole d'économie de Paris. Pages 2 and 21 of that report are particularly relevant: wid.world/document/climate-change-the-global-inequality-of-carbon-emissions-1990-2020-world-inequality-lab-working-paper-2021-21/ (last retrieved: 1 June 2022).

17 For a summary of the research which explores this issue using models, see the website of the anthroecology lab at the University of Maryland, anthroecology.org/project/anthroecology/. For an article summarising this research and the patterns it is based upon, see link.springer.com/article/10.1007/s11625-017-0513-6 (last retrieved: 1 June 2022).

18 Protected areas refers to areas of land and sea, and it is not just a proposal made by academics, but is now a political demand, for example from the EU Parliament www.europarl.europa.eu/news/en/press-room/20210604IPR05513/biodiversity-meps-demand-binding-targets-to-protect-wildlife-and-people (last retrieved: 1 June 2022).

19 Christoph Möllers: *Freiheitsgrade* (*Degrees of Freedom*), Suhrkamp, Berlin 2020, p. 58.

20 Cf. Martin Schürz, Überreichtum (*Overrich*), Campus, Frankfurt 2019.

21 Ibid., p. 52.

22 The World Inequality Lab's *World Inequality Report 2022* gives an overview of the developments in taxpayer behaviour and taxation policy in recent decades, as well as the distribution of income and property, and illustrates the fact that a system is developing which is similar to pre-twentieth-century feudalism: wid.world/document/world-inequality-report-2022/. The entire World Inequality

Database (WID) is available online at wid.world (last retrieved: 1 June 2022).

23 See the nuanced report in the *FAZ* of 16 January 2014, on the various kinds of 'golden passport' approved by Malta at that time, www.faz.net/aktuell/politik/malta-eu-parlament-ruegt-verkauf-von-staatsbuergerschaften-12754797.html; see also the EU Parliament's current efforts to stop the practice, which have been bolstered by the sanctions imposed on oligarchs, www.rnd.de/politik/staatsbuergerschaft-kaufen-eu-parlament-will-europaweites-verbot-von-goldenen-paessen-E2HN52TARKYYB-CCXACGKUHAZ6Y.html (last retrieved: 1 June 2022).

24 Eisler, *The Real Wealth of Nations*, p. 30 ff.

25 Ibid., p. 30.

26 Ibid.

27 Production of the vaccine began in November 2020, and by December 2021 the various manufacturers had already produced almost 11 billion doses. For an evaluation of the data, see globalcommissionforpost-pandemicpolicy.org/Covid-19 -vaccine-production-to-december-31st-2021/ (last retrieved: 1 June 2022).

28 Cf. Asher Mullard, 'Reiche Länder sichern sich Corona-Impfungen', in *spektrum.de*, 3 December 2020, www.spektrum.de/news/der-Covid-19-impstoff-wird-ungleich-verteilt-werden/1803563 (last retrieved: 1 June 2022).

29 'It is especially costly to be poor in times of crisis' said Achim Steiner, head of the United Nations Development Programme (UNDP), in an interview on this issue. He went on to explain why national isolationism and self-reliance without negative consequences is no longer possible in a complex, networked world. www.zeit.de/kultur/2022-05/achim-steiner-russland-ukraine-krieg-vereinte-nationen-ernaehrungskrise-multilateralismus/seite-2 (last retrieved: 1 June 2022).

30 See *Our World in Data*, vaccination figures ourworldindata.org/covid-vaccinations (last retrieved: 1 June 2022).

31 Cf. the International Chamber of Commerce's report on vaccine nationalism from 25 January 2021, iccwbo.org/media-wall/news-speeches/study-shows-vaccine-nationalism-could-cost-rich-countries-us4-5-trillion/ (last retrieved: 1 June 2022)

32 By January 2022, Canada, for example, had delivered less than half the agreed amount of vaccine to the WHO's COVAX initiative, while it ordered enough doses to vaccinate every adolescent and

adult in its own population three times over. Cf. *Die Zeit*: www.zeit.
de/wissen/2022-01/weltweite-impfstoffverteilung-corona-pandemie-
ungleichheit (last retrieved: 1 June 2022).

33 Cf. Maxence Peigné, 'EU Unable to Cap COVID-19 Vaccine Prices
in Secret Deals', in *Investigate Europe*, 23 September 2021, www.
investigate-europe.eu/en/2021/eu-negotiators-Covid-19 -vaccine-
price-moderna-pfizer/ (last retrieved: 1 June 2022).

34 The relevant excerpt from this interview can be viewed on the
YouTube channel of the Global Citizen platform, www.youtube.
com/watch?v=erHXKP386Nk (last retrieved: 1 June 2022).

35 For a short summary of the way commons are defined and allocated,
see the German Federal Agency for Political Education, www.bpb.
de/kurz-knapp/lexika/lexikon-der-wirtschaft/20244/oeffentliche-
gueter/ (last retrieved: 1 June 2022).

36 This explains the heading 'Cooperation is the new realism' that
appears in the 2022 annual report, *Environment of Peace*, from the
Sipri Institute in Sweden, which specialises in studying global risks
and conflict. Cf. www.sipri.org/media/press-release/2022/world-
stumbling-new-era-risk-concludes-sipri-report, (last retrieved:
1 June 2022). The report outlines five principles for policymaking
which are also applicable to other organisational contexts: 1. Think
fast, think ahead, act now. Establishing an environment of peace
requires a far-sighted vision, but also swift, short-term action.
2. Cooperate to survive and thrive. The new era of risk demands a
new mode of cooperation to address common threats. 3. Expect the
unexpected—be prepared to adapt. Continuous horizon scanning,
far-sighted analysis and adaptive implementation are needed to keep
ahead of unpredictably changing risks. 4. Only a just and peaceful
transition will succeed. In making the transition to environmentally
sustainable societies, we must avoid creating new risks to peace. 5. By
everyone, for everyone. Decision-making processes from the United
Nations down to community projects should include the people most
affected.

37 Meadows, *Thinking in Systems*, p. 97.

38 Katharina Pistor, *The Code of Capital: how the law creates wealth and
inequality*, Princeton University Press, Princeton 2019.

39 See the Wyss Academy For Nature's annual report, www.
wyssacademy.org/ (last retrieved: 1 June 2022).

40 See Architects for Future's statement, www.architects4future.de/
forderungen (last retrieved: 1 June 2022).

41 See Cathrin Zengerling's expert study for the WBGU, *Rethinking Land in the Anthropocene: from separation to integration. Strengthening climate rrotection and development through international trade law*, Berlin 2020, www.wbgu.de/fileadmin/user_upload/wbgu/ publikationen/hauptgutachten/hg2020/pdf/Expertise_Zengerling_ EN.pdf (last retrieved: 1 June 2022).

42 See the Advisory Council on the Environment's 2019 report, *Democratic government within environmental limits. On the legitimation of environmental policy*, www.umweltrat.de/SharedDocs/ Downloads/EN/02_Special_Reports/2016_2020/2019_SR_ Government_within_environmental_limits_KF.html (last retrieved: 1 June 2022).

43 See Josefine Koebe, Claire Samtleben, Annekatrin Schrenker, and Aline Zucco, 'Systemrelevant und doch kaum anerkannt. Das Lohn- und Prestigeniveau unverzichtbarer Berufe in Zeiten der Coronakrise', 2020, www.diw.de/de/diw_01.c.792754.de/ publikationen/diw_aktuell/2020_0048/systemrelevant__aber_ dennoch_kaum_anerkannt__entlohnung_unverzichtbarer_berufe_ in_der_corona-krise_unterdurchschnittlich.html (last retrieved: 1 June 2022).

44 See Rupert Neat, '"Raise my taxes—now!': the millionaires who want to give it all away', in *The Guardian*, 3 April 2021, www. theguardian.com/news/2021/apr/03/raise-my-taxes-now-the- millionaires-who-want-to-give-it-all-away (last retrieved: 1 June 2022).

45 Graham Leicester's short book *Transformative Innovation* is a treasure trove of insights and concrete suggestions for everyday practice, especially in the public sector.

46 Leicester, *Transformative Innovation*, p. 31.

47 Ibid.

48 Although this quote is often ascribed to Viktor Frankl, it seems actually to have come from his student, Stephen Covey, author of the *Seven Habits* books. He recounts having discovered it in a book from a library in Hawaii, and found it apposite to Frankl's theories. See: www.viktorfrankl.org/quote_stimulus.html. (last retrieved: 16 July 2023).

Part III: Who are 'We'?

1   Eric Young, quoted in Frances Westley et al., *Getting to Maybe: how the world is changed*, Vintage Canada, Toronto 2007, p. xiv.

Chapter Eleven: Heads together

1   Bertrand Russell, *What I Believe*, Routledge Classics, London, New York 2014, p. 16.

2   For information on Leipzig Zoo and its cooperation with the Max Planck Institute for Evolutionary Anthropology, see www.zoo-leipzig.de/artikel/grosses-jubilaeum-20-jahre-pongoland-menschenaffen-wissenschaft-und-forschung-unter-einem-dach-1091/ (last retrieved: 1 June 2022).

3   Alexander Mäder, 'Experimente zu sozialen Fähigkeiten', in *Stuttgarter Zeitung*, 24 November 2011, www.stuttgarter-zeitung.de/inhalt.schimpansen-im-test-gescheitert-aber-trotzdem-schlau-page1.224621b3-ce27-43f8-89c3-4578546e21ca.html (last retrieved: 1 June 2022).

4   The Smithsonian Museum of Natural History's website has very accessible information on the genetic differences between humans and other primates. See humanorigins.si.edu/evidence/genetics (last retrieved: 1 June 2022).

5   Cf. Michael Tomasello, *The Cultural Origins of Human Cognition*, Harvard University Press, Cambridge (Mass.) 1999, p. 2.

6   Michael Tomasello gave a speech on the question *What Makes Us Human?* at the annual convention of the US Association for Psychological Science in 2019, cf. www.psychologicalscience.org/observer/tomasello-keynote (last retrieved: 1 June 2022).

7   In a study published in the journal *Science* in 2007, Michael Tomasello and his team compared the cognitive abilities of children aged two and a half with those of chimpanzees and orangutans when completing mostly identical tasks. Cf. www.science.org/doi/10.1126/science.1146282 (last retrieved: 1 June 2022).

8   Video recordings of this series of tests are included in Tomasello's speech at the Association for Psychological Science referenced above, www.psychologicalscience.org/observer/tomasello-keynote (last retrieved: 1 June 2022).

9   Michael Tomasello, *Becoming Human: a theory of ontogeny*. Harvard University Press, Cambridge (Mass.) 2019.

10 Cf. Michael Tomasello, *The Cultural Origins of Human Cognition*, Harvard University Press, Cambridge (Mass.) 1999, p. 5.

11 The internet platform *The Inspiration Journey* presents scientists from different disciplines, along with their findings. The anthropologists Alice Roberts and Michael Tomasello are featured in the video titled *What Makes Us Human*, vimeo.com/theinspirationjourney.

Chapter Twelve: Heroes

1 Hannah Arendt, *The Life of the Mind*, Harcourt 1971, p. 7.

2 Cf. Nicholas Kulish and Rebecca R. Ruiz, 'The Fortune of MacKenzie Scott', in *The New York Times*, 10 April 2022, www.nytimes.com/2022/04/10/business/mackenzie-scott-charity.html (last retrieved: 1 June 2022).

3 Cf. Nicholas Kulish, 'Giving Billions Fast, MacKenzie Scott Upends Philanthropy', in *The New York Times*, 20 December 2020, www.nytimes.com/2020/12/20/business/mackenzie-scott-philanthropy.html (last retrieved: 1 June 2022).

4 Cf. Guido Mingels, 'Sie verschenkt ihre Milliarden—'bis der Safe leer ist", *Spiegel*, 19 February 2021, www.spiegel.de/wirtschaft/unternehmen/mackenzie-scott-die-frau-die-ihre-milliarden-verschenkt-bis-der-safe-leer-ist-a-00000000-0002-0001-0000-000175447381 (last retrieved: 1 June 2022).

5 Cf. Kristin Stoller, 'The Top 10 Richest Women in the World', in *Forbes*, 2020, www.forbes.com/stories/billionaires/the-10-richest-women-in-the-world-2020/ (last retrieved: 1 June 2022).

6 Guido Mingels, 'Sie verschenkt ihre Milliarden—'bis der Safe leer ist", *Spiegel*, 19 February 2021, www.spiegel.de/wirtschaft/unternehmen/mackenzie-scott-die-frau-die-ihre-milliarden-verschenkt-bis-der-safe-leer-ist-a-00000000-0002-0001-0000-000175447381 (last retrieved: 1 June 2022).

7 MacKenzie Scott published the names of the recipient organisations in July and December 2020 on medium.com, mackenzie-scott.medium.com (last retrieved: 1 June 2022).

8 Cf. Maria Di Mento and Ben Gose, 'Jeff Bezos, MacKenzie Scott, and Michael Bloomberg Top List of America's 50 Biggest Charity Donors' in *The Chronicle of Philanthropy*, 9 February 2021, www.philanthropy.com/article/jeff-bezos-mackenzie-scott-and-michael-bloomberg-top-list-of-americas-50-big-gest-charity-donors (last retrieved: 1 June 2022).

9 Cf. Nicholas Kulish and Maria Cramer, '$12 Billion to 1,257 Groups: MacKenzie Scott's Donations So Far', in *The New York Times*, 23 March 2022, www.nytimes.com/2022/03/23/business/mackenzie-scott-philanthropy.html (last retrieved: 1 June 2022).

10 The Giving Pledge website has background information on the history of the initiative, portraits of its members, and statistics on

their countries of origin and areas of business: givingpledge.org (last retrieved: 1 June 2022).

11 From the letter of 25 May 2019, in which MacKenzie Scott announced her membership of the *Giving Pledge* initiative, givingpledge.org/pledger?pledgerId=393 (last retrieved: 1 June 2022).

12 This quote is taken from the 1913-founded organisation's own mission statement, www.rockefellerfoundation.org/about-us/ (last retrieved: 1 June 2022).

13 Cf. Chuck Collins and Helen Flannery, *Gilded Giving 2020: how wealth inequality distorts philanthropy and imperils democracy*, August 2020, Institute for Policy Studies, Washington 2020, p. 3, inequality.org/wp-content/uploads/2020/07/Gilded-Giving-2020-July28-2020.pdf (last retrieved: 1 June 2022).

14 According to documents obtained by the non-profit organisation ProPublica, the 25 richest Americans paid less than 4 per cent tax on their wealth between 2014 and 2018. Cf. Jesse Eisinger et al., *The Secret IRS Files: trove of never-before-seen records reveal how the wealthiest avoid income tax*, 8 June 2021, www.propublica.org/article/the-secret-irs-files-trove-of-never-before-seen-records-reveal-how-the-wealthiest-avoid-income-tax (last retrieved: 1 June 2022).

15 Cf. Collins and Flannery, *Gilded Giving 2020*, p. 8, inequality.org/wp-content/uploads/2020/07/Gilded-Giving-2020-July28-2020.pdf (last retrieved: 1 June 2022).

16 For an article summarising the findings of research into the size of donations and a very welcome explanation of the way different methods influence those results, see Michaela Neumayr and Astrid Pennerstorfer, 'The Relation Between Income and Donations as a Proportion of Income Revisited: literature review and empirical application', in *Nonprofit and Voluntary Sector Quarterly*, 2020, vol. 50, no. 3, pp. 551–77, journals.sagepub.com/doi/full/10.1177/0899764020977667 (last retrieved: 1 June 2022).

17 MacKenzie Scott, 'Seeding by Ceding', in *medium*, 15 June 2021, mackenzie-scott.medium.com/seeding-by-ceding-ea6de642bf (last retrieved: 1 June 2022).

18 Cf. Collins and Flannery, *Gilded Giving 2020*, p. 7 f., inequality.org/wp-content/uploads/2020/07/Gilded-Giving-2020-July28-2020.pdf (last retrieved: 1 June 2022).

19 For example, David Beasley gave an interview on the issue

to the news broadcaster CNN and posted excerpts of it on Twitter on 27 October 2021. See twitter.com/ WFPChief/ status/1453398212837052422 (last retrieved: 1 June 2022).

20 A summary of the planning and the funding necessary to prevent millions from starving in each region was published by the World Food Programme on 3 October 2021. See www.wfp.org/stories/ wfps-plan-support-42-million-people-brink-famine (last retrieved: 1 June 2022).

21 The American business magazine *Forbes* publishes a real-time rolling update of the estimated wealth of a number of rich people. For Elon Musk, see: www.forbes.com/profile/elon-musk/?sh=5294e1b87999 (last retrieved: 1 June 2022).

22 For Elon Musk's tweeted response to the request from the WFP chief Beasley to donate for the starving, see twitter.com/elonmusk/ status/1454808104256737289 (last retrieved: 1 June 2022).

23 Cf. Jerry Hirsch, 'Elon Musk's growing empire is fueled by $4.9 billion in government subsidies', in *Los Angeles Times*, 30 May 2015, www.latimes.com/business/la-fi-hy-musk-subsidies-20150531-story. html#page=1 (last retrieved: 1 June 2022).

24 The entire exchange between the two men can be found on Twitter: twitter.com/ WFPChief/status/1456041431051735040 ?refsrc=twsrc%5Etfw (last retrieved: 1 June 2022).

25 Cf. Dieter Thomä, *Warum Demokratien Helden brauchen. Plädoyer für einen zeitgemäßen Heroismus* (*Why Democracies Need Heroes: an argument for a contemporary form of heroism*), Ullstein, Berlin 2019.

26 Ibid. p. 233 f.

27 Ibid. p. 234 f.

28 Ibid. p. 233.

29 Ibid. p. 179.

Chapter Thirteen: You Matter

1 This is one of the quotes published on the BBC web page on the occasion of Angelou's death: www.bbc.com/news/world-us-canada-27610770 (last retrieved: 1 June 2022).

2 Karen O'Brien, *You matter more than you think. Quantum social change for a thriving world*, Oslo 2021, p. 102.

3 Ibid.

4 Ibid. p. 103.

5 Cf. Garrett Hardin, *Filters Against Folly: how to survive despite economists, ecologists and the merely wloquent*, New York 1985, pp. 15 ff.

6   These three questions are based on Hardin's three kinds of filter, which he calls Literacy, Numeracy, and Ecolacy. Cf. Hardin, *Filters against Folly*, p. 25.

7   Stuart Kauffman, *Investigations*, Oxford University Press 2000, p. 22.

8   Nassehi, *Unbehagen* (*Discomfort: theory of the overwhelmed society*), pp. 318 and 325.

9   Jonas Salzgeber, *The Little Book of Stoicism: timeless wisdom to gain resilience, confidence, and calmness*, self-published 2019.